Atheism Explained

IDEAS EXPLAINED™

Atheism Explained

From Folly to Philosophy

DAVID RAMSAY STEELE

OPEN COURT
Chicago and La Salle, Illinois

Volume 5 in the Ideas Explained™ Series

Publishers' Note. This book is inerrant. Every statement of fact asserted by the author in the original manuscript of this book is guaranteed to be literally true, except where it is obviously intended figuratively, and then it is true in the sense obviously intended. Every statement of fact in the first printed edition of this book is true, except where editors, typesetters, or printers have introduced departures from the original manuscript. Every statement of fact in subsequent printed editions of this book is true, except as qualified above, and except where editors, typesetters, or printers have introduced departures from the first printed edition.

To order books from Open Court, call toll-free 1-800-815-2280, or visit our website at www.opencourtbooks.com.

Open Court Publishing Company is a division of Carus Publishing Company.

Copyright © 2008 by Carus Publishing Company

First printing 2008

Printed and bound in the United States of America.

Library of Congress Cataloging-in-Publication Data

Steele, David Ramsay
    Atheism explained : from folly to philosophy / David Ramsay Steele.
        p. cm.
    Summary: "Explains and evaluates the principal rationale for and against belief in God, and argues in favor of atheism" — Provided by publisher.
    Includes bibliographical references (p.) and index.
    ISBN-13: 978-0-8126-9637-0 (trade paper : alk. paper)
    ISBN-10: 0-8126-9637-9 (trade paper : alk. paper)
    1. Atheism. I. Title.
    BL2747.3.S7255 2008
    211'.8—dc22
                                                                2007042691

To David McDonagh

"Honesty is an achievement."

Contents

Preface

There are many books explaining atheism and arguing for it. Most of them fall into one of two types. The first type takes for granted a lot of technical language in philosophy of religion and soon loses the ordinary reader. The second type is usually personal in tone, seething with moral indignation against atrocities committed in the name of God, unsystematic in approach, and occasionally betraying ignorance of just what theists have believed.

Several books of both types are really excellent in their way, but I'm trying something different. I explain atheism by giving an outline of the strongest arguments for and against the existence of God. My aim is to provide an accurate account of these arguments, on both sides, in plain English.

Following a Christian upbringing, I became an atheist by the age of thirteen. For a few years, it seemed axiomatic that I ought to do my bit to help convert the world to atheism. Then I became more interested in social and political questions.

Over the years since then, the whole issue of atheism gradually sank into comparative insignificance. It seemed clear to me, and still seems obvious today, that there is no God. But it has also gradually become apparent that this issue has less practical urgency than I used to imagine.

Most people who say that they believe in God live their lives pretty much as they would if they did not believe in God. They are nominal theists with secular outlooks and secular lifestyles. They would judge it to be at best a lapse of taste if any mention of God were to intrude into their everyday lives.

Whether or not a person believes in the existence of God seems to have no bearing on what that person thinks about war, globalization, welfare reform, or global warming (there are of course statistical correlations, but these seem to be due to mere fashion, not to any logical necessity). The social and political positions taken up by Christian churches, for example, are merely a reflection of ideological currents generated in the secular world. The landmark papal encyclicals on social questions, of 1891 and 1931, tried to steer a middle course between socialism and free-market capitalism—just one illustration of the fact that, since the eighteenth century, secular social movements have made the ideological running; the churches flail about trying to come up with some angle on socal questions that they can represent as distinctively religious.

It's true that believers in God are usually gratified to discover that the Almighty sees eye to eye with them on many practical issues, but theists can be found on all sides of any policy question. There is no distinctively 'theist view' or 'Christian view' on anything of practical importance. Still less does belief or disbelief in God have any relevance to whether a person is considerate, courageous, kind, loving, tolerant, creative, responsible, or trustworthy.

In recent years I have spent a good portion of my energies on combating the ideas of two atheists: Karl Marx and Sigmund Freud. This bears out my view that atheism is purely negative, like not believing in mermaids, and is in no way a creed to live by or anything so grandiose. I view belief in God as like belief in the class struggle or belief in repressed memories—just a mistake. The issue of theism or atheism is something to get out of the way early, so that you can focus your attention on matters more difficult to decide and more important.

Today my view of atheism is very different from what it was in my teens. Then I thought that the existence of God was a vitally urgent question. Now, I still believe there's no God, but I do not think this is as consequential a matter as I used to suppose. I am struck by three considerations.

First, the existence of God seems preposterous, but so do some of the things quantum physics tells me, and I do accept quantum physics. (I do not accept quantum physics *because* it seems preposterous, but because it tests out well; its predictions are borne out by numerous experiments.) While this does not make me directly more disposed to believe in God, it does make me more acutely aware of how complicated the world is and how little I know about it. And this makes me entertain the possibility of some future shifts in human knowledge that might conceivably make some kind of God's existence a more promising hypothesis than it seems to be right now. (I say "some kind of God" because, as you'll see if you keep reading, God as strictly defined by Christianity and Islam is an incoherent notion which can be demonstrated not to correspond to anything in reality.)

Second, I have come to recognize something that was once unclear to me: that the bare existence of a God, if we accepted it, would not take us even ten percent of the way toward accepting the essentials of any traditional theistic system. For example, every human would have to possess an immortal soul—something that might be true if there were no God, and might be false if there were a God. God would have to decree a major difference to people's lot in the afterlife according to whether those people believed in his existence in this life. And usually, some uneven collection of ancient documents, such as the *Tanakh*, the *New Testament*, or the *Quran*, would have to be accorded a respect out of all proportion to its literary or philosophical merit. Even if we were to accept the bare existence of God, these additional elementary portions of traditional theistic religion would remain as fantastically incredible as ever. If I were to become convinced tomorrow of the existence of God, I would be no more inclined to become a Christian or a Muslim than I am now.

Third, so many horrible deeds have been done by Christians and Muslims in the name of their religions that a young Christian or Muslim who becomes an atheist often tends to assume that there is some inherent connection between adherence to theism and the proclivity to commit atrocities. The history of the past one hundred years shows us that atheistic ideologies can sanctify more and bigger atrocities than Christianity or Islam ever did. The casualties inflicted by Communism and National Socialism vastly exceed—many hundredfold—the casualties inflicted by theocracies. In some cases (Mexico in the 1930s, Soviet Russia, and the People's Republic of China), there has been appalling persecution of theistic belief by politically empowered atheists, exceeding any historical atrocities against unbelievers and heretics.

I don't conclude that atheism is particularly prone to atrocities, as the historical rise of secular social movements coincides with the enhanced efficiency of the technological and administrative means to commit atrocities. The mass murderer Torquemada would have done as much harm as the mass murderer Mao, if only he'd had the means at his disposal. (For those who doubt that extraordinary brutality of a 'modern' sort could be perpetrated by devout theists, I recommend a look at the activities of the Iron Guard in Romania or the Franco regime in Spain.)

I do conclude, sadly, that atheists are morally no better than Christians or Muslims, and that the propensity of people to commit atrocities at the behest of unreasonable ideologies is independent of whether those ideologies include theism or atheism.

In light of all the above, why take any interest in the question of the existence of God? The primary reason is intellectual curiosity: as Aristotle said, we humans have an appetite to find out the truth about things. Just as I would like to know whether there are advanced civilizations in other solar systems (and whether they have discovered Texas Hold'em), whether the universe is infinite, and who really wrote the works attributed to Shakespeare, so I would like to know whether there is a God (and in this case I think I do know).

I believe in confronting opposing points of view at their strongest. Therefore I give more attention to Richard Swinburne and William Lane Craig than to C.S. Lewis or Lee Strobel. However my choice of topics to which to devote space is partly determined by those issues which the ordinary non-academic reader will encounter in considering whether or not God exists. My general procedure is to begin with extreme positions, then move on to more moderate positions, unless these have already incidentally been refuted in considering the extreme positions.

Since this is an introductory survey with endnotes kept to a minimum, mention of an idea without a citation does not imply any claim to originality. The bibliography includes all the sources cited and all those directly drawn upon in the writing of this book. In quoting from the *Quran* and the *Bible*, I always compared numerous different English translations. Biblical quotations always follow the divisions by chapter and verse standard in Protestant translations.

Open Court's Publisher, André Carus (whose great-grandfather
Paul Carus famously styled himself "an atheist who loves God")
considered that American culture was ripe for a fresh restatement
of atheism and therefore encouraged me to knock off this little
pamphlet.

I hereby thank the following people for reading drafts of the
manuscript and giving their valuable comments, though I have not
followed their advice in every instance: David Gordon, Jan Lester,
David McDonagh, Victor J. Stenger, Martin Verhoeven, and Lisa
Zimmerman.

I

Mere Atheism

HOLDEN: Oh my God! . . . Oh well, you know, not my
God, because I defy him and all his works, but—does
he exist? Is there word on that, by the way?

BUFFY: Nothing solid.

—*Buffy the Vampire Slayer*
(Season 7, 'Conversations with Dead People')

1

One Kind of God—
and a Few Alternatives

Every newborn baby is an atheist. An atheist is a person without any belief in God.

Atheism is the absence of a certain type of belief. We do not have a special word for lack of belief in psychic spoon-bending, unicorns, cold fusion, or alien abductions, but we do have a special word for lack of belief in God. This usage arose because for many centuries deeply devout theists were in control of the state and used it to assault people whose opinions they found distressing. For a person to admit to being a non-believer in God could easily result in that person being vilified, tortured, and killed.

Since atheism is merely a negative aspect of people's beliefs, atheists are not united in any of their other beliefs. To illustrate this diversity, here's a handful of notable atheists (though not all notable for being atheists):

Lance Armstrong	George Orwell
Isaac Asimov	Pablo Picasso
Dave Barry	Ayn Rand
Béla Bartók	Jean-Paul Sartre
Warren Buffett	Thomas Szasz
Penn Jillette and R.J. Teller	Mark Twain
Katherine Hepburn	H.G. Wells
H.L. Mencken	Joss Whedon

As you can see, atheists are a mixed bunch,[1] and you must not expect them all to agree on anything except their atheism. An atheist, as I have defined it, may not even prefer to be called an atheist, and atheists don't even agree on what to do about atheism.

God's Ten Qualities

Different people have many different ideas of what 'God' Means. But there is one quite precise conception of God, traditionally held by Christian, Muslim, and Jewish theologians. I will refer to this as the God of 'classical theism'.

According to classical theism, God is:

1. a person
2. a spirit
3. all-powerful (omnipotent)
4. all-knowing (omniscient)
5. everywhere at once (omnipresent)
6. all-good (omnibenevolent)
7. interested in humans
8. creator of every existing thing other than himself
9. unchanging (immutable)
10. necessary.

Any Christian, Jewish, or Muslim religious leader who questioned any one of these ten qualities would not be considered entirely orthodox.

Such lists of the qualities of God have often been compiled, and they do not seriously disagree. For example, the Christian philosopher Van Inwagen (2006, pp. 20–32) provides a list which includes all of the above with the exception of 2 and 7, though his discussion makes clear that he takes 2 and 7 for granted. His list also includes God's "eternality" and his "uniqueness," and his discussion of #3 suggests that he may not accept God's omnipotence in the traditional sense. Other lists include God's 'perfection', his 'freedom', his indivisible simplicity, or his 'all-merciful' quality, but I think it's most convenient to omit these from my list.

Since reference to these ten qualities of God will keep cropping up in my discussion, I will now briefly expand upon each of them.

1. God is a person. A person behaves purposively—acts to achieve desired ends he or she has mentally preconceived. God has conscious preferences and behaves intelligently to bring about what he prefers. God thinks, imagines, chooses, calculates, and plans. In traditional accounts he experiences emotions, though some theologians repudiate this.

Theists usually say that referring to God as male is just a manner of speaking. God really has no sex. Albeit, the plumbing of the virgin birth would have aroused more comment if a virgin Joseph had been selected to impregnate an unembodied female God.

2. God is a spirit. This means that God is not physical. He is not made of atoms or quarks, or superstrings, or of energy. He cannot be detected by the naked senses or by scientific instruments. No flickering needle on a dial could ever cause some research worker to say 'Hey, we've got some God activity here'.

3. God is almighty, omnipotent. This means he can do anything he likes, as long as it's logically possible. Most theists say that God cannot do anything which is logically impossible, such as make a square circle. But with that restriction, he can do anything. For example, he could wipe out the entire physical cosmos in an instant, completely effortlessly. He could then bring a new cosmos into existence with entirely different physical laws, again completely effortlessly. Or he could intervene piecemeal in the cosmos, in a trillion different ways simultaneously, again without effort, and without his attention being distracted in the slightest from other matters.

4. God is all-knowing, omniscient. God knows everything every human has ever known, and a lot more besides. There's nothing that can be known that God does not actually know. He knows every detail of the past. Some say he also knows every detail of the future, though this is disputed.

5. God is everywhere at once. He is not localized in space. God is, for instance, in the room with you as you read these words. As the *Quran* puts it (50:16), he's closer to you than your jugular vein. And he's just as fully present in the center of the Sun, on the icy surface of Pluto, and in every particle of the Horsehead Nebula, 1,600 light years away.

For all practical purposes, the claim that God can accurately perceive what is going on everywhere and can actively intervene everywhere is equivalent to the claim that he *is* everywhere.

6. God is perfectly good. He does no wrong and never could do any wrong. Theologians don't agree on whether good is good and bad is bad because God has decided it that way, or whether good and bad are defined independently of God. But they do agree that, one way or another, God is entirely good and never commits evil.

7. God is interested in humans. He is usually reported to be intensely concerned about the life of each individual human. For example, he cares whether individual humans believe in his existence and, if they do, whether they have the appropriately awestruck attitude. Many people assume that God's interest in individual humans follows automatically from his perfect goodness, but I think it's so remarkable that it deserves a separate listing here.

8. God made the entire physical universe. If there's more than one universe, God made the whole lot of them. And if there's a spiritual universe, apart from God himself, God made that too. He made the universe, or all universes, out of nothing ('ex nihilo').

9. God never changes. He is "the same, yesterday, and today, and forever" (*Hebrews* 13:8). This at least means that his character never changes, but it's usually taken to mean more than that, for example that he cannot learn from experience because he already knows everything. Theologians differ somewhat on this point.

They also differ quite sharply on a related point, whether God has existed for all of infinite time, or whether instead time is finite and God is 'outside time'.

10. God is necessary. What this means is that it's inconceivable that God could not exist: he *has* to exist. Why would anyone think this about God? We'll look at some reasons in Chapters 6 and 7.

The God of Classical Theism and Other Gods

Today classical theism dominates the world of organized religion. Over half the world's population is classified as Christians or Muslims. You will occasionally find individual Christians or Muslims who disclose in conversation that their conception of God is not quite the same as classical theism, but the leading spokesmen of these religions are all committed to classical theism. Several other major religions, including Judaism, Sikhism, and Baha'ism, also embrace classical theism or something very close to it.

Anyone reading that list of ten qualities will probably notice that it's difficult to reconcile some of them with others. And it's hard to reconcile some of them with observable facts about the world. Most obviously, it's tricky to reconcile God's all-powerfulness and his all-goodness with the existence of the amount of evil we can observe in the world. (We'll take a look at these difficulties in Part III.)

I find it natural to help the theist out by explaining these ten qualities as poetic exaggerations, and to develop some notion of a limited God or gods. After all, in most stages of history, people who have believed in anything that might loosely be called a god have not believed in any entity with these ten qualities. The Sumerian gods, Egyptian gods, Germanic gods, Greek gods, Roman gods, or Aztec gods do not possess these ten qualities, or even a majority of the ten. And to this day, no Buddhist, Daoist, Confucian, or Jain believes in a God with a majority of these ten qualities. The current predominance of belief in the God of classical theism is a product of the evolution of human culture over the last two thousand years.

But most theologians don't want my help and they don't want a limited God or a godling. They want a God with the ten qualities. So it wouldn't be of much use for me to take up most of this book developing a more defensible concept of God, in order to assemble a stronger hypothesis to attack. Most of the time, since I want to respond to the predominant kind of belief in God that is actually out there, I have to focus on the theologians' God, and that means the God of classical theism, the God with these ten qualities.

However, some of the arguments can also apply to other kinds of gods. For example, John Stuart Mill entertained the notion of a Creator, who was very powerful by human standards, very knowledgeable, and fundamentally benign, yet limited in his power, his knowledge, his wisdom, and his benevolence towards humans. Mill accepted the possibility of such a God because he gave some weight to the Design Argument, which has always been the most popular argument for any kind of God, including the God of classical theism. If I can show that the Design Argument fails (and I do show just this in Chapters 3 and 4), then I refute one major argument for the God of classical theism, and I also incidentally refute Mill's argument for his more limited God.

Before we get into the main discussion, let's take a quick look at some concepts of God which do not comply with classical theism. These are gods who lack some of the ten qualities.

Alternatives to Classical Theism

A Stupendously Great but Strictly Limited God

Just imagine a God who has qualities vastly greater than those of any human, or of any conceivable evolved animal, but not almighty. He is millions of times more powerful than any other intelligent entity, but not unlimited in his power. He may have a benign feeling for humans, but is not greatly concerned about their welfare. Olaf Stapledon's "Star Maker" is dissatisfied with this universe and hopes to do better next time.

The arguments for and against this kind of God are very similar to those for the God of classical theism. It's not so easy to show that the limited God doesn't exist, because the believer in a limited God is claiming much less. But I can't see any reason to take seriously the hypothesis that such a God exists.

The God of Process Theology

Process theology is a fairly new trend in the thinking of some theists. Creation is going on now and we are participating in it. In opposition to classical theism, process theology holds that God is powerless to act except through his creation, which includes you and me.

Process theology has made serious criticisms of classical theism but has not done anything to develop a new case for God's existence. Like belief in a limited God, process theology is not as easy to refute as traditional theism, simply because its claims are weaker.

Godlings

By a godling I understand some being like the Buddhist devas, or like the god Thor, or like Galactus in the early *Fantastic Four* comics.[2] A godling is superhuman but not supernatural. The universe is a big place and we can't rule out the possibility that such evolved beings with powers vastly greater than ours might exist somewhere. But if they do, it's almost certain that our paths will never cross.

PANTHEISM

Pantheism is the theory that God *is* the universe. It's very hard to see any difference between pantheism and atheism. Though there are all kinds of pantheists, and there is no pantheist party line, most pantheists don't claim that the universe thinks or acts. Perhaps the idea is that we ought to worship the universe, but atheism has nothing to say about what, if anything, we ought to worship, only about what exists, and we all agree that the universe exists.

The universe is so big compared with the human world that if the universe could have preferences or interests, we wouldn't be able to affect their realization one way or the other. So even if the universe does have purposes or goals, that's no concern of ours.

PANENTHEISM

Panentheism isn't always opposed to classical theism. I mention it here because it could be confused with pantheism. Process theologians are radical panentheists, but most panentheists are not process theologians.

The distinctive view of panentheism is that the universe is not God but is part of God. This doesn't seem to lead anywhere interesting. My fingernails, lungs, and brain are part of me, but my fingernails are more expendable than my lungs, which are more expendable than my brain.

DEISM

Like pantheism, deism comes in various colors and chest sizes. Deism usually sees God as a benign force, rather than truly a person, and it sees God as having set things off a long time ago, and then left them alone to work themselves out. This theory doesn't have any advantages over the theory that there is no God.

Deism was popular in the eighteenth century—most of the Founders of the United States were deists. The *name* 'deism' doesn't have much of a following today, but deism itself seems to be fairly popular in an unorganized grassroots fashion.

The religious assumptions of the *Star Wars* movies are deist, and therefore incompatible with classical theism. Everyone knows that Albert Einstein believed in 'God'. However, Einstein was emphatic in rejecting the personal God of classical theism, and we can classify him as a deist. In 2004 it was widely reported that the well-known atheist philosopher Antony Flew had come to believe in 'God', though the God he had come to accept was deist rather than classical theist.

This may seem like a whole lot of nit-picking, but look at it this way: Today's Christians are very ready to appeal to the fact that some notable people believe in 'God', while yesterday's Christians would have burned at the stake anyone who upheld the God of Einstein, Flew, or George Lucas—not to mention François-Marie Voltaire, Tom Paine, or Thomas Jefferson.

2

Religion Can Do Without God

Religion and belief in God are mutually detachable. If you grow up in an Abrahamic (Christian, Muslim, or Jewish) culture, you will tend to suppose that religion involves God, and that belief in God is one of the most vital aspects of religion. In fact, religions vary considerably on these points. Some religions reject belief in God. Others, while not rejecting it, do not require it. Others do involve some kind of a god or gods, without this being regarded as one of the most important elements in the religion.

The idea that *belief* itself—belief in anything—is the touchstone of religious commitment is itself a peculiarly Christian and Muslim idea. Christianity, in particular, has defined itself by creeds (from the Latin 'credo', 'I believe'), and called its enemies 'infidels' (from the medieval Latin for 'unbeliever'). Many religious communities have placed much more emphasis on rituals and other observances, and have not cared so much about whether members of the community mentally assented to the truth of any particular proposition.

When Maimonides (1135–1204 C.E.) made a list of propositions Jews must agree to if they were to be considered true Jews, this drew objections from some Jews. It seemed very alien to them to compile something almost like a creed in the manner of the Christians. Judaism has still not lost its quality of being (by contrast with Christianity) more a way of life than a list of things a person must believe.

Religions Without God

Here are some religions which do not believe in the God of classical theism:

11

- **Buddhism**. None of the sects of Buddhism accepts the existence of an all-powerful Creator God. Most Buddhists believe in the existence of devas, beings with powers far more exalted than anything human, and having little to do with humans. Like humans, devas may misbehave and be reincarnated as lower life forms. Buddhists have traditionally held that the universe has existed and will exist for ever.

- **Jainism** has about fifteen million members, in several different sects. It's an old religion dating back to ancient India, though most members are now outside India. Jains have always been noted for strict morality, asceticism, and dedication to learning. They explicitly reject the concept of a Creator or controller of the universe. They hold that the universe has existed for infinite time, going through repeated cycles which will continue for ever. Jains will not usually reject the word 'God', but will define it in terms of abstract qualities rather than a conscious agent. Similarly, they appear to worship their tirthankaras (great sages of the past), but will always insist that they do not worship these individuals, only the virtues they embody.

- **Daoism** is a traditional Chinese religion. Its two main scriptures are the *Daodejing* and the *Juangzi*. Daoism is concerned with human life, personal and social. The *Dao* (or 'way') is the natural flow of things. Daoism has no concept of worship and no concept of salvation. Its central tenet is *wu wei* or non-interference: violent, invasive action will produce more problems than it solves.

- **Confucianism** is a system of beliefs in which a very vague reference to 'heaven' plays a small part, nothing like the central part of 'God' in the Abrahamic faiths. Confucians emphasize right conduct, which to Westerners often seems more a matter of etiquette than of morality.

- **'Chinese traditional religion'** refers to beliefs currently held by most Chinese (nearly a fifth of the world's population). It's largely an amalgam of Confucianism, Daoism, and Buddhism, along with some 'folk beliefs' that are not specifically Confucian, Daoist, or Buddhist. What is called 'ancestor worship' is an element in traditional Chinese thinking, but it does not necessarily commit its followers to the theory that the deceased ancestors are still conscious.

- **Falun Gong** is a new religion, with about one hundred million followers, based on the writings of 'Master' Li Hongzhi. It has been banned in China since 1999. Most of the beliefs concern qigong, the traditional breathing exercises associated with Buddhist and Daoist meditation. Li has expressed views about the malign influence of aliens and about distant and finite 'gods', but these views are not paid much attention by rank and file practitioners of Falun Gong, who are mainly concerned with raising their consciousness, improving their health, and behaving morally.

- **Shinto** is the traditional folk-religion of Japan. Most Japanese follow both Buddhism and Shinto to some extent, often merely ceremonial (at weddings and funerals). Even today, more than ninety-five percent of Japanese have no contact with classical theism or anything close to it. Shinto involves recognition of numerous gods—"the eight million gods"—though 'nature spirits' might be a more accurate rendering of the Japanese word 'kami'. As in many forms of non-Abrahamic religion, there are virtually no demands on what an individual personally believes. Shinto has little in the way of a distinctive morality: elaborate traditional Japanese morality comes mainly from Confucianism.

- **Christian atheism** is something that springs up from a hundred different places. The Death of God Theology of the 1960s has been influential, but mainly confined to theologians. The best expression of popular Christian atheism is Don Cupitt's book, *Taking Leave of God*. Christian atheists work within many traditional denominations, though many find themselves most at home in the Unitarian Universalist churches.

- **Unitarian Universalists** have their historical roots in Christianity. Unitarians were Christians (such as Arius, fourth century C.E.) who denied that Christ was God and rejected the Trinity. Universalists (such as Origen, third century C.E.) were Christians who believed that all souls, even Satan himself, would eventually be saved. In the U.S., Unitarians

and Universalists united in 1961. However, they also accepted
into their ranks people who did not believe in God or an afterlife. They no longer define their denomination as specifically
Christian. A recent survey of the labels Unitarian Universalists
choose to apply to themselves (respondents were permitted to
give more than one answer) came up with the following per-
centages: Humanist, 54 percent; Agnostic, 33 percent; Earth-
centered, 31 percent; Atheist, 18 percent; Buddhist, 16.5
percent; Christian, 13.1 percent; Pagan, 13.1 percent.

I mention these examples of non-theistic or doubtfully theistic
religion, not to recommend them—I personally feel not the slightest urge to go to church, sing hymns, or spend time performing
picturesque rituals—but to illustrate that religion need not involve
belief in God.

In his book, *The God Delusion*, Richard Dawkins begins by
using the term 'religious' in a favorable sense, but then settles on
equating religion with belief in God. This is a bit parochial.
Religion in all its diversity is a fascinating arena of human conduct,
and we can't begin to understand it if we keep on relating it to the
peculiar Abrahamic worldview. In this book, I have to focus on
classical theism, but please bear in mind that *theism is not religion*,
and atheism is not essentially opposed to religion.

God and Immortality

Two of the three Abrahamic religions now dominate the world of
organized religion. Christianity still has by far the biggest following of any religion, and Christianity is still growing worldwide.
Fertility rates are falling in every country, but more slowly in the
poorest countries, so Christianity and Islam are increasing their
share of world population. The big story is the rapid conversion of
many millions of people to Pentecostalism—often, but not exclu-
sively, from Catholicism. Both Christianity and Islam are strongest
among the low-income populations of the Third World: both
wither on the vine when exposed to modern capitalism.

In the Abrahamic cultural world, rejection of one component
of the Abrahamic religions tends to go along with rejection of others. For example, the atheist George Orwell had very strong senti-
mental emotions associated with Anglican Christianity, and was

buried, at his own request, in a country churchyard. Orwell considered that belief in God and other Christian tenets was out of the question for any intellectually honest and tolerably well-informed person. He also maintained that the loss of belief in God is necessarily wrenching and traumatic. Surprisingly, then, a close study of Orwell's writings reveals that he never had the slightest affection for God. He reports that when he did believe in God's existence— up to the age of fourteen—he felt contempt for God.[3]

What upset Orwell was that he was going to die. He loved life and therefore would have preferred to live for ever, or at least, for a lot longer than the customary human lifespan. He evidently never considered that these two beliefs are separable—that one can believe in God, but not in an afterlife (as the writers of *Genesis* did) or believe in an afterlife but not in God (as Buddhists do). There's no logical connection between these two beliefs, but they are both components of Christianity and Islam, so many people tend to assume that they go together.

Can You Prove It?

If you get into a discussion about the existence of God, especially with people who are not accustomed to such discussions, you will usually find that the word 'proof' is tossed around freely. Pretty soon, someone starts making assertions about what can or cannot be proved. People will often solemnly tell you that you cannot deny the existence of God until you can disprove it, though the same people would consider it quite loopy to say that you can't deny the existence of leprechauns until you can disprove it.

At one time the English word 'prove' meant what we now mean by 'test'. So, the sentence translated in the *King James Bible* (1611) as "Prove all things" is now best translated as "Test everything" (*1 Thessalonians* 5:21). (This would be excellent advice if we had unlimited time and other resources. Since we have to economize, it should be replaced with something like 'Hold nothing immune from possible testing'.) The meaning of the word 'prove' has gradually shifted so that 'prove' has come to mean 'demonstrate' or 'substantiate'.

In today's English, 'prove' has several distinct meanings. The strictest meaning refers to a proof in mathematics or logic. Given a few premises (assumptions we start from) we can prove such results as Pythagoras's theorem in geometry. This kind of proof is entirely a matter of reasoning, and it can be laid out very clearly, step by step. If you can't find a flaw in the reasoning, you have to accept the result of the proof (that is, you have to accept that the conclusion does follow from the premisses; where you get your premisses is another matter).

In U.S. courts of law, there are two main conceptions of proof, which we saw being appealed to in the O.J. Simpson trials. Simpson was first tried for murder in a criminal court, where the standard of proof of guilt is 'proof beyond any reasonable doubt'. When he had been acquitted, there was a civil trial, which requires a lesser degree of proof: 'proof on the preponderance of the evidence'.

When scientists talk about proof, they may be referring to a purely mathematical and logical exercise, showing that a certain result follows from certain assumptions. Or they may be using the term in a more loose way, where 'prove this theory' means 'find some evidence that tells in favor of this theory'.

Science proceeds by accepting or rejecting hypotheses. A hypothesis is a guess, a stab at the truth, preferably one which has been so precisely formulated that it can be tested by definite observations. The existence of God is a hypothesis, but it is not the kind of hypothesis that can be tested by definite observations. It's difficult to imagine someone looking into a microscope or a telescope and exclaiming: 'Wow! This means there is a God after all!' Discussion of the existence or non-existence of God usually doesn't turn on particular observations; it most often turns on more general considerations of the kind we call 'metaphysical'.

Both theists and atheists often assert that, on some particular point, their opponents have 'the burden of proof'. I think that making any such claim, in this context, is a mistake. 'Burden of proof' is a useful concept in legal trials, where, as a matter of practical administration, we have to let the defendant go or hang him. I can see no place for it in discussion of a factual question like the existence of God.

Three Types of Unbelief

Someone who does not believe in the existence of something—and the something can be leprechauns, kangaroos, global warming, alien abductions, or God—may or may not assert the nonexistence of that something. If the person fails to believe in the existence of something while not believing in its nonexistence, we can call that person an 'agnostic'.

'Agnostic' is a word deliberately invented by T.H. Huxley in 1869 to refer to anyone who, like Huxley himself, had no belief in God but was not prepared to deny God's existence. Prior to that date all 'agnostics' had been recognized as atheists. 'Atheist' comes from two Greek words meaning 'without God' and 'agnostic' comes from two Greek words meaning 'without knowing'. An agnostic, then, is someone who 'does not know' whether there is a God or not.

To the Victorian ear, 'agnostic' sounded a lot less threatening and more respectable than 'atheist'. However, a number of avowed and notorious 'atheists' have been agnostics by Huxley's definition, including the celebrated nineteenth-century atheist Charles Bradlaugh.

Some people classify agnostics as distinct from atheists while other people classify agnostics as atheists. I prefer the latter usage: I use the term 'atheist' to include 'agnostic',[4] although I am not an agnostic and my arguments in this book don't favor agnosticism. Recently some people have started using the term 'nontheist' to cover both those who merely fail to believe in God's existence and those who believe in God's nonexistence. In this book 'atheist' means the same as 'nontheist'.

So there are three types of non-believer in something:

1. The agnostic, who refuses to render a verdict on whether that thing exists.

2. Someone who denies the existence of the thing, but does not believe that the thing's non-existence can be conclusively demonstrated.

3. Someone who denies the existence of the thing and believes that its non-existence can be conclusively demonstrated. (When applied to the God question, this third kind of non-believer is called a 'disproof atheist'.)

Which of these three is the best attitude to take to God? My answer depends on what kind of God is being considered. On the subject of the Abrahamic God, the God of classical theism (omnipotent, omniscient, omnipresent, and so forth), I am a disproof atheist. I think this kind of a God can be demonstrated to be an incoherent notion, an absurdity, that cannot correspond to reality. Several such demonstrations are outlined in Part III of this book.

With respect to a limited God (such as John Stuart Mill considered) or godling (such as the god Thor or a Buddhist deva), I don't think a strict disproof can be offered. I place these entities in the same category as alien abductions, the Loch Ness Monster, and leprechauns. Many attempts have been made to detect them, without success, so it's reasonable to conclude that they don't exist.

I do allow that agnosticism is a reasonable attitude to some questions, especially questions to which someone has given little thought. For example, I'm agnostic on the question of whether there ever was a castle called Camelot—though because I'm temperamentally the sort who makes up his mind, at least provisionally, on disputed issues, if I spent a weekend researching the Camelot question, I guess I would provisionally come down on one side or the other. I do not think that agnosticism is a reasonable attitude to the God hypothesis. The issue just isn't that close.

II

The Arguments for God

General Napoléon Bonaparte liked to encourage evening discussions on set topics among his officers. One night (according to a popular anecdote) the topic was materialism, and the discussion showed that most of his officers disbelieved in any spirit world. After listening for a while, the general pointed up at the stars and said, "That's all very well, gentlemen, but who made those?"

3

Paley's Challenge to Atheism and Darwin's Answer

William Paley's argument goes like this. If you find a watch lying on the ground, you immediately know that it had to have been designed and built by an intelligent person. The watch must have existed in someone's mind before it could exist as a physical object. You can be sure of this because it has many complicated parts, which all fit together to serve the purpose of the watch: to tell the time. The watch is not like a stone, something you might also find lying on the ground, which shows no signs of having been designed and manufactured.

Now, says Paley, if you look at the human eye, you must come to the same conclusion. The eye has a lens, a pupil, and a retina, it can focus, it has lids to protect it and tears to wash it clean. It's obvious and indisputable that the eye is for seeing with, just as a watch is for telling the time with. Therefore, the eye, just like the watch, and unlike the stone, *must* have been designed and built by an Intelligent Designer and Creator.

This is the most popular argument for God's existence. Similar arguments go back to Plato and earlier, but Paley's is the classic statement.

Paley develops this argument in some detail, and answers in advance several objections. He points out that it is no answer to say that a human being with eyes was born and not built. If we found that watches were capable of making new watches to replace themselves, we would be even more impressed by their ingenious construction, and just as convinced that the first watches, the ancestors of all watches, must have been designed.

Although Paley introduces his argument by the example of the watch, which we can see must have the purpose of telling the time, he's quite well aware that in general we do not have to know the purpose of some instrument in order to conclude that it must have been designed. Paley surely knows that if we had always found watches littering the ground and had no knowledge of their man-ufacture—if for example we knew nothing of metal-working or numerals—we would have concluded that watches were natural products, like flowers, or insects, or like the human eye.

The real point of Paley's argument is that complex organization adapted to some end or purpose (such as seeing or telling the time) is proof of design. And the reason for this is that complex organi-zation directed to an end or purpose could not have come about by pure chance. It's just too improbable.

In 1831 a young man named Charles Darwin, a convinced Christian who was planning to become a clergyman, read Paley's book, *Natural Theology*, and was bowled over by it. He admired Paley's argument immensely, was completely convinced by it, and read Paley's book repeatedly until he almost knew it by heart.

Years later, Darwin began to have doubts about Paley, and eventually, in 1858, Darwin was to offer the world the theory that answers Paley, the theory of evolution by natural selection.

Darwinism and Atheism

Most people who have studied biology agree that Darwinism is true. Nowadays most theists accept some kind of evolution but they often hold back from full-blown Darwinism, which maintains that the evolution of life has been a purely spontaneous and undi-rected sequence of events.

Darwinism does not imply atheism. Yet Darwinism is tremen-dously important for atheism because Darwinism refutes what is far and away the most popular argument for theism: Paley's Design Argument. In the absence of Darwinism, Paley's argument would have been quite strong, and would have become steadily stronger since Paley's lifetime, because the complex organization of living things has been found to be even more amazingly elaborate than was suspected at the time Paley wrote.

Who was right, Paley or Darwin? Let's find out.

Paley's Argument Is Narrow and Specific

Paley's argument is about little bits of the universe: animals, plants, or parts of animals and plants. In Chapter 5, we'll look at a different kind of argument, that the universe as a whole, or the laws of nature, must have been designed. Although Paley thinks the laws of nature are instruments of God, he doesn't claim that natural laws alone provide evidence of design. The stone is just as much subject to laws of nature as the watch, and as a Christian Paley thinks they were both designed by God, but he accepts that the stone does not count as *evidence* for design in the way that the watch does.

If we could show that animals and plants could have arisen by spontaneous processes in accordance with the laws of nature, without having been designed, then we would have completely answered Paley's argument.

Paley's argument is powerful—*given one crucial assumption*. Paley's crucial assumption is that there are only two possibilities to consider: design or chance; if something could not have come about by pure chance, then Paley concludes that it must have come about by design.

What if Paley Were Right?

Suppose that Paley's argument were entirely correct. What would follow? It would follow that living things were at least partly designed. We would have to acknowledge some design input into the construction of living things.

But as soon as we accept that, all kinds of fascinating questions pop up and cry out to be answered.

- **When did this design take place? Or is it going on all the time?**

- **Were all the nasty things about the world of living things designed as well as all the nice things? (Presumably so, since these nasty things are often just as complex and well-adjusted to their evident purpose as the nice things.)**

- **How many designers were there and were they all acting according to a common program?**

- Were the designers successful in making actual living things conform to their preconceived models, or were there errors of implementation of the original blueprints?

- What were the goals of the designers—for example, why did they build so much carnage, bloodshed, and pain into the animal kingdom? Or was this a case where 'mistakes were made', and things didn't turn out as the designers had planned? Or were the designers so restricted in their powers that this was the only way they could do it?

- Once a living organism exists according to its prior design, is there something that keeps it from straying from that design over the generations, or can it evolve away from that design?

- Why were so many organisms built which lasted for a comparatively long time and were then completely wiped out? (Was this a colossal series of unanticipated snafus? Or was it intentional? And if so, with what conceivable purpose in mind?)

Paley himself noticed the objection later voiced by John Stuart Mill: if we infer a Designer from the wonderful mechanisms found in nature, then this doesn't point to an *omnipotent* designer. An omnipotent Designer would have no use for wonderful mechanisms, being able to accomplish anything he wants directly. Paley's answer is that the wonderful mechanisms are put there for our benefit, to display to us the existence of the Creator.

Although Paley did attempt to show that the facts of nature imply the God of classical theism, most people who relied on Paley's argument were generally not interested in such questions. They were content that Paley seemed to show there was evidence for the existence of a designer and maker, who might be God. Christianity already had its creation story, and Paley's readers were chiefly interested in supporting this story. But if we're to seriously consider the theory that God created the world and everything in it, we have to consider just how and when he did all this.

Young Earth Creationism

If you read *Genesis* Chapter 1 in a straightforward and perhaps naive fashion, you're likely to conclude that according to *Genesis* the Earth and humankind are both about six thousand years old. Chapter 1 of *Genesis* seems to be saying that God created Heaven and Earth in six days, the sixth day's work including the creation of humankind in the form of Adam and Eve. After this burst of activity, God rested from his exertions on the seventh day.

Genesis goes on to give dates for the lifespans of the three sons of Adam and Eve, their sons and grandsons, and many subsequent descendants. By following up clues of this sort in *Genesis* and *Exodus*, we eventually arrive at historical events which can be dated without much controversy: their dates are pretty much agreed upon by archeologists, historians, and fundamentalist theists. Working backwards from these dates, we can date the six-day creation of the world. Most estimates are not much earlier than 4,000 B.C.E.

The theory that the Earth and all living things were created in one six-day period just a few thousand years ago is known as Young Earth Creationism. Young Earth Creationists maintain (and more or less have to maintain) that all fossils were formed during Noah's Flood, which lasted just over a year. This theory of fossils is called Flood Geology, and is practically equivalent to Young Earth Creationism.

According to *Genesis*, Chapter 1, the Earth was created in a period prior to the six days of creation. Day and night were created on the first day. The Sun, Moon, and stars were created on the fourth day. Thus, day and night were created before the creation of the Sun, which occurred after the creation of the Earth. This contradicts the findings of modern science, which tells a story of stars coming into existence before planets, the Earth's Sun being a star just like billions of other stars.

To anyone who reads the first chapters of *Genesis* attentively, it's surely clear that the authors of these passages were ignorant of a number of elementary facts, accepted today even by Creationists. These authors did not know that the Earth spins and that this causes night and day. They did not even know that day and night are caused by the position of the Sun relative to a given point on the surface of the Earth.[5] They had no idea that the fixed stars are like the Sun, only a lot further away, or that the wandering stars are like the Earth.

But there's worse. Physicists now believe that the stars we can see in the sky are many light years away. Some are millions of light years away. A light year is the distance light travels in a year. Therefore, when we see these stars, we are seeing them as they were millions of years ago. Young Earth Creationists hold that the stars were created only a few thousand years ago. How do they account for this?

One possibility is to deny that the stars are millions of light years away, though I don't know of any Creationists who now deny this. Another is to deny that light always travels at 186,000 miles per second. There are Young Earth Creationists who argue that the speed of light has fallen over time: The speed of light, they say, used to be much faster than it is today. An enormous and recent decline in the speed of light is not indicated by any observations; it is merely invoked in an attempt to square *Genesis* with astronomy.

Other Young Earth Creationists hold that when God created the stars, he created them already fixed up with millions of past years of radiated light. This makes sense, as *Genesis* seems to suggest that the stars were created for the benefit of people on Earth, so there would be no point in putting the stars there if their light would reach Earth only long after humans had become extinct.

And yet it follows that if astronomers today witness an event, such as an exploding star, that appears to have occurred millions of years ago, this observed event is just part of a bogus history of the cosmos. For God to have given the stars radiated light as if they had been there for billions of years, he also had to fake up a deceptive history of the cosmos, as if it were some billions of years old. Fundamentalists deny that there was ever a Big Bang (because this contradicts *Genesis*), but in that case God must have rigged the universe to look as if there had been a Big Bang.

God must have made an impressively thorough job of this fakery. Many more stars can be seen with the aid of telescopes than can be seen with the naked eye, so God must have rigged up this elaborate illusion for the benefit of modern scientists, beginning with Galileo, who have had increasingly powerful telescopes at their disposal. As part of this charade, God also installed the cosmic background radiation: microwave radiation that seems to be an 'echo' of the Big Bang.

Old Earth Creationism: The Gap and Day-Age Theories

A different approach is to accept *Genesis* while also accepting that the Earth is many millions of years old, thus rejecting Young Earth Creationism. There are two standard ways to do this. One is to suppose that there is a Gap, perhaps of many millions of years between Verse 1 and Verse 2:

1. In the beginning God[6] created the Heavens and the Earth.

2. And the Earth was void and without form . . .

Proponents of the Gap theory believe that there was an earlier creation, and even an earlier civilization, destroyed by God when the angel Lucifer rebelled, resulting in an Earth which had become void and without form. Whereas Young Earth Creationists have to claim that humans and dinosaurs lived at the same time, Gap theorists can say that the dinosaurs were destroyed long before Adam and Eve.

Another way is to interpret the 'days' of creation not as literal days, but as much longer periods of time. This is known as the Day-Age theory. People new to these discussions often suppose that Young Earth Creationism is the traditional Christian position, and that the Day-Age theory is a recent compromise. It's not that simple. The idea that the 'days' of creation were really much longer periods of time was entertained by, among others, Augustine in the fourth century C.E. The narrow reading of *Genesis*, giving a Young Earth, and the looser reading, permitting an Old Earth, have both had adherents among Christians from very early on.

For thousands of years people have been finding fossils in the earth, things that look like living organisms. For a long time people disagreed on how these things came to be there. But by the eighteenth century C.E. scholars had become convinced that these were the petrified remains of long-dead living organisms, both plants and animals. Miners and civil engineers as well as scientists also noticed that different fossils were strictly separated according to the various layers of rock. In the oldest rocks, fossils were often unlike anything still alive, whereas in the newest rocks, they were much more like animals and plants that could still be found alive.

And so the science of geology came into being. In the early nineteenth century, the different geological epochs were identified and given the names still in use (triassic, jurassic, and whatnot). These geologists were nearly all Creationists, that is, they accepted the conventional assumption that God had miraculously created the different species of living things. They also believed in Noah's Flood, and tried to fit their knowledge into the theory that Noah's Flood had occurred. But the more they found out about fossils, the more difficult this turned out to be.

Although they were Creationists, these geologists all came to accept that the Earth was vastly older than the six thousand years suggested by a naive reading of *Genesis*, Chapter 1. While, in the mid-nineteenth century, there were still people who read the Bible and believed in a six-thousand-year-old Earth, there was no dramatic confrontation between these people and the geologists, because they all accepted that God had created living things, including humans.

What transformed this situation, and led to the emergence of a militant movement for Young Earth Creationism was the impact of Darwin's *Origin of Species* (1859) and *Descent of Man* (1871). Darwin combined the vast age of the Earth with a picture of living things changing very slowly by a spontaneous, unplanned process, explicable in accordance with ordinary laws of nature. Once life had begun in a simple form (something that Darwin, in *Origin of Species*, still attributed to "the Creator"), it could evolve over millions of years, without any interference from God, into the rich diversity of life as we now know it.

Quite suddenly, toward the end of the nineteenth century, believers in the literal truth of *Genesis* found themselves confronted by an influential ideology which quickly captured all the major seats of learning. This ideology,[7] Darwinism, combined belief in an Old Earth with belief in the non-miraculous emergence of living things by natural processes.[8] An Old Earth was no longer just an alternative form of Creationism, Creation at a more leisurely tempo, but was now an essential component of the rejection of Creationism. For the first time, because of the intellectual triumph of Darwinism, those who wanted to retain belief in God's deliberate creation of separate kinds of living organisms had a strong motive to deny the vast age of the Earth.

In reaction to Darwinism, Young Earth Creationism came into existence. As a self-aware ideology and an organized movement, it is largely a product of the late nineteenth century and especially of the early twentieth century, more particularly of the period after about 1920 (Numbers 1993).

The Gap and Day-Age theories are able to combine an acceptance of *Genesis* with a very old Earth. There are several other ways of trying to effect a reconciliation.[9] One approach would be to reason as follows—and thousands of devout Bible students have reasoned precisely along these lines:

> Not everything in the Bible is meant as a straightforward factual assertion. For instance, the parables of Jesus are obviously meant to convey hidden, symbolic truths, and in the book of *Proverbs*, we sometimes find one proverb followed by a flat-out contradictory proverb. How, then, are we to understand the first chapter of *Genesis*? It can hardly be seriously meant as a historical report of what happened. Why, for instance, is the creation of male and female humans described in 1:27 and then differently in 2:7–22? (Leave aside whether they can be reconciled—why begin the story again?) Remember, *Genesis* was written before quotation marks, section headings, or footnotes were invented, so things like that had to be implied. . . .

You see where this is going. We'll arrive at an interpretation of the early chapters of *Genesis* in which we see them as exhibiting stories about creation, which may be inaccurate as to concrete fact, but which are assembled because they convey edifying or enlightening truths of a broader and deeper nature.

Since *Genesis* clearly indicates that the Earth is six thousand years old, you may be puzzled as to why most Young Earth Creationists say it is ten thousand years old. Where did the extra four thousand years come from? The answer is that *Genesis* equally clearly tells us that the worldwide Flood occurred less than five thousand years ago. Several great civilizations were already old by that time, keeping copious records, and they fail to record any interruption of their normal business. This evidence is so crushing that even most fundamentalists have to find a way to interpret *Genesis* less than literally. They do it by accepting that the post-Flood genealogies (in *Genesis* 11) are telescoped,[10] with many generations not mentioned. (Ah, the slippery slope of compromise!) This enables them to push the Flood back to just before recorded history. It also helps them to reconcile the conflicting genealogies of Jesus given in *Matthew* and *Luke*.

Noah's Flood

Let's suppose that by a broad reading of *Genesis*, that book can be reconciled with the Earth being billions of years old. There's still no way to get round the very clear insistence by *Genesis* that *humans* have been on the Earth for just a few thousand years. Not only that, but all humans with the exception of precisely eight survivors were wiped out in a great Flood.

It's difficult to interpret the account of the Flood as anything other than a purported historical account. Its literal truth is endorsed in the *New Testament* (*Matthew* 24:37–39; *2 Peter* 3:6–7). If we're to set it aside, then almost anything in the *Bible* which looks like a historical report might just as easily be set aside.

According to this account, the Andes and the Himalayas must have been simultaneously under water (unless, as some Creationists say, such high mountains did not exist before the Flood). The Flood must have exterminated all land animals except those who came onto the Ark in pairs. Platypuses and armadillos, tigers and skunks, ostriches and tarantulas, must all be descended from the animals, collected in the 450-foot wooden Ark by Noah, and then kept at sea for over a year.

Housing all those animals and providing for their varied diets, sewage disposal, and need for exercise seems like a major engineering challenge for a level of technology that would build a giant ship entirely of wood. Creationists have gone to amazing lengths to argue that Noah's Ark was practically feasible.[11]

Any theory that there was a local flood in the Near East, wrongly taken by the authors of *Genesis* to be a worldwide Flood, has to concede that the writers of *Genesis* were fallible and not guaranteed against error by God. The *Genesis* account is similar to an earlier Sumerian story, even down to striking details like the appearance of rainbows as the promise that there would be no more worldwide floods. Fundamentalists have to maintain that the Sumerian story was derived from the one which much later became incorporated in *Genesis*.

If Biblical Creationism is correct—in its Young Earth or Old Earth forms—then either we have to accept the Gap theory, or we have to accept that all fossils without exception were created in just one year, the year of Noah's Flood, which means that prior to the Flood, all the living things now preserved as fossils were alive at the same time. The majority of biblical inerrantists reject all scientific techniques for dating rocks. These techniques indicate that Earth is four and a half billion years old and that life is over three billion years old.

Different fossils are found in different rocks of different ages. For example (to take just one of many thousands of such examples) you never find fossilized horses or elephants in the same rocks as fossilized dinosaurs, but always in higher-level rocks. Creationists have come up with three explanations for this remarkable fact (Whitcomb and Morris, pp. 271–76).

First, when all the animals fled from the Floodwaters in the time of Noah, some would be drowned before others because they couldn't run so fast. It's difficult to see why every single dinosaur would be drowned before every single elephant. Some dinosaurs could run faster than elephants, and even among very fleet-footed animals, some individuals might be having an accident-prone day. Aside from that, what's true of fossilized animals is true of fossilized plants. According to the evidence of the rocks, non-flowering plants existed for a very long time before flowers appeared. In rocks dated earlier than 130 million years ago, not only do we never find elephants, rabbits, or birds, but we never find flowering plants. This cannot be because flowering plants could gallop away from the Floodwaters faster than non-flowering plants.

Second, Creationists appeal to hydraulic sorting, the action of the Floodwaters in burying smaller objects deeper than more massive ones. Again, why would this be so very precise? And again, how does it account for plant fossils? (You might think that plants would float to the surface and there form a fermenting mush, and so would not be fossilized at all.) Furthermore, there are animals of similar sizes—but very different characteristics in other respects—in many different layers of rocks.

Third, Creationists argue that some particular habitats would be flooded before others. The lowest rock layers have only marine animals, which Creationists (rather oddly) say would have been killed and deposited first by the Flood. But why only invertebrate marine animals? And why, above that, vertebrate and invertebrate marine animals, but no sea turtles, with sea turtles appearing only at higher levels still?

There are numerous other problems with the Flood story. For instance, in order to make enough room on the Ark, Creationists say that aquatic animals did not have to be taken on board (though aquatic animal fossils are differentiated into precise strata just like land-dwelling animals). But if the Floodwaters were salty, the freshwater animals would have perished, or if they were fresh, the saltwater animals would have perished. Or again, what did the carnivorous animals eat, the day, week, or month after they left the ark when the Flood was over? In cases like these, Creationists have to resort to miraculous intervention by God. But then, why have an Ark at all, and why go to such lengths to show that it was a feasible engineering project?

Darwin's Theory of Natural Selection

The theory now accepted by biologists as the correct explanation of the evolution of living things was thought of by Charles Darwin in 1838 and independently by Alfred Russel Wallace in 1858.[12] It was made public by both of them jointly in 1858, and expounded at length in Darwin's book, *Origin of Species*, published in 1859. *Origin of Species* is still a tremendously exciting book that everyone should read.[13] *Darwin's Ghost* by Steve Jones is a restatement of *Origin of Species* drawing upon much evidence that has accumulated since Darwin. It is, to the present-day reader, even more riveting than *Origin of Species*, and makes a marvelous introduction to Darwin's great work.

The idea of evolution had been discussed since ancient times. The idea of natural selection was known prior to Darwin, but was used mainly to explain why species remained the same.[14] We can see that abnormal or deformed individuals leave fewer offspring than individuals typical of the population. Nature culls the freaks, and tends to prevent departures from the norm.

Biologists still accept this role for natural selection. Over a short time period of a few thousand years, the main effect of natural selection is to prevent random (and mostly deleterious) departures from the norm. What Darwin saw was that, given longer time periods, natural selection would bring about very slow, very gradual changes in the norm for any given breeding population. The same mechanism, natural selection, eliminates the freaks in the short term and brings about, in the long term, a very gradual change in what constitutes the norm and what constitutes a freak.

How does natural selection answer Paley's argument? Paley says that the human eye is constructed for the purpose of enabling its owner to see things. We can leave aside the precise meaning of 'serving a purpose'. Paley's point is that the eye is so organized and constituted as to enable its owner to see, and we cannot begin to explain the existence of the eye without understanding that it is 'for seeing with'. And the way in which the eye is structured for the purpose of 'seeing with' is so elaborate and complex that it could not possibly have come into existence by chance.

All this is entirely correct. Where Paley went wrong was in supposing that the only alternative to chance is deliberate design. Darwin's theory offers an explanation which is neither chance nor design: natural selection.

The world is full of orderly phenomena which are caused by neither chance nor design. For instance, on any pebbly beach, we can see that the bigger pebbles are further away from the water, the smaller pebbles closest to the water. This is not due to chance, which would distribute all the pebbles randomly according to size. But equally obviously, it is not due to design. No intelligent being is consciously moving the large pebbles inland and the smaller ones towards the water. Order can appear spontaneously, by the blind operation of natural forces.

It's much harder to explain the production of living things by natural forces. For something like an eye to emerge, two conditions are needed which are lacking in the example of the pebbly beach. First, there must be the possibility of building on past results, of accumulating changes in a particular direction. This condition is met by the mechanism of heredity. DNA copies itself, with only rare errors. The other condition is vast periods of time in which this accumulation of change can proceed. This condition is met by the immense period of time elapsed since life began on Earth: about three and a half billion years.

Given hundreds of millions of years, it is possible to imagine that an animal might have a patch of skin slightly sensitive to light-and-heat, and the animal might also have a tendency to move towards the source of light-and-heat. If this increased the chances of that animal having offspring, then individual animals with more of that ability would leave more offspring. Once there was an animal whose behavior was linked with its responsiveness to light coming from a particular direction, it would be advantageous for this responsiveness to become steadily more accurate. Those animals with a more accurate awareness of the source of light would leave more offspring than those animals with a less accurate awareness of light.

Do you think this theory is convincing? Let's look at the reasons people have for rejecting it.

4

The Objections to Darwinism

The standard objections to Darwinism have not changed since 1859. Biologists accept Darwinism because, having become acquainted with a lot of relevant evidence, they think these objections can be answered. Still, the biologists could be wrong; we should take nothing for granted. I will now deal quickly with all the objections to Darwinism you are likely to encounter.

Objection #1:
There Hasn't Been Sufficient Time

Darwin's theory requires many millions of years. Is the Earth that old? By 1800 all geologists, though they were Creationists, accepted that the Earth was many millions of years old. This conclusion was forced upon them by the evidence of the rocks. To mention just one factor, it became clear that in some locations, there had been enormous changes, such as long periods with a totally different climate.

But there was a huge problem. Physicists said that the Earth just could not be older than twenty or thirty million years. In any greater period of time, the Sun would burn out and the Earth would freeze. There was no known type of combustion that could keep burning for a hundred million years, and the idea of any such unknown type of combustion would have been considered utterly fantastic. Early critics could truthfully declare that both Darwin's theory and geology contradicted elementary physics, and stood condemned by 'established scientific fact'.

Then, in 1895, Wilhelm Roentgen made an x-ray photograph
of the bones in his wife's hand. Physics soon woke up to the existence of nuclear radiation and nuclear energy. It became clear that
there was indeed a type of combustion that could keep a star like
the Sun burning for many millions, or even billions, of years—
nuclear fusion. Geology was saved and Darwinism was saved. Or,
looking at it another way, physics was saved.

Objection #2:
We Don't See Evolution Occurring Today

Perhaps the most common objection among people who have
never opened a book on evolutionary biology is that 'we don't see
evolution going on today'. The Darwinist will reply that we do
indeed witness evolution going on today. An example would be a
strain of bacteria which acquires immunity to an antibiotic, or rats
who acquire immunity to a particular type of rat poison. There are
numerous examples of this kind of thing.

The skeptic about Darwinism will say that this isn't at all what
he was getting at. What he means is that we don't see apes turning
into men, we don't see fish turning into land animals, we don't see
animals which have never flown taking to the air.

The simple answer to this is that such transformations take
place gradually over millions of years. Darwinism tells us that we
must not expect to witness any such major transformations, from
start to finish, because we're just looking at a few decades, or if we
consult historical records, a few thousand years.

Objection #3:
We Don't See Half-Evolved Features of
Living Organisms

A related argument is that we don't observe any half-evolved features. Scott Adams makes this objection to evolution in *God's
Debris*: he says evolution must be wrong because we don't see any
partly evolved aspects of animals.[15]

This, however, misunderstands evolution. There never were any
half-evolved features and there never will be. If we were transported back in time to the Earth thirty million years ago, and our

memories of modern living organisms erased, what we would see would not look 'half-evolved'. Everything would look just as complete and finished as things do today, though *different*.

The paleomastodon, ancestor of the elephant, had a long nose but nothing as spectacular as an elephant's trunk. The paleomastodon would look quite 'finished', and if we were then shown a picture of an elephant, with its amazingly long and versatile trunk, and told that this was where the paleomastodon was headed, we would probably feel that such a preposterous beast as this 'elephant' was a bizarre product of opium-induced fantasy.

But, some objectors will say, if we have eyes, there must have been a time when our ancestors had half-eyes. Why don't we ever see anything like that? First, the eye does not have to be reinvented for every kind of animal. Humans inherit the basic model of the eye from our ape ancestors. All mammals inherit the eye from reptiles, and all reptiles inherit the eye from fish.

Second, there are many living organisms still around today that do indeed have 'half-eyes', or even 'one-tenth eyes', that's to say, they have eyes that are a lot more primitive than ours, for example lacking a lens and lacking eyelids (and having only a single eye, rather than two working together). Are these evolving more advanced eyes? Quite possibly some of them are, but we can't say for sure.

Objection #4:
Dogs Don't Turn into Cats

A standard feature of Creationist thinking is that the 'kinds' of living things are fixed. Dogs don't become cats and giraffes don't turn into elephants.

This sounds very straightforward, but it's actually a bit tricky for the Creationists. Creationists cannot deny that some modification of a living population is possible. Creationists will usually accept that basset hounds, beagles, and dandy dinmonts have all been bred from the same original stock of wolves domesticated by humans thousands of years ago. Among many marvels of selective breeding in agriculture, we now have seedless fruits (propagated by humans, who take cuttings of the trees) and cows with such an immense capacity to produce milk that they would soon get sick and die if humans were not there to milk them regularly. So we know that there is nothing keeping a population of living things exactly the same: it can change over the generations.

If all humans today are the descendants of eight individuals who boarded Noah's Ark somewhere between four thousand and nine thousand years ago, then there must have been quite rapid transformations to produce all the modern races of humankind. The barrel-shaped body of the Eskimo, the lithe physique of the Nilotic tribes, the tiny stature of the pygmies, the abundant body hair of the Caucasian—such physical differences are minor compared with the overall similarity of humans by contrast with other species, yet they are remarkably divergent if we are to suppose that they all evolved from eight people within the last four to nine thousand years. And to make room for all kinds of animal on Noah's Ark, 'kinds' of animal has to be defined very broadly. All the hundreds of thousands of land-dwelling animal species must have evolved from a comparatively few 'kinds' within a few thousand years.

Creationists find themselves compelled by the logic of their own Biblical argument to accept that a whole lot of very rapid evolution has occurred. But they also have to claim that there are limits to this process. While a wolf can be turned into a poodle, and a single human family can quickly evolve all the present-day human races, there is some barrier that prevents a wolf or a poodle from being turned into a cat, or an ape into a man, or a fish into a reptile.

Until about 150 years ago, the basic mechanism of heredity had not been discovered, and the precise chemical mechanism was not discovered until around fifty years ago. We now know that there is no barrier keeping evolutionary change within any specific limits. A gene is a gene is a gene. A rat, a limpet, a pineapple, and an *Escherichia coli* bacterium have exactly the same basic method of reproduction. It's purely a matter of chemistry, and nothing has been discovered—no 'barrier' exists—which would prevent any one of these from being gradually transformed into any other, given immense periods of time.

The mere fact that all organisms share the same hereditary mechanism is itself a startling and brilliant corroboration of Darwinism. If God had separately created various kinds of living organisms, he need not have given plants, animals, and bacteria the same reproductive mechanism. Furthermore, by looking at the

DNA of various animals and plants, we can see how closely related they are—and this information meshes well with the evidence from fossils.

Objection #5:
New Forms Would Be Swamped

A more subtle and difficult objection to Darwinism is to ask how segments of a single population could diverge at all. If the elephant and the hippopotamus have a common ancestor (as they do), how could that population of common ancestors have split into two populations, one proto-elephant, the other proto-hippopotamus? Surely, as they started to evolve distinctive differences, these differences would promptly be diluted away by interbreeding.

The quick answer is: geographical separation. If two parts of a single population are somehow prevented from interbreeding, they may evolve in different directions. The most obvious candidate for such a prevention of interbreeding is geographical separation. Two populations become separated geographically. Later, the descendants of these two populations may meet again. But possibly, in the interim, they will have become sufficiently different that they no longer readily interbreed. Now that they are again occupying the same territory, but not interbreeding, this actually accentuates the pressure for them to become more dissimilar, for each to specialize in a mode of life that the other population is less favored at.

Biologists now believe that the divergence of one population into two separate species can sometimes occur without geographical separation. But geographical separation is a process, easy to grasp, which sufficiently answers the objection that no such divergence would be possible.

Objection #6:
Apes Are Still Here

Larry King has stated on his TV show that evolution is doubtful because we still have monkeys around today. The implication is that if some monkeys—actually apes[16]—evolved into humans, then all apes should have done so. What's holding them back?

Darwinism certainly tells us that present-day apes could evolve into humans, or could be artificially bred into humans. If we were to take a population of apes, sterilize the ones with the least human-like characteristics and multiply the offspring of those with more human-like characteristics, we could eventually turn them into humans. It would probably take us many thousands of years, but if Darwinism is correct, we could do it—even despite the fact that no modern ape is the same as the population of apes from which humans evolved. This doesn't mean, though, that surviving populations of wild apes today have the slightest tendency to become more human.

Larry King was probably assuming that the theory of evolution presupposes some inbuilt tendency for advancement or progress, and that therefore there is something in apes that tends to make them more human. There is nothing in evolution that automatically makes a population 'better' or 'more advanced', though this is not ruled out, either. The great majority of individual living organisms today are bacteria, and no doubt in the distant future, bacteria will survive long after all mammals have become extinct. The great majority of species (as opposed to individual members of species) are insects. By any crude measure, bacteria and insects are immensely more 'successful' than humans will ever be, and this is no surprise to a Darwinist.

If you could go back in a time machine a few million years and look at the Australopithecines like 'Lucy', comparing them with apes, you would not be struck by any dramatic sign that the Australopithecines were on a fast track to greatness. The Australopithecines were walking upright, but their brains were small, and they were no more intelligent than apes. Australopithecines and apes had diverged, they were different, but one was not 'superior' to the other. Very likely at that time there were far more chimpanzee-like animals than Australopithecines, so by that crude measure of 'success', our ancestors weren't terribly successful.

Objection #7:
There Are Gaps in the Fossil Record

Fossils found since Darwin's time strongly bear out what Darwin claimed. Many fossils of animals intermediate between apes and humans have been found, as well as animals intermediate between reptiles and birds, and between fish and land vertebrates.

Darwin's theory that humans are descended from apes gave rise to the cliché expression, 'the missing link', an animal midway between an ape and a human. This expression has fallen out of use, because paleontologists, digging in East Africa and elsewhere, have found several different kinds of 'missing link'. There's continuing debate about precisely which of these animals, if any, is the direct ancestor of humans, but there's no question (among those acquainted with these old bones) that, from six to two million years ago, populations of animals existed which were physically intermediate between apes and humans.

Although there are some examples of living things that have barely changed in many millions of years, still, many of today's living things did not exist sixty million years ago, and many of the living things of sixty million years ago have died out. The fossil record, for example, completely bears out the Darwinian theory that all land vertebrates (animals with backbones) are descended from fish, and that mammals and birds are both descended from reptiles. In other words, we find fish in early strata where there are no land vertebrates. Then later we find land vertebrates as well as fish. In rocks of just the right age, we find animals transitional between fish and land vertebrates. And we find reptiles and amphibians before we find mammals or birds. Later we find both mammals and birds, alongside reptiles and amphibians.

If we were to find fossils of animals with backbones living on land, older than the earliest fossils of fish, or if we were to find mammals and birds in strata earlier than reptiles, or if we were to find whales in strata earlier than land mammals, these would be major shocks to biological theory. They would probably not lead to the abandonment of evolution itself, but would upset some very well-established views about the specific course evolution has taken. If fossils of living things were found randomly in all ages of rocks, with rabbits, birds, and flowering plants in the earliest strata, evolution itself would have to be abandoned as an account of how the different kinds of living organisms came into existence.

Creationists often say that there are gaps in the fossil record, and that therefore the fossil record does not bear out the Darwinian theory that all adaptations arose very gradually. Creationists very frequently go further, and make outrageously false claims. In just a few seconds I found these statements on Creationist websites: "not a single transitional form has been uncovered" and "The gaps in the fossil record are today actually worse than in Darwin's time."

Hundreds of transitional forms have been discovered, just as Darwin predicted, including animals intermediate between apes and modern humans, fish and amphibians, reptiles and mammals, reptiles and birds, and land animals and whales. And these fossils are *always* in the appropriate layer of rock.

But when the false claims of Creationists have been disposed of, there's a residue of truth in these allegations about 'gaps'. Only a handful out of many millions of living organisms are fossilized. To be fossilized, and for the fossils to remain intact through subsequent disturbances, and to be in a place likely to be found by paleontologists, is a freakish accident. For example, less than a dozen specimens of *Archeopteryx* (an animal intermediate between reptiles and birds) have been found, and only two of these are complete. Yet various species of *Archeopteryx* must have lived over at least hundreds of thousands, and more likely millions, of years. Some living organisms are known by only one fossil specimen, and we can be sure that millions of species have left no fossils that have been found or ever will be found.

Critics of Darwinism often point out that, although we do see, with many types of animals and plants, a gradual change of forms in the geological record, this gradual change is jerky, not smooth. What we often see is a succession of similar forms, each one slightly different to its predecessor, but still, if looked at in close detail, decidedly different. But this is what we might expect to see, for a couple of reasons.

First is the rarity of fossilization and fossil preservation just mentioned. The other reason is that rapid evolution is most likely to occur in fairly small populations. If one of these small populations (probably a geographically isolated variety of a much bigger population) hits upon some very successful innovation so that this population expands to compete with its more numerous relatives, it is exceptionally unlikely that the original location of that small population will have left any fossils. What will appear in the fossil record, if we're lucky, is one or two specimens of that expanding smaller population as it invades a larger territory.

Because of the rarity of fossilization and the vastness of geological time, what occurs in just a few thousand years is invisible. To a paleontologist, fifty thousand years is like a single instant, and yet distinct though slight differences in anatomy can easily appear in fifty thousand years.

Can the jerkiness of the fossil record be explained by everything I have just said? Biologists are not all agreed on this. Some theorists of evolution believe that the usual scenario is for populations to stay roughly the same for very long periods. Dramatic evolution, involving major anatomical changes, takes place in rapid spurts—though remember that 'rapid' means anything from fifty thousand to a few hundred thousand years.

If someone objects to Darwinism because there is no smooth transition in the fossil record we can ask this person what they think is going on. (To test any theory, we compare it with a rival theory.) Either there is some natural force in evolution that makes populations take a little jump every now and then, or some Intelligent Designer is intervening by giving these populations a little push in 'the right' direction—thought 'the right direction' is one which will soon be terminated by extinction. Working out a good theory for either of these, the one without God or the one with God, seems like a daunting task, and the people who object to Darwinism don't seem at all interested in taking up this task.

By the way, paleontologists are expert at reconstructing an entire animal from one or a few bones. A paleontologist may be able to infer from one leg bone or jawbone what an entire skeleton most probably looked like. Some pictures in books on evolution are the results of such reconstructions. Paleontologists have sometimes drawn pictures of what certain animals would have looked like when alive, based on a large amount of deduction from very few bones, combined with some guesswork. In some cases, such pictures have had to be drastically revised, when the later discovery of a more complete skeleton has refuted the assumptions made by the paleontologist-artist who drew those pictures.

Creationists have gotten wind of the fact that such imaginative reconstruction sometimes goes on, and they often mention this in their arguments for Creationism. They claim that many of the pictures of extinct life forms found in biology textbooks are made up and therefore 'fraudulent'.

So it's worth mentioning that, with some of these intermediate forms there are several whole specimens of complete fossilized skeletons. This is true of *Archeopteryx* and it's true of *Tiktaalik*.

These animals are not imaginative reconstructions by paleontologists, but animals whose entire skeletons have been excellently preserved in several different specimens. These critters really did live and breathe, and they certainly are intermediate 'links' between broad 'kinds' of living things.

Objection #8:
Irreducible Complexity Cannot Arise by Gradual Stages

Intelligent Design (ID) became a watchword and—in non-fundamentalist circles—a scareword, in the early 1990s. I'm looking at arguments for and against the existence of God, so I'm strictly concerned with ID only to the extent that it yields an argument for the God hypothesis.

ID proponents themselves insist that there's no talk about God in the theory of ID. They contend that the best scientific explanation for some features of living things is that these were 'intelligently designed'. At that point, Intelligent Design says no more: if someone wants to take the conclusions of ID further and argue for a God, they are stepping beyond ID theory itself. If living things have been designed, we may still debate whether the designer or designers has to amount to God, but at least Darwinism would be false.

Once we strip ID of its political and religious associations, ID is nothing more nor less than one of the old standard objections to Darwinism, dating back to 1859. The objection is as follows:

> There are some adaptations in living things which could not possibly have come about by natural selection, because all the parts would have to be in place before any of them could be advantageous to the organism.

ID advocates call such a state of affairs "Irreducible Complexity." Just suppose, for example, that some essential organ of a living thing consists of five parts, and removal of any one of those parts would cause that organ to cease to function, and the organism to die. Since all five parts are indispensable to the operation of that organ, no one of them could evolve until the other four were in place. In that case, then, the organ could not have

Sidebar: It Doesn't Matter Much Whether Creationism Is Science

Creationists like to say that they are scientific, and Darwinists dispute this. But from the point of view of the factual issues (rather than the politics of public education), it doesn't matter much whether Creationism is science or not.

In one sense, that of science as a social institution, Creationism is not science: if you look at Creationist publications you don't find reports of Creationist research generating new knowledge about living things, or even proposals for any such research. Creationist writers display little interest in extending our knowledge of the world of living organisms. All you find in Creationist publications are criticisms of evolution. The detailed evidence is taken entirely from the work of evolutionists.

However, I don't see scientists as a new priesthood, to be protected from criticism by non-scientists. Science as an actual institution can go off the rails, as Soviet biology did in the Lysenko affair or as several branches of science did under National Socialism. People who criticize the current conclusions in a branch of science are perfectly entitled to do so, and the fact that they do so from outside that branch of science is no guarantee that they are wrong. Nor does the fact that they do so from religious motives discredit them. One's motives are immaterial to the strength of one's arguments, and religiously motivated people have often made outstanding contributions to human knowledge (as when Kepler identified the elliptical orbits of planets, Maxwell discovered magnetic fields, or Lemaître proposed the Big Bang). Science is never sharply separated from the broader culture, and science has always taken some of its hypotheses from outside the institutional arena of science.

We humans find ourselves engaged, willy-nilly, in the vast intergenerational project of discovering truths about the universe and our place in it. This project always takes the form of disputes or debates. The first rule of this project is that no opinions or conjectures are to be ruled out of court or excluded from the general public debate (though, as a matter of economizing on time and other resources, they may reasonably be excluded, provisionally and subject to review, from specialized professional journals or scholarly venues).

The best response to Creationism is not to label it pejoratively or exclude it from discussion, but to argue against it by explaining the evidence that leads biologists to accept the truth of Darwinism.

evolved at all, because the appearance of that organ would require all five parts to be gradually evolving for a long period before the organ could work. If each of the five parts depends for its effectiveness on the existence of the other four parts, then it's impossible for those five parts to have evolved gradually. It's essential to Darwinism that evolution cannot look ahead and generate some change because there will be a pay-off later.

This argument doesn't work. Just because removal of any one of the five parts would *now* be fatal doesn't show that this was the case in the past, in the ancestry of that organism. It could be that the contribution of Part #5, for instance, was made in the past by a different part, call it Part #5a. Then Part #5 evolved, in association with Part #5a. Then Part #5a disappeared, leaving only Part #5. And in its turn Part #5a could have originally evolved to serve another function before it became a part of the organ in question. So at least one of Parts #1 through #4 could have evolved before Part #5 appeared. And what holds for Part #5 holds for each of the other four parts.

This had been pointed out by Darwinists before the emergence of the ID movement. For example, in his classic popular discussion of the origin of life, *Seven Clues to the Origin of Life*, first published in 1985, A.G. Cairns-Smith discusses what he calls "essential complexity," precisely the same concept as ID's later "irreducible complexity." He gives the example of stones arranged to form an arch. It's difficult to see how stones could become arranged like that by incremental trial and error, because the whole arch won't hold up unless all the stones play their part. However, Cairns-Smith points out that it becomes easy to imagine such an outcome if we suppose that the stones forming the arch was first supported by other stones, which later disappeared.[17] When we look at a product of evolution, we may be seeing something which originally had a scaffolding, even though the scaffolding has long gone. (The scaffolding was not in place *because* it was a scaffolding. It just happened to act as a scaffolding.)

To address just such a possibility, Behe (the leading proponent of ID) concedes that it would not be impossible for irreducible complexity to evolve "by an indirect circuitous route. However, as the complexity of an interacting system increases, the likelihood of such an indirect route drops precipitously" (Behe 2001, p. 94). This last assertion is surely false. One aspect which would make the "indirect circuitous route" more likely would be if organisms rely upon several different methods to achieve the same outcome, and perhaps such an aspect is more likely with the most highly complex systems. Living things do often achieve the same functions in several different ways simultaneously: something called redundancy. It's like wearing both suspenders and a belt—on pants that already have elastic sewn in the waist.

Irreducible Complexity Is Not Paley's Argument

Although it's often stated that the Irreducible Complexity Argument is similar to Paley's Design Argument, they are actually quite distinct. Some people may advance both arguments, or may even slip without noticing from one to the other, but they are different. Paley's argument is that adaptations are too complex to have come about by chance. The ID argument is that *some* adaptations possess a special kind of complexity that could not have come about *gradually*. Notice that, following the logic of the ID argument, even an Intelligent Designer could not have brought about these adaptations *by the accumulation of minute alterations*, but only by an instantaneous 'back to the drawing-board' redesign (unless the minute alterations were accompanied by miraculous protection from competition, so that initially useless organs could develop).

Although ID supporters are reticent about this, and many in the lower ranks might repudiate it, the position taken by the intellectual leaders of ID (Behe and Dembski) implies that the vast majority of adaptations could have come about by Darwinian natural selection, and only a small minority require the intervention of a Designer. Behe, the movement's most distinguished author, has said that he sees no reason to repudiate the descent of all living things from a single ancestor. Biblical Creationists have noticed this aspect of the ID movement and now regularly criticize it.

Paley died over fifty years before Darwin's *Origin of Species* appeared. Paley could not comment on Darwin's theory and although Paley's argument is directed against pre-Darwinian theories of evolution, he never gets into the nuts and bolts of how evolution might occur. Because Paley wasn't looking at Darwinism, he sees no great difference between a complex adaptation coming into being instantaneously and doing so by gradual stages: both appear to him equally unlikely. But the Irreducible Complexity Argument tries to show that some aspects of living things could not have come about by gradual stages. It is specifically a response to Darwinism.

Closer to Paley's argument is the argument from Specified Complexity advanced by ID theorist William Dembski. Dembski's argument is based on the sheer improbability of certain combinations coming about by chance, so it assumes that Behe's argument from Irreducible Complexity is correct—that these combinations could not have emerged by natural selection.

Getting Here from There

Irreducible Complexity says that some adaptations exist for which there is no possible evolutionary route. 'You can't get here from there'. The whole question of whether you can get here from there has constantly preoccupied theorists of evolution.

If we start to wonder whether we could have gotten here from there by gradual evolution, three possibilities may occur to us:

1. **It's just impossible to get here from there.**

2. **It's puzzling to see how we could have gotten here from there.**

3. **We don't know the precise route by which we got here from there.**

The ID movement has tended to announce what seems like #1, then slide to #2 or #3. There are many, many examples of #3 and quite a lot of examples of #2, but no demonstrated examples of #1.

The wings of an eagle are complex and superbly adapted to the eagle's hunting habits. But there's no suspicion of Irreducible Complexity in this case. There's really no problem for us to conceive of wings developing from front legs, by gradual stages over immense periods of time. We know that there are some animals that cannot fly, but can glide to a greater or lesser extent. An animal that climbs high trees might have its life saved by even a very slight tendency to glide with the aid of its feet, and we do know of many animals with varying degrees of partial flying or gliding ability. So the wing doesn't have to be complete before it can help a particular type of animal. There's no part of a wing that's indispensable to the process of flight. And once a wing has developed, there's no problem about its developing into a highly specialized wing for a swooping predator.

An eagle's wings might have been cited by Paley (though they weren't). An eagle's wings are more complex than a watch and they are obviously 'for flying and hunting with'. But an eagle's wings would never be cited as proof of design by an ID proponent, or by anyone after Darwin, because they clearly lack Irreducible Complexity. Similarly, there's no Irreducible Complexity in Paley's famous example, the human eye. The eye is not made up of components each of which just had to be in place before any of the others could work.

There are examples where a quick glance evokes puzzlement. Some fish are able to deliver a powerful electric shock, which they employ as a weapon, either to stun their prey or as a defense against predators. It doesn't look as if there is any way this weapon could possibly have developed gradually. A lot of complex apparatus has to be in place before an animal can deliver a powerful electric shock to its enemies, and, it seems, a very *mild* electric shock would be useless. This example might have been cited by Creationists (though I have not come across any such use of it).

However, there's an easy solution to this one. Many fish use very weak electric currents as means of communication and others use them as a way of sensing features of their environment. There is no problem therefore about understanding how organs could develop to fulfill these functions, and then evolve to make the electric current somewhat stronger. It might then occur that an electric current used for communication or sensing could have the incidental effect of stunning or deterring another animal, and natural selection could take it from there.

Some kinds of bacteria have tails with which they can swim. These tails or 'flagella' have quite a complex structure. When ID began, this was Exhibit A in the case against Darwinism. Thirty proteins are involved in the creation of the flagellum and, the ID people argued, all thirty had to be in place before the flagellum could work.

No sooner was this claim made than it was refuted. It was discovered that ten of these thirty proteins were responsible for forming the secretory organ of some bacteria. So it's not true that all thirty proteins had to be in place before any of them could be.[18]

What ID proponents wish would happen, and sometimes erroneously imply has happened, just could imaginably happen. Scientists looking at the evolution of complex systems might begin to be baffled by inexplicable examples of Irreducible Complexity, and might begin to consider the hypothesis of intervention by a Designer.

Some people have claimed that science cannot consider this possibility, but ID proponents have quite correctly pointed out that this is mistaken. Science does not exclude considerations of possible design. For example, SETI, the program looking for evidence of intelligent life elsewhere in the cosmos, analyzes signals to determine whether any of them signify intelligent life. SETI is trying to determine whether any signals show evidence of design. Hypothetically, it's entirely possible that, for instance, metal objects might be found floating in space or resting on the ocean floor, and scientists would be called upon to decide whether these were natural formations or intelligently designed products of a sentient civilization.

What's wrong with ID is not that science rules out in advance the possibility of an Intelligent Designer—science does no such thing—but that the evidence so far is against any such possibility.

The Designer's Limitations

If we accept Intelligent Design theory, we accept the existence of an Intelligent Designer, or several intelligent designers, intervening on many thousands, or millions, of separate occasions, to help along the process of evolution. But this is where Charles Darwin came in.

Years before Darwin developed the notion of natural selection as a force capable of generating exquisitely complex adaptations, he was struck by the fact that, given the results of geological dating, Creationism required a Creator who intervened piecemeal and repeatedly, over many millions of years, with no indication of any overall plan, and creating many organisms only to see them become extinct. At first a Creationist, Darwin considered this kind of repeated and undirected intervention so dubious that a purely natural explanation began to seem more appealing to him, and this eventually led him to consider natural selection.

Intelligent Design theory makes no attempt to analyze the character of the Designer from the data of the Designer's performance. It is merely concerned with accumulating examples suggesting that there is a Designer, and that Darwinism can be rejected—and there the theory of Intelligent Design stops.

There are many cases where we don't know the path evolution actually might have taken. It's always possible to point to some adaptation, assert that it could not possibly have come about by accumulated gradual adjustments, and reiterate this assertion for as long as biologists have not come up with any specific evolutionary pathway.

However, this is to look at only half the evidence relevant to the design hypothesis. We also have to consider those many aspects of living organisms which appear, from a design point of view, to be botched and incompetent. If the Designer is so Intelligent, how come he keeps screwing up?

Examples of outrageously bad 'design' can usually be explained by the path evolution has taken. There really are cases where 'you can't get here from there', or at least it's too improbable. Since natural selection cannot look ahead and try a radically different approach to solving a particular problem, but always has to move by slow increments from something which has worked in the recent past, there will sometimes be cases where the outcome is just hopelessly inefficient.

There are innumerable such examples. One is the fact that human babies naturally have to be born through the bone-enclosed pelvic opening. Untold billions of babies and their mothers have died in childbirth because of this elementary 'design flaw', which arose because humans are descended from animals that scampered on all fours. In many cases today, the birth opening which idiot nature failed to hit upon is provided by a surgeon, in a caesarian section. This saves the lives of millions, and in many more cases reduces brain damage to the infant or hours of discomfort to the mother. Any intelligent designer planning the human body from scratch would have installed a birth opening in the lower abdomen, where there is no tight constriction by bones. But natural selection could not accomplish this clear and obvious improvement, because there was no way to get 'there from here' by minute adjustments.

The human body is an exhibition of engineering disasters.[19] The routing of the optic nerve through the front of the retina, so that there is a 'blind spot' in each eye, and the routing of the male testis around the ureter, when it would be so much simpler and more efficient to take a direct route, are other instances.[20] These sorry failings do not contradict the proposition that many features of the human body display marvelous construction, sometimes far exceeding what could have been accomplished by human ingenuity. The two aspects exist side by side: dazzling sophistication and crude sloppiness. ID theory has no explanation to offer for the latter. Darwinism tells us to expect both. A striking example occurring in all mammals is the routing of the recurrent laryngeal nerve, which instead of going directly from the brain to the larynx, makes a completely pointless detour to loop around a lung ligament. In the giraffe, whose neck lengthened in the course of evolution, this nerve is twenty feet long, instead of the required one foot.

Why can't evolution itself take care of these problems? Why can't evolution create a new birth canal in humans, reroute the optic nerve into the back of the retina, or shorten the routes of the male ureter and the recurrent laryngeal nerve in the giraffe's neck? The answer is that once a highly complex 'basic plan' for an animal's body is in place, there are some improvements that cannot be accomplished by slight changes, but only by a radical redesign. There are indeed cases where you can't get here from there, and precisely in such cases, very obvious and simple improvements don't come about in nature, exactly as Darwinism leads us to expect.

Aside from cases of bad design, there are also aspects of the actual process of evolution which are difficult to explain from a Design point of view. Why did life for at least a billion years consist of nothing but single-celled organisms such as bacteria? Why were all plants non-flowering until 130 million years ago, when flowering plants proliferated into thousands of diverse forms? This doesn't give the impression of a Designer who had any idea where he was going. Facts like these are puzzling if we assume there's a Designer. If there's no Designer (or a designer of strictly limited powers), these facts fall naturally into place: they are what we would expect.

If there were some complex adaptations which could not be explained by natural selection, there would still be the possibility of some non-Design explanation. A few biologists believe that natural selection needs to be supplemented not by design but by self-organization. Some arrangements of matter spontaneously form themselves into organized shapes. For example, water vapor freezing in the atmosphere forms itself into intricate six-pointed crystals—snowflakes. Stuart Kauffman argues that self-organization tends to create complicated structures in living things, and that natural selection works on improving those structures. Kauffman's intriguing theories have appealed to some scholars in several disciplines, but have not so far been adopted by mainstream biology.

Did God Create through Evolution?

As long as God is accorded a hands-off and self-effacing role, Darwinism doesn't contradict God's existence. People who believe in both God and Darwinism insist that theism and Darwinism can be reconciled but they usually don't offer any distinctive reasons for believing in God.

The Christian biologist Kenneth Miller spends about two-thirds of his justly admired book, *Finding Darwin's God*, arguing that Darwinism is true and that Creationism is untenable. Most of the remaining third is devoted to showing that Darwinism is compatible with theism. Very little indication is given as to why theism should be supposed to be true. Miller thinks that quantum indeterminism favors the existence of God, though his reasoning here is unclear. He also appeals to the Improbable Universe Argument, which we'll be looking at in Chapter 5.

Theists who embrace Darwinism often retain the ten qualities of classical theism. So they usually believe that God *could have* directly created living things, but chose instead to set up a universe in which living things would probably emerge, in some tiny corner or other of that universe, after billions of years of the blind working out of the initial conditions. Such theists usually also retain the theory that God made the universe for the benefit of humans or other intelligent creatures. Miller specifically says that God had to leave it up to chance whether the intelligent creatures which would emerge would be human or something very different.

This theory naturally raises the question why God chose to create intelligent animals in such an indirect way. It seems more promising to speculate that God set up the universe to achieve some purposes unknown to us, and that the possible emergence of intelligent life is just a curious little bonus, or perhaps a contamination, like a yeast infection in a winery. But theists, and especially theologians, show no interest in that kind of thinking. A contemplative cockroach might conclude that the entire ensemble of human artifacts has been built solely for the benefit of cockroaches (or for the elect of cockroaches who will be saved), and theologians tend to think in that fashion.

When they discuss these issues, Darwinist theists often lapse into the tacit denial of God's omnipotence. If God is omnipotent he could have brought about any of the results of evolution without evolution. Therefore any attempt to surmise that the reason God created by means of evolution was because of some of the good qualities emerging from evolution implies God's lack of omnipotence. Often, theists apparently don't notice this.

Francisco Ayala is a superstar of evolutionary biology who has retained the Roman Catholic beliefs of his childhood. In *Darwin's Gift to Science and Religion*, he follows the same pattern as Miller: he explains the reasons why evolution by natural selection is true and Creationism false, without offering any arguments for God. Oddly, he describes the discovery of evolution as a relief, apparently because we don't need to blame God for the evils of nature. However, the Catholic conception of God requires that (even if evolution were true) God could have created life, including humankind, without evolution. Thus, if such a God exists, he made the deliberate choice to have life evolve with all its evils, when he could have just as easily chosen to create equally diverse and wonderful life without such evils. The basis for Ayala's sense of relief is hard to make out.

John Haught advances an "evolutionary theology," accepting Darwinism and a kind of process theology, in which Creation is unfinished. Again, there is a demonstration that theism and evolution are compatible without much in the way of arguments for theism. The only two I noticed are the Improbable Universe Argument and the Argument from Consciousness.

Where Did the First Life Come From?

Theists sometimes claim that, even if all life has evolved from simple organisms like bacteria, the beginning of life itself couldn't have occurred naturally. Therefore, God was needed to kick off the whole process of evolution.

In recent decades there has been a transformation of our understanding of the very meaning of 'life'. As recently as fifty years ago, it was common for theists to assert that living organisms are separated from non-living matter because they contain some 'vital essence' in addition to their physical structure. With advances in molecular biology, this claim has now been completely abandoned. No one now disputes that living things are alive purely because of their physical composition. Just get the right chemicals in the right arrangement, and you have something alive. In that sense, the 'mystery of life' has vanished.

The puzzle about the *origin* of life is to find what kinds of circumstances, that could have arisen on the early Earth, could have led to the right chemicals coming together in the right way. Several rival theories for the origin of the first life are proposed by different biologists, but none of them yet commands general acceptance.

Although I mentioned all existing life developing from "simple organisms like bacteria," I meant "simple" by comparison with more elaborate organisms like centipedes or dandelions. Bacteria are actually very complicated (if we compare one of them with, say, an auto assembly plant). Evidence currently suggests that some of the bacteria that lived on Earth three billion years ago are closely similar to some of those around today.

All life that we know today reproduces by the same chemical method (using DNA), but this method is itself highly complex, and was therefore (if there was no designing intervention by a God, a godling, or a space-alien Johnny Appleseed) itself the end-product of a long process of evolution. The challenge for theorists of the origin of life is to reconstruct that process of evolution, by showing a possible route from the lifeless Earth as it existed four billion years ago to the emergence of 'simple' organisms like bacteria three billion years ago. It will then be possible to test such a theory in two ways: by finding actual fossil traces of simple pre-DNA life and by setting up artificial laboratory conditions as they were on Earth before DNA and watching for various stages of this pre-DNA evolution to occur.

The first thing we need for life to emerge is the existence of molecules which, in the right chemical environment, can make copies of themselves. Such molecules do exist in non-living matter (the process is called 'autocatalysis'), and would have existed in abundance on the Earth before life emerged. Several stages are needed to get from simple autocatalysis to DNA, and the puzzle is to reconstruct those stages.[21]

The outlook for a convincing story of precisely what happened is currently less rosy than it seemed half a century ago. In 1953 Stanley Miller put together in a glass container the gases that were then thought to compose the atmosphere of the early Earth (mainly ammonia and methane), along with boiling water, and subjected this to electrical sparks. Amino acids (the basic building blocks of all proteins) and other complex organic chemicals spontaneously appeared within a week. Subsequent experiments also generated nucleic acids, the molecules that organize into DNA and RNA. Many people in the 1960s supposed that the details would soon be worked out and we would have an adequate theory of life's origin. As it turned out, the evidence now suggests that conditions on the early Earth were less favorable: instead of an atmosphere of methane and ammonia, there was probably an atmosphere of nitrogen and carbon dioxide, with some traces of oxygen (which would have been destructive to the first living things).

Experiments recreating these early conditions still generate amino acids. In fact all twenty amino acids actually found in today's living organisms will spring into existence if the atmosphere of the early Earth is recreated in the laboratory, though not as readily as in Stanley Miller's experiment. Some amino acids have even been detected in meteorites and in the dust in outer space. The theory that life itself came to Earth from outer space is currently not favored, but very likely some organic chemicals which would be part of the first living things did arrive in this way.

However, other difficulties have been noticed. Before living organisms had generated the present atmosphere, chemicals on Earth would have been subject to lethal doses of ultra-violet radiation. Some scientists have therefore suggested that life might have arisen, not on the surface, but in deep sea volcanic vents.

Is Life Just Too Improbable?

One argument for God's existence is that the coming together of 'the right chemicals' is so improbable that it could never have happened by chance. Theists who advance this argument routinely make mistakes in their calculations.[22] They assume that molecules found in today's living organisms must have come together by chance, whereas scientists all agree that these are the results of a long evolutionary process. The earliest living thing would be simpler than anything still around today. Even within the present-day molecules, Creationists often wrongly assume that the chemicals we do find are the only ones that would work at all.

Creationists also usually assume, in calculating their probabilities, that there is only one sequence of trials. In effect, they assume that there is just one molecule and we are calculating the probability that this would develop in a specific way. But in fact there would be trillions upon trillions of such molecules—and the beginning of life only has to happen once.

It's imaginable that biologists working in this area might one day find that all routes to the emergence of life by ordinary physical processes are fantastically improbable. If this happens, it will lend support to the hypothesis that some outside intervention was needed to start life on Earth. But (as far as I have been able to determine) not one of the biologists working in this area now expects that this is at all likely.

5

Did Someone Set the Dial?

We've now seen that living organisms—tiny portions of the universe—were not designed. They evolved. But what about the universe as a whole? Did the universe require a God to design and build it?

In explaining the evolution of life by natural selection, we have assumed that there are laws of nature. If life originated and developed by matter blindly operating in conformity with natural laws, then there's no need to imagine a person designing living things. But some theists say that since there are *laws* of nature, there must be a law maker and a law giver.

Laws of nature are attempts by scientists to formulate statements which are universally true as well as being helpful in explaining what we observe. The theist will insist, however, that although the scientific laws we know are drawn up by scientists, they are attempts to capture real laws, the true laws which actually do prevail in nature, independently of the activities of scientists. It's these true laws, independent of human activity, which require a law giver.

Although I agree that scientists are on the track of objectively true 'real laws', and have even found some of them, this line of argument comes to nothing, because a law of nature is not like a law in the juridical or legal sense. What scientists call 'laws' could easily be called something else, for instance 'regularities'. It's just an accident of the way our language has evolved that we call natural regularities by the name 'laws'.

Laws of nature and juridical laws are very different. A scientific 'law of nature' can *never* be 'broken'. Any clear breach of a proposed law merely demonstrates that it is *not a law at all*. The proposed law would be refuted and discarded.[23] A proposed law of nature is an attempt to describe the way things actually happen. A law passed by the U.S. Congress is nothing of the kind. Quite the contrary: the legislators and everyone else fully expect that any such law will be broken, and they write into their legislation instructions on what is to be done on the occasions when their new law is broken.

Even human laws of the kind appealed to in courts of law do not require a law giver. All great 'law givers' throughout history, like Hammurabi, Justinian, or Napoléon, started from pre-existing legal rules. Powerful monarchs, or people working for them, harmonized and codified those pre-existing rules. These rules first emerged as the customs of local communities. When tribal villages came into contact by means of trade and imperial rule, people had to devise ways of settling disputes between individuals from different communities. They also noticed that there were similarities as well as differences among the different traditional customs for settling disputes, common principles which could be identified. This is what actual historical 'law givers' did.[24] There has never been a law-giver without a pre-existing system of law. And even when a law is 'given' by a political ruler, it always evolves after that because of decisions in courts, decisions never anticipated by the law-giver. It's impossible to prevent this evolution of new law.

The theist may try a different approach. 'The fact that there are universal regularities—laws of nature, and especially laws of physics—is something that requires explanation. The atheist cannot explain it, whereas it can be explained by saying that it comes from the mind of God'. The theist is not saying here that the specific type of universal regularity could have been different and is improbable (I'll get to that next). The theist is instead saying that *any regularity at all* requires a further explanation.

This claim rests on the assumption that if there were no God, we should expect there to be no regularities in the universe. But I can think of no reason why we should make that assumption. Furthermore (and this is a point I will return to several times in this book), the existence of God itself presupposes regularities. Whether there's a God or not, we're just stuck with the fact that there are regularities. God cannot account for all the regularities that prevail, because God could not exist if there were no regularities.

There certainly do seem to be universal regularities (or at least, regularities which hold for several billion galaxies, together constituting a tiny speck within the whole universe), though we should bear in mind that there's also a huge amount of disorder and chaos in the universe, or what we can see of it. What we can see of the universe is generally characterized by a whole lot of empty space, and by chaotic violence and—as far as we can discern—utterly pointless occurrences on a vast scale.

Theists generally claim that natural laws are all determined by God, who could have chosen entirely different laws. Swinburne maintains—and in this he is typical of theologians—that all laws originate from God, who is not governed by laws. Thus all impersonal regularities, such as existing laws of nature, have a personal source: the free choice of God.

Suppose that God did decree all the physical laws of our universe. Still, there must be other natural laws that apply to God. Any general truth about the way reality operates is a natural law. If it's true that everything God wills comes about, then that is a natural law. If it's true that God can think, then there must be laws governing his mental processes. So even if there is a God, and even if God determined the laws of nature for our universe, God himself must still be subject to impersonal natural law. But if there must be natural laws to which God is subject, then we cannot say that any natural laws demand an explanation in terms of God, and this goes for the natural laws of our universe.

The Anthropic Coincidences

The Improbable Universe Argument—sometimes misleadingly called the Fine-Tuning Argument— is derived from facts about the universe revealed by modern physics. I believe it's now the strongest argument for the existence of some kind of God.

It may be worth pointing out that this argument cuts no ice with most physicists, who are generally atheists.[25] I mention this, not because I think physicists are expert authorities in the area of philosophy and that we ought to accept their judgments on matters such as the existence of God—I think just the opposite—but simply to head off a possible misunderstanding about this particular Argument. Physicists, mostly non-theists, have developed various theories about the universe, and theists, mostly non-physicists, have adapted these theories to make the Improbable Universe Argument. Only a few physicists buy the Improbable Universe Argument, though they get a lot of press.

We humans can only exist because the universe has certain characteristics. For example, if planets had never come into existence, and had not then continued to orbit stars for billions of years, the emergence of humans would have been impossible.

It turns out that there are certain laws (or 'constants') prevailing in our universe which, if they had been different by only a few percentage points, would have meant that the conditions for human life could never have arisen. These laws have been called *anthropic coincidences.*

For example, if the 'strong' nuclear force had been slightly weaker, no element other than hydrogen could have come into existence. And if the strong force had been slightly stronger, stars would have quickly burned themselves out, without surviving for the billions of years needed for life to evolve.

Another example is the resonance of carbon. The only way in which carbon could have been formed within stars was by the collision of three helium atoms producing one atom of carbon. For this process to be effective, carbon had to possess a specific resonance; if that resonance had been somewhat different, the collision of three helium atoms would not have produced an atom of carbon.

A third example is the weakness of the force of gravity. The strength of electromagnetism between charged elementary particles is vastly greater—by a factor of 10^{39}—than the strength of gravity. If gravity were much stronger than it is, then stars would quickly collapse in upon themselves and planets would never have been produced.

The Improbable Universe Argument claims that if the laws of nature had been even slightly different from what they are, then the universe would not permit the development of life and consciousness, such as has evolved on planet Earth. Of all the imaginable laws of nature the universe might have, the vast majority would not have permitted life and consciousness to appear. According to some proponents of this Argument, the odds of natural laws being such that life and consciousness might appear are only one in many billions.

For a universe with the actual natural laws to have come into existence is therefore so improbable that it cannot have happened by chance. It requires a special explanation. That explanation can only be that someone—some intelligent agency—selected the laws. Obviously anyone capable of doing this has to possess stupendous powers that we can only consider godlike.

This Argument is sometimes referred to as a Design Argument, but it is very different from Paley's Design Argument. It is frequently called the Fine Tuning Argument, but this is misleading. 'Tuning' is making adjustments to an already functioning apparatus to enhance its efficiency. Precisely this is what we are pretty sure has *not* happened with laws of the universe. If it had happened, the Improbable Universe Argument would be undermined: it is only because the Designer is not going to give the system periodic tune-ups that it is considered so vital to get the conditions exactly right from the getgo. Pickover likens this idea to the Creator adjusting a dial before setting off the reaction that would create the universe. Dial-setting is a more accurate metaphor than fine-tuning.

The Improbable Universe Argument does not dispute that, given the existence of the universe as it is, with its actual laws of nature, life and consciousness could evolve spontaneously, without direction or intervention by a conscious intelligence. The Argument maintains, however, that a conscious intelligence must have chosen the actual laws of nature—and must have done so with the aim of permitting life and consciousness to evolve.

Notice that this Argument goes against various types of Design Argument often deployed in favor of God. For instance, the claim that life could not have arisen naturally on the Earth because that would be too improbable implies that our universe is extremely inhospitable to the emergence of life. There's obviously some awkwardness in proposing both of these arguments, though some theists manage to do it.

I don't think the Improbable Universe Argument is convincing, given the present state of physics, but I can imagine future developments in physics that might strengthen it so that it would become more persuasive. For reasons I explain in Part III, this could not show the likely existence of the God of classical theism, because the God of classical theism is an incoherent notion and logically cannot exist. But it is imaginable that future findings of physics might cause us to entertain the hypothesis that a powerful intelligent being, or association of beings, set the dial for our universe.

Some physicists have questioned whether the anthropic coincidences are as highly improbable as is often claimed.[26] Here, however, I'll assume that they are, and offer some objections to the Argument on that basis.

Objection #1:
We Don't Know that Our Universe
Is Improbable

The Improbable Universe Argument rests on the assumption that our universe could have had entirely different physical laws, and that any imaginable laws were just as likely to hold for the universe as any others. It therefore assumes that there are more fundamental laws above and beyond the physical laws of our universe, and according to those more fundamental laws, any other laws could just as easily have been true in our universe. This is a bold claim about the nature of physical reality. Unless we accept such a claim, we cannot assume that these other, imaginary laws are just as probable as the ones we have.

A true die, as used in gambling, will show any given number from one to six (for instance, three) on any throw, with probability one sixth. This is because the six sides of the die are equally likely to turn up on top, if the die is properly thrown. A loaded die will show a three with (let's assume) a probability one-fifth. Whether various results of throwing a die are equally probable or not is a matter of the shape and density of the die, and of physical laws. As we see from the case of the loaded die, the probability of the loaded die showing a three does not become one-sixth just because we can list six possible outcomes. The claim that our universe 'could just as easily have had different laws' is a claim about physical facts more fundamental than any laws which we attribute to our universe, and therefore it is a claim about natural laws which hold for all possible universes.

To claim that the laws of our universe are highly improbable is to claim that any other set of laws would have been equally probable. It is to claim that the die determining the laws of the universe, a 'die' with billions of sides rather than just six, was not loaded. We are currently not able to look at a random sample of universes to find out how the die might have landed in other cases, and neither are we able to examine the conditions determining the probability of any throw of this die. The probability that our universe has precisely the laws it has could be 1 (one hundred percent), or it could be $\frac{1}{2}$ (fifty percent), or any other fraction of 1.

Objection #2:
The Improbable Conditions May Not Be Independent

Suppose the laws of our universe could have been any other imaginable laws. It's still possible that the actual laws of our universe are not as improbable as claimed by the Improbable Universe Argument. These long odds against the universe having laws allowing life to emerge are arrived at by multiplying each of several probabilities. One of the standard elements of probability theory is that while we may multiply probabilities to arrive at a compound probability of two 'events', we may not do this if the events are not independent.[27] There is still so much to be discovered about physics that it would not be surprising to find that some of the laws and conditions are not fully independent of each other. In that case, it would be mistaken to multiply them, and the probability of the universe having the laws it has could be much higher (or possibly much lower).

Objection #3:
The Argument Assumes Existing Laws

Gilbert Fulmer has pointed out (Fulmer 2001) that any conclusion that life would be impossible under certain conditions can only be derived from assuming the laws of our universe. The Improbable Universe Argument proceeds by looking at just one or a few laws or constants different from those in our universe, assuming that all the other laws would be the same. If we assume that all laws might simultaneously be different, the conclusion does not follow. No attempt has been made to show that the emergence of life is improbable, given that all logically possible combinations of laws are possible.

Objection #4:
There May Be Many Universes

But suppose that it's true that the probability of the universe having the laws required to permit life is just as tiny as the Argument claims—for any one universe. Still, the Argument must assume that there is just one universe, or perhaps only a few. If there are, or have been, a great many universes, perhaps an infinite stream of them, then it would not be improbable for some of those universes to have the laws required. It would be certain. Exactly this has been proposed by some physicists. Given enough universes with different laws (in succession, or simultaneously, or related in a way where they cannot be compared in a common measure of time), for some of them to have the laws of our universe would be virtually certain.

Some atheists argue that life and consciousness may well exist in other universes under completely different conditions than in our universe. This strikes me as weak. Although 'life' in the bare sense of self-replicating molecules may exist in non-carbon chemistry, I believe it would be very rudimentary compared with carbon-based life, and even so, all elements heavier than helium would only exist in abundance in a universe with laws very much like ours. Hoyle (*The Black Cloud*) imagined a great cloud of gas in space that could think and Herbert (*Whipping Star*) imagined stars that could think, but probably once we have found out more about the physical conditions required to generate consciousness (given the laws of our universe) we will find these about as convincing as a block of wood that can think. If we ever find intelligent non-human life, I expect it will be carbon based.

Objection #5:
There May Be Natural Selection of Universes

Lee Smolin has suggested that universes may reproduce, in the sense that events in one universe may give rise to other universes. If, for example, universes produce new universes by generating black holes, and if universes tend to generate new universes in some respects like themselves, then there would be natural selection of universes likely to form black holes, and therefore there would be natural selection for universes having laws very much like ours. Universes with black holes, as it happens, are universes likely to have solar systems with planets rich in carbon and other elements essential to life as we know it.

Objection #6:
Dial-setting Does Not Imply God

Supposing that the laws of our universe are indeed due to dial-setting, still that does not imply the God of classical theism. Perhaps our universe was given its laws by a very powerful but less than omnipotent God, or perhaps by the final supreme collective effort of a dying association of godlings in another universe. We might call that association 'God', but it could be that this 'God' is long gone, or has no way of communicating with us or influencing us now that our universe exists.

There are even some physicists investigating the possibility that new big bangs, generating new universes, may be initiated in a laboratory run by humans. If this were possible, a laboratory-generated new universe would have its own spacetime, and would therefore probably not get in our way.

Objection #7:
Would God Choose to Create Our Universe?

Much discussion of the Improbable Universe Argument takes for granted that if God exists, then he would have some incentive to bring into being a Universe like the one we live in.

If this were true, it would not, by itself, be much support for the existence of God. The fact that if A occurs then B is highly probable does not imply that if B occurs it is highly probable that A has occurred. If for the past hundred years the U.S. government had been permeated from top to bottom by a super-dedicated, super-secret conspiracy which had the object of bringing it about that the U.S. comprised precisely fifty states, then it's very probable that the U.S. would now comprise precisely fifty states. But given that the U.S. comprises precisely fifty states, this does not make the existence of such a super-dedicated, super-secret conspiracy highly probable.

Nonetheless, the assumption that God would have such a motive and will is required by the Improbable Universe Argument. And surely this assumption is quite reckless.

Let's suppose that there is a God but there is no physical universe. We're angels at an angel seminar. Topic of the seminar is 'Possible Things God Might Do'. We know all about physical universes on the theoretical level (these are the kinds of fantastic hypotheticals we angels like to debate in our abundant spare time, when we're not dancing on the points of needles[28]). Would we conclude that God might set the dial for a physical universe like ours? It's hard to see why.

Why would God want physical life to evolve at all? By hypothesis, something we can only call life already exists, in spirit form. We angels are one species of this spirit life. This spirit life has highly developed consciousness, and if we believe that the Devil started out as an angel, then these living entities have free will. What is it that's so wonderful about physical life that is unattainable in the spirit world? Given the things theists tell us about spirits, I have no idea of the answer to this. (Don't forget that if the answer is 'Only a physical universe would enable *x, y,* or *z* to occur', then *whatever x, y, or z may be*, that implies that God is subject to prior natural law, and the whole argument self-destructs, at least insofar as it is an argument for the God of classical theism.)

Assume, however, that biological life is desirable to God because it can evolve higher consciousness like that of humans (even though this higher consciousness already exists in the spirit world and does not therefore require the evolution of biological life). At least, then, an angel at the seminar would have to know that once the physical universe got going, life and conscious intelligence would both evolve by the operation of purely physical laws within that universe.

Yet surprisingly, many advocates of the Improbable Universe Argument reject this. Swinburne, for example, fully accepts Darwinian evolution and a completely physicalistic origin of life, yet he claims that the emergence of consciousness can never be explained by science. Consciousness requires special intervention by God. God has to intervene miraculously to make certain arrangements of matter the bearers of consciousness.

Given Swinburne's view, despite what Swinburne himself concludes, it's not obvious that the existence of a physical universe is necessary, or even helpful, to achieve anything God wants to achieve. A population of disembodied minds could exist (according to all Christians and Muslims, *does* exist) prior to a physical universe, and even given a physical universe, there has to be (in Swinburne's view and in that of many theists) special intervention to make a population of conscious minds possible.

When theists try to explain what purpose it would serve God to arrange for a universe like ours, they tacitly abandon God's omnipotence. When proponents of the Improbable Universe Argument assert that the various fundamental physical laws could be anything, this is in one sense far too sweeping (because we have no data on whether they 'could be' any different to what they are). But in another sense it's far too modest: a God who could merely set the dial for an infinity of different physical constants would be a cripple of a God.

God's omnipotence implies that there is no law of physics independent of God's will, and thus the most fundamental laws of physics would be limited only by the laws of logical consistency. For example, God could just as easily have created a universe without fundamental particles, in which any type of substance could be divided infinitesimally, or he could have created a universe with several time dimensions as well as several spatial dimensions. He could have created a universe in which water was not H_2O and heat was not mean kinetic energy. Suppose that 'string theory' is all wrong. There are no superstrings. Still, God could have created a universe in which string theory was true. It's surely clear that a truly omnipotent God could have created an infinity of different types of physical universe in which conscious life could evolve.

Christian apologists such as Bruce Reichenbach and Richard Swinburne, when they discuss cosmology, tacitly (and no doubt unwittingly) assume that God is subject to physical law (even though this law may be much more general than the laws of our universe). They tacitly give up God's omnipotence.

Theists may respond that God might have motives, such as esthetic ones, for arriving at conscious life by the roundabout method of arranging for a Big Bang. That can't be disproved. I'm not confident I can say much about the esthetic preferences of an omniscient and omnipotent God. But surely the point of the Improbable Universe Argument is to suggest that something which seems odd and inexplicable (laws of nature permitting the emergence of life and consciousness) can be made more comprehensible by supposing a God who started the universe and fixed its laws with the objective of bringing humans into being. This gain in comprehensibility, if it exists, must be lost if we have to start adding all sorts of *ad hoc* speculations about God's otherwise unknown motives or limitations.

The Improbable Universe Argument hinges on the instigation of the universe being a means to God's end. However, an omnipotent God would not and could not have means to ends: he could directly attain any desired ends. And if the instigation of the universe is not a means to God's supposed end at all, but just something God did for inexplicable reasons, then the dial-setting hypothesis doesn't help us.

Some atheists have proposed that if God wanted to create a universe which would enable conscious life to come into existence by the blind operation of natural laws, he would not have 'wasted' so much space just to produce *us*. The universe is quite big, and almost none of it has anything to do with humans. This isn't a very good argument against God.

First, since God is omnipotent he faces no opportunity costs. Therefore no resource is 'wasted' because there's always any amount more where that came from—and where that came from, according to classical theism, is nothing (nihil). Second, God may have numerous other plans not involving humans. We might be a very tiny part of all God's reasons for creating the universe. Most theists would indignantly deny this, and insist that the universe is all there for our benefit. But that's not essential to theism, and we ought to criticize an opposing position at its strongest.

6

Does God Explain Why Anything Exists?

A simple argument for the existence of God goes like this:

1. **Everything has a cause.**

2. **Therefore the universe must have a cause.**

3. **That cause can only be God.**

We immediately think of three obvious objections:

1. **Why must the universe have a cause? Couldn't it be uncaused?**

2. **If everything must have a cause, then God must have a cause. Saying that God is the cause of the universe doesn't get us very far. What's the cause of God?**

3. **If we accept that the universe must have a cause, and that this cause of the universe does not itself require a cause, what's that got to do with 'God'? Let's call the uncaused cause *x*. Why would we suppose that *x* has the ten qualities of God— or any three of them? Why couldn't *x* be, for example, some kind of blind force, aimless, incapable of caring about humans or anything else, and morally neutral?**

This kind of argument is called a Cosmological Argument. There are many varieties of Cosmological Argument, some of them far more elaborate than this one (and too many to explore in this little book). Yet when we look at all these more elaborate forms, we find that they never manage to get away from the same three simple objections.

The First Cause Argument

The Cosmological Argument holds that the universe requires an explanation outside of itself, and that explanation has to be God. The Cosmological Argument is not based on any particular feature of the universe, such as that life exists, or that the universe is orderly, but on the mere fact that there is any universe at all.

The many different forms of the Cosmological Argument can be grouped in two broad types: those concerned with the succession of events in time (usually called First Cause Arguments) and those not concerned with the succession of events in time (usually called Arguments from Contingency). The first type of argument usually denies that there can have been an infinity of past time, while the second type of argument usually grants that there might have been an infinity of past time.

One form of the First Cause Argument goes like this:

1. Either the universe has been going on for ever or it began at a certain point.

2. The universe cannot possibly have been going on for ever.

3. But if it began at a certain point, then something must have brought it into being, and that something is God.

Our three obvious objections apply to this form of the Argument. We do not know of any reason why the universe could not have been going on for ever, and if it has been going on for ever, then it certainly cannot have had a cause in the sense of a thing or event pre-existing it in time.

If the universe began at a certain point, then either there was a time before the universe existed or there was no such time. If there was no such time, then all of time is part of the universe.[29] If all of time is part of the universe, then the beginning of the universe is the beginning of time. In that case, there was no cause of the universe in the sense of events earlier than the universe (since there was nothing earlier).

One view of God is that he is outside time, and one view of causation is that causes are (or can be) instantaneous with effects, rather than preceding effects in time. If we put these two views together, we get the possibility that God, a being outside time, could have caused the universe, including time, by instantaneous action.

However, in Chapter 16 I point out that the God of classical theism cannot be outside time, because any entity outside time cannot think or act. A 'God' outside time cannot therefore be a person. A growing number of theistic philosophers and theologians have come to a similar conclusion, so that the theory that God is outside time has lost support among them over the past hundred years.

Furthermore, if the cause of the universe is outside time, and therefore does not itself require a cause, then there is no reason why this cause outside time has to be God, as opposed to some kind of blind force.

The Kalam Argument

A slightly different version of the First Cause Argument is the Kalam Argument (from the Arabic 'kalām', meaning 'speech'), popularized by the Christian philosopher William Lane Craig.

The distinctive feature of this argument is that it claims to demonstrate the impossibility of an actually existing infinity of items. For example, it asserts that there cannot be an infinite number of physical objects. From this, it concludes that there cannot have been an infinite past time, or an infinite number of past events. But suppose that the universe is limited in extent (that is, in spatial distance and in matter-energy content) and therefore cannot contain an infinity of any type of physical object. This doesn't prevent it having existed for an infinite period of past time or continuing to exist into an infinite period of future time.

To refute the theory of an infinitely old universe, Craig imagines someone counting down through all of past time up to now, then concluding with '. . . three, two, one, zero'. Craig asserts that this is impossible, and he is surely right. If the universe has existed for an infinite period of time, then the universe had no beginning. Counting, however, is an operation that must have a beginning. So it's just absurd to suppose someone counting for an infinite period of past time, but not absurd to suppose that *something or other* has been going on for an infinite period of past time. It's quite easy to imagine someone starting to count now, and counting for an infinite time period: this just means that this person will never stop counting. There will never be a time when they have finished and can say: 'I have been counting for an infinite time'.

If the universe has been going on for ever, then an infinite amount of time has already elapsed. So we may take the present moment (or any moment) as the termination of an infinite series. On a number line, there's an infinity of negative whole numbers and an infinity of positive whole numbers. We can take the negative numbers to represent past moments, and the positive numbers to represent future moments.

... -5 -4 -3 -2 -1 0 1 2 3 4 5 ...

If we add the absolute values of these two infinities together, we get an infinity, encompassing both positive and negative numbers. This seems weird, but that's infinity for you. The fact that, conceivably, something that has always been going on could now stop (or could be arbitrarily declared to have ended) does nothing to call into question the possibility that that something has always been going on, and that the aggregate of everything that has been going on had no beginning.[30]

Maybe what Craig is getting at is that if something has been going on for ever until now, and then stops, it has been going on for an infinity of time, yet if it had stopped a billion years ago, it would also have been going on for an infinity of time. And however far back we go, it would always have been going on for an infinity of time. If something has been going on for an infinity of time, then for every second of an infinity of past time, it was already the case that it had been going on for an infinity of time. There was never a point where it 'reached' an infinity of time by adding up the time elapsed.

If you've never thought about infinity before, there's something startling about this, but nothing illogical, and I see no reason to discount the possibility that the universe is infinitely old. Craig accepts that an infinity of time is not logically impossible, but claims it is "metaphysically absurd." The appearance of absurdity seems to arise from the ridiculous scenarios conjured up by his arguments, not from the bare notion of infinite duration. Of course no one has been counting for all past time, and of course no one is going to go on counting for all future time, but this doesn't go against the possibility that something or other has always been going on or that something or other always will be going on, or both.

Another possibility is that time neither goes back for ever nor begins at a certain point. This possibility was mentioned by Hawking in *A Brief History of Time.* It's no longer so relevant, because most physicists no longer think that there was no time before the Big Bang. But I mention it here to show that an infinitely old universe and a universe with a beginning are not the only alternatives.

Beginning Without a Cause

But what if Craig is right in saying that the universe has not existed for an infinitely long time? Craig further asserts that "everything that begins to exist has a cause." This wording includes the universe and excludes God. The universe must have a cause but God needn't have a cause.

Craig offers two possible interpretations of this: 1. that God never began to exist because he is outside time; 2. that God never began to exist because he exists in a different type of time, an 'undifferentiated' time. The reason Craig offers this second possibility is because he sees the problems with accepting a God outside time, and yet if God has always existed in our familiar kind of time, this would contradict the Kalam Argument, as God would have lived through an infinite number of hours.

But does it make any sense to suppose God living without cause or beginning, through endless 'undifferentiated' time, lacking an infinite succession of units of duration? In these vast eons of undifferentiated time, did anything happen? If yes, that undifferentiated time is not undifferentiated, and must be divisible into units of duration. If no, then undifferentiated time appears much the same as timelessness, with all the drawbacks of that concept. Surely, if there is time, then successive moments can be identified and counted, just as, if there is space, it can be measured in units of distance.

Aside from that, the God of classical theism would have to contain an infinite number of items, for example, items of knowledge. Therefore 'an actual infinity', which Craig claims cannot exist, must exist. As I explain in the next chapter, either God knows all the decimal places of *pi*, that is, he is aware of an infinite number of ordered numerals, in which case an actual infinity is possible and the Kalam Argument falls, or he knows only a finite number of decimal places of *pi*, in which case he is not omniscient and not the greatest being conceivable: it's possible to conceive of someone who knows more than God.

We needn't accept Craig's claim that everything that begins to exist has a cause. According to quantum mechanics, this statement is false. Things begin to exist without any cause all the time. Craig offers no argument for his claim that nothing can begin without a cause, only his sense of conviction. Physics and biology explain why conditions on the surface of the Earth are such that we would tend to evolve such intuitive senses of conviction, which are a good enough guide to practical affairs in that local environment. Craig asks:

> Does anyone in his right mind really believe that, say, a raging tiger could suddenly come into existence uncaused, out of nothing, in this room right now?[31]

Of course not! My informed judgment tells me that anything like a raging tiger has to be a product of millions of years of evolution on the surface of a planet. By contrast, a shift in the orbit of an electron has no cause at all, in the sense of a pre-existing set of conditions which determined that it had to occur. When it comes to the universe around the time of the Big Bang—unimaginably hot, unimaginably dense, unimaginably disorderly, and unimaginably tiny—is this more like the raging tiger or the shift in an electron's orbit? It strikes me as very unlike a raging tiger, mainly because it is so disorderly.

If the universe began and its beginning had a cause outside time, we still can't reasonably conclude that this cause was God. But for the sake of completeness, we should note that we haven't heard any good argument for why the universe could not have begun to exist without a cause.

Suppose that there was nothing. Why couldn't a universe have sprung into existence without cause? According to speculations by physicists, a universe might have exploded into being in a quantum vacuum. But a theist might say that a quantum vacuum isn't really, really nothing, and that such a universe would have been caused—probabilistically—by the prior state of a quantum vacuum. 'True nothing' must lack even the properties of a quantum vacuum. A quantum vacuum already has laws of nature, those laws governing the probable commencement of a universe.

But let's pursue this a bit further. If it's a requirement of 'true nothing' that it lacks any properties and any laws, then true nothing must lack any law prohibiting the appearance of something. The assertion that, given true nothing, a universe could not pop into existence is therefore self-contradictory. If nothing does not permit something, such as an expanding universe, to start existing for no reason at all, then it's a fact about this nothing that the probability of something coming into existence is zero, and such a general fact would be a law, thus the nothing in question could not be true nothing.

A theist might respond that the inability of something to pop into existence where there was nothing is not a law of nature but a metaphysical necessity. But in the relevant sense, a law of nature is the same as a metaphysical necessity. Laws of nature are regularities prevailing in reality. Empirical science looks for laws of nature which can be tested by observation. If a law of nature can't be tested by observation, the assertion of such a law is metaphysical. What is metaphysics and what is empirical science is relative to the situation of the observers. No doubt we can't test by observation the assertion that true nothing prohibits or doesn't prohibit the coming into existence of something, but this doesn't stop that assertion being a hypothetical law of nature.

The Argument from Contingency

The First Cause Argument is easy to grasp. The Argument from Contingency is more elusive, and has carried more weight with philosophers and theologians.

Many things we observe are contingent, that is to say, although they exist, we can easily imagine them not existing. This seems to be true of all specific arrangements of matter: the Taj Mahal exists,

---

Sidebar: Aquinas's Five Ways

Thomas Aquinas (1224–1274) laid out Five Ways of proving the existence of God. The first three of these are forms of the Cosmological Argument, yet Aquinas never endorsed a First Cause Argument. Catholics are obliged to believe that the existence of God can be proved by reason alone, and this Aquinas accepted. But he maintained that it is impossible to prove the finite duration of the universe (though he accepted it because the Church taught it). Aquinas therefore intended all three of his Cosmological Arguments to work even if the universe has been going on forever.

    The classic detailed examination of Aquinas's Five Ways is by Anthony Kenny (1969). He concludes that all five arguments, as Aquinas framed them, fail, and this verdict is now generally accepted even by most Christian philosophers. More credence has been given to the Cosmological Argument as propounded by Leibniz and by Samuel Clarke, both improved versions of Aquinas's Third Way. This approach is called the Argument from Contingency.

---

but there seems to be no problem in supposing that it did not exist.

The Argument goes on to assert that a full explanation of contingent things cannot be given purely in terms of contingent things. For example, suppose the entire universe were just an evolving collection of contingent things. Each contingent thing could perhaps be explained in terms of other contingent things, but the whole universe would lack an explanation.

At this point the Argument appeals to something called the Principle of Sufficient Reason, a principle that used to be accepted by many philosophers but is now accepted by very few. The Principle of Sufficient Reason says that nothing can exist without a sufficient reason for its existence.

Therefore, the Argument continues, there has to be at least one necessary thing, and there are no prizes for guessing who that's going to turn out to be.

Everyone who makes a distinction between contingent and necessary things, agrees that the difference between necessary and contingent is the difference between 'the way things have to be' and 'the way things happen to be'. But what does this really mean?

Is it true that all objects are either contingent or necessary, and if so, how do we tell the difference? How do we know that the Taj Majal is not necessary? Suppose that determinism were true, in which case the Taj Mahal (and every other existent object) would be strictly required by the Big Bang. The proponent of the Contingency Argument would *still* deny that the Taj Mahal was necessary.

But if the Taj Mahal is not necessary, regardless of whichever theory of causation we adopt, then how can there be such a thing as a necessary thing? We can easily imagine the Taj Mahal not existing, but we can just as easily imagine God not existing.

There is indeed one neat way to make this distinction. It solves a lot of problems. But it turns out to be devastating for the Argument from Contingency. This is the division between matters of logic and matters of fact not decidable by logic alone. It is a matter of logic that a white rabbit is a rabbit, but it is a question of fact which logic alone cannot settle, whether there is a white rabbit in downtown Chicago. David Hume pioneered the view that what is necessary is what is logically necessary, and nothing else is necessary at all. If what is necessary is what is logically necessary (what it would be self-contradictory to deny), then what is contingent is what can be asserted or denied without self-contradiction.

If we adopt this approach, then strictly speaking, necessary or contingent do not apply to things but only to statements (because logic applies only to statements). However, these terms can be extended to things by applying them to the statements that such and such a thing exists. So, if the Taj Mahal is contingent, this means that the statement that the Taj Mahal exists is not a truth of logic—which is certainly correct. If God is necessary, this means that the statement 'God exists' is a truth of logic, which means that if you deny it, you contradict yourself. This is what the Ontological Argument tries to show. But, as we will see in the next chapter, the Ontological Argument is a failure: there is no self-contradiction in denying that God exists.

It does not look as if 'God exists' is a truth of logic; certainly, no one has yet shown this. It might even be a truth of logic that every existing entity exists contingently. Most people who still adhere to the Contingency Argument would dispute that 'necessary' is confined to 'logically necessary'. They would say that there

Sidebar: Is God Part of the Universe?

The word 'universe' is often taken to mean 'everything that exists'. This strictly implies that, if there is a God, then either God is the universe or God is part of the universe. If there's a spirit world, in addition to physical reality, then this spirit world would have to be part of the universe (and God, if he does not include the physical universe, either is this spirit world or is part of this spirit world).

This way of talking would be clear and consistent but, perhaps unfortunately, almost no one adheres to it all the time. People talk of 'parallel universes', 'alternate universes', and 'multiple universes'. Physicists, philosophers, science fiction fans, and theologians have all picked up the habit of talking like this. As soon as we start talking about more than one universe co-existing, or about anything that might exist outside the universe, then the word 'universe' cannot mean everything that exists.

In order to maintain clarity, it would be useful to have a word that is defined to mean everything that exists, and I propose the word 'metaverse'.[32] It's part of the definition of 'metaverse' that there can never be more than one metaverse, and there can never be anything outside the metaverse. If there are many universes, they are all by definition parts of the metaverse. If there's a God, then by definition either he is the metaverse or he is part of the metaverse.

The ambiguity of the word 'universe' is a great help to theists. It rhetorically insinuates the assumption that after we have taken account of everything that exists, there might possibly be something else left over. If we stick to talk of the metaverse, our simple form of the Cosmological Argument can hardly even be formulated without appearing silly. We simply can't say: 'The metaverse must have a cause. That cause is God'. Or if we do say it, and try to make sense of what we're saying, we're merely saying that part of the metaverse is the cause of all of the metaverse—and why would anyone seriously entertain this suggestion? And if God is the metaverse, then we would flatly contradict ourselves by saying that the metaverse cannot cause itself and yet the metaverse does cause itself (for if there was a time when only part of the present metaverse existed, then at that time that part of the metaverse would be the whole metaverse).

If 'metaverse' is defined as 'everything that exists or ever has existed, including God if he exists or ever has existed', then we have to say that the metaverse cannot possibly have a cause outside of itself. Either the metaverse has no cause or, what might amount to the same thing, it is its own cause. (One state of the metaverse causes a subsequent state of the metaverse.)

If God is defined as part of the metaverse, then the Argument would have to take this form: part of the metaverse requires a cause outside itself, and that cause has to be another part of the metaverse. The part of the metaverse which requires a cause outside of itself is (or includes) that part of the metaverse of which we have direct observational evidence. It is that part of the universe which both theists and atheists acknowledge to exist.

People who propose an argument like this one usually take 'universe' to mean 'everything physical that exists'. God is not physical. They therefore assume that everything physical has to have a cause, while anything that exists but is not physical does not have to have a cause.

Here 'physical' must be given quite a broad meaning. For example, subjective experiences such as thoughts or feelings are, at least in one sense, not physical. But no one wants to deny that they are components of the universe. Abstract relationships, such as obligations, are also part of the universe. They're therefore physical from the viewpoint of the Cosmological Argument: they belong to the non-spirit universe.

---

are additional, metaphysically necessary truths. I'm not sure that any good candidates have been proposed for these, but like truths of logic they would presumably be very general. It's difficult to see how the existence of a specific entity, like a disembodied person, could be metaphysically necessary.

If, all the same, we want to say that the universe might not have existed, and depends for its existence on something else that could not fail to exist, then matter-energy or a quantum vacuum, or some even more fundamental physical condition, looks like the best bet.

The Ultimate Explanation of What There Is

The Argument from Contingency just doesn't work. But it leads us to a different argument, or what looks like a different argument. Theists maintain that God is the ultimate explanation of the universe. Asked what is the ultimate explanation of God, they respond that God is the kind of thing that needs no further explanation. For theists, the stopping-point of explanation is God, while for atheists the stopping-point of explanation may be the universe itself. This atheist attitude has frequently been described as accepting the universe as 'a brute inexplicable fact'. What often motivates the Cosmological Argument is a feeling—or an intuition—that it's unsatisfactory to accept the universe as a brute inexplicable fact, whereas it's perfectly okay to accept God as a brute inexplicable fact.

Some physicists are looking for what they call a Theory of Everything—one theory which will unite quantum theory, relativity theory, and all observable facts. But if they ever come up with such a theory, and it's so successful that all physicists accept it, then it will still be possible to ask why physical reality is such that this theory is true. Or: Is there some deeper theory that explains why the Theory of Everything is true?

However, even if such questions continue to arise indefinitely, I can see no reason why the entire debate should not proceed on the assumption that non-spirit reality is sufficient unto itself. Both the atheist and the theist agree that there's a realm of existence which has to be accepted as a brute fact. To the atheist it is non-spirit reality, to the theist it is the hypothesized spirit world. Non-spirit or physical reality exists—there's no disagreement about that— whereas the very existence of the spirit world is controversial.

Swinburne has argued that one of the qualities of a good scientific theory is simplicity, and that the God hypothesis is favored because of its extreme simplicity. Yet he also argues that appeal to God as an explanation arises where science is unable to explain: it's a radically different type of explanation. And so, while protesting that theism is outside science, he proposes to take one element of scientific method—simplicity—and make it the basis for a metaphysical argument for theism.

In the history of science a simpler explanation has often been dropped in favor of a less simple one. For example, Einstein's theory of gravitation is less simple than Newton's, and each successive theory of atomic structure, over the past couple of hundred years, has been more complex than its predecessors. In empirical science, a simple theory gives way to a less simple theory if the less simple theory better fits the observations.

That thunder is caused by a god's anger is far simpler than an explanation in terms of electromagnetism. But by comparison it is a pathetically bad explanation. It looks to me as if 'simplicity' is not an unqualified virtue in a theory, but acquires merit only in conjunction with testability. The way I see it, science tries to come up with theories that fit observations, subject to certain constraints. Simplicity is one of these constraints. It is not a stand-alone virtue in a theory.

Does Physics Change the Cosmological Argument?

In 1929 the astronomer Edwin Hubble observed that distant stars seem to be rushing away from us. He quickly realized that what seems to be the case viewed from Earth would also look that way viewed from anywhere else: the universe as a whole is expanding: the distances between the galaxies are rapidly increasing. As our universe expands, it cools. If the universe has been expanding for a long time, there must have been a time in the past when it was much smaller by comparison with its present size, and much hotter.

Evidence has accumulated to support the theory that, about fourteen billion years ago, what we think of as our universe was so compressed together that there could be no stars, no galaxies, and no atoms. There were just particles of matter, anti-matter, and light, with a temperature of at least one thousand trillion degrees Centigrade. After a few hundred thousand years, this universe had expanded and cooled to the point where atoms came into existence, but only atoms of hydrogen and helium. Gravitation pulled these atoms together into stars and galaxies, and inside stars, heavier elements like oxygen, carbon, nitrogen, and iron were generated.

Physicists are now unanimous in accepting this theory of the Big Bang. The few remaining doubters gave up when cosmic background radiation was measured in 1964, an 'echo' of the early stages of the Big Bang. Fundamentalist Christians reject the Big Bang, because it contradicts *Genesis*. Non-Fundamentalist Christians and other theists have welcomed the Big Bang theory, because it seems to harmonize with the idea that there was a single event which started our universe off. The universe, it now appears to some, has not existed indefinitely, but exploded into existence about fourteen billion years ago.

Does 'our universe' mean all of physical reality? This is a matter on which physicists are not agreed, and it is highly speculative (meaning that at present there is not much evidence from observation to test it). When the Big Bang theory was first popularized, the theory that it began with a Singularity, a point where all space and all time began, was popularized along with it. But the notion of a Singularity has now been abandoned by many physicists, and so has the theory that there was nothing earlier in time than the Big Bang. It's now widely accepted that something preceded the Big Bang. One theory entertained by some physicists is that there have been a vast number, perhaps an infinite number, of Big Bangs.

Inflationary cosmology, developed by Alan Guth and by Andrei Linde, sees our universe as a tiny part of a bubble, there being an indefinitely large number of such bubbles. The inflationary theory has returned cosmology to the notion of a universe (or in my recommended terminology, the metaverse) which, once started, goes on for ever, and which could possibly be infinitely old.

In recent theories of physical cosmology, we can discern three possibilities about the beginning of the whole universe (the metaverse):

1. Our universe (the one which results from the Big Bang) is the only universe there is and it began about fourteen billion years ago. Time only exists in this universe and so time began when this universe began.

2. Our universe is the only universe there is, but it had no beginning. As you get back in time to about fourteen billion years ago, you find that time and space are unbounded.

3. Our universe is a tiny part of a bubble, which is one of an immense number, perhaps an infinity, of bubbles. The whole agglomeration of bubbles is infinitely old.

It's probably true that most theists feel very comfortable with #1 while atheists feel more comfortable with #2 and most comfortable of all with #3. But strictly speaking none of the three implies that there is or is not a God.

Why Is There Anything (Instead of Nothing at All)?

One form of the Cosmological Argument arises from the question, 'Why is there something instead of nothing at all?' Some people have claimed that the fact that there is anything at all, and not absolutely nothing, is in itself evidence for God's existence.

Many people have found the question 'Why is there something rather than nothing?' baffling. But I don't see that God would make it less baffling. Just suppose that a God exists. Then we would have the question 'Why is there a God instead of nothing?' This is at least as baffling as the former question, and I would say a bit more so.

This point applies to other baffling questions too. Sometimes, God will be offered as the answer to some baffling question when in fact the existence of God would not make the question any less baffling.

For instance, imagine a cosmos very like the one we know, but bereft of consciousness. Would such a cosmos contain numbers? This is a genuinely difficult metaphysical issue. Numbers do not seem to be objects in the cosmos, like stars or love affairs or electrons or thoughts passing through someone's mind. Yet it seems clearly wrong to say that numbers are nothing more than a mental administrative technique, file folders of the human mind. It appears that numbers would enjoy a kind of objective existence even if no one were there to become aware of them. Among philosophers of mathematics, there is nothing close to agreement as to what numbers are.

Craig has offered abstract objects like numbers as evidence for the existence of God. But the difficulty of supposing that numbers exist in God's mind is no less than the difficulty of supposing that they exist only in human minds. If they do not exist only in minds, but exist in arrangements of physical stuff, independent of any thoughts about them, then they exist whether or not there is a God. Supposing that there might be a God does not get at the root of the puzzlement. It does not help us to understand what numbers are.

One reason that the question 'Why is there something instead of nothing?' seems baffling is that we tend to suppose that the existence of something calls for an explanation, whereas the nonexistence of anything would be more natural, somehow easier, or even self-explanatory.

> It is extraordinary that there should exist anything at all. Surely the most natural state of affairs is simply nothing: no universe, no God, nothing. (Swinburne 1996, p. 48)

"Extraordinary" is a comparison with the ordinary. Since it's almost impossible to imagine there being nothing (not even space or time or a quantum vacuum), that state of affairs can hardly be ordinary. And if the existence of both God and universe is unnatural, yet we know that the universe, at least, does exist, it seems to follow that the nonexistence of God must be natural, though that was not the conclusion Swinburne was looking for.

From Rest to Nothingness

The early forms of the Cosmological Argument, as found in Plato, Aristotle, and Aquinas, are motivated by the conviction that immobility is more natural than change. Change or motion requires a special explanation, whereas stasis or immobility does not.

This conviction was killed by Galileo. Since Galileo, we understand that immobility is impossible even to define, except in a very local sense, and where it's observed at a local level, it is just as much requiring an explanation as change—perhaps more so.

Later forms of the Cosmological Argument came to terms with Galileo. Nobody now believes that stasis is the default, while change requires a special explanation. But now, the conviction still prevails that nonexistence is the default, while existence requires a special explanation. Perhaps the theory of quantum gravity will do for existence what Galileo did for motion. It may come to be recognized that the nonexistence of everything is impossible even to define or clearly conceive, and that it is much more problematic for this state of affairs to prevail than for there to be something. Or as Frank Wilczek has proposed, nothingness is unstable (Stenger 2007, p. 130).

That may be just speculation. However, I can make the more modest claim: we don't know of any good reason why the nonexistence of anything would be the default. It's unwarranted to suppose that nonexistence is more natural than existence. No good theory, physical or metaphysical, tells us to expect there to be nothing.

So it's quite reasonable to respond to the question, 'Why is there something rather than nothing?' with 'Why not?'

7

Can We Prove God Exists by Pure Logic?

Some people used to think we can prove the existence of God by pure logic. The argument they thought could do this trick is called the Ontological Argument.

The Ontological Argument is terrific fun. In its simplest form, it goes like this:

1. Nothing greater than God can possibly be thought of.

2. A God who exists is greater than a God who does not exist.

3. Therefore: God exists.

At a quick glance, this argument seems to work! Conclusion 3 does seem to follow from Premisses 1 and 2. If it's part of the definition of God that we cannot possibly think of anything greater, then apparently a God who does not exist must be ruled out, as a God who exists appears to be obviously greater than a God who does not exist.

I'm going to criticize this argument on three grounds:

a. The Argument is unsound because it relies on switching the meaning of the word 'greater'.

b. The greatest thing we can possibly think of cannot be God without the universe, but must be the whole universe. However, even the claim that the whole universe, including God, could be the greatest thing we can possibly think of is a bit dubious.

c. The greatest thing we can possibly think of, if it could exist, would have to contain an infinite collection of items. There are reasons for not accepting the existence of such an entity, and most theists wouldn't want to accept it.

The Argument is sometimes worded in terms of 'most perfect' instead of 'greatest'. This makes no difference. The Ontological Argument, as I have phrased it, does not explicitly state that the greatest thing we can possibly think of is a person, but this is taken for granted by everyone who wants to defend the Argument. The Argument in effect assumes that we can think of nothing greater than an all-powerful, all-knowing person.

A Flaw in the Ontological Argument

Suppose someone were to say, 'Sherlock Holmes is certainly a great detective, but he would be so much greater if he had actually existed'. Either this is a joke or it's a muddle. Someone who wanted to persist with this might say, 'But look, if Sherlock Holmes really existed, he would be able, in the real world, to solve crimes. The fictitious Sherlock Holmes has never *really* solved any crimes at all, because, poor thing, he is fictitious. It's indubitably the mark of a great detective to be able to solve real crimes in the real world. So you have to admit that a real Sherlock Holmes would be a greater detective than the fictitious Sherlock Holmes.'

However, if we adopt that way of talking, then the fictitious Sherlock Holmes has *no* claims to greatness as a detective, or even to being a detective at all. If we want to say *both* that the fictitious Holmes is greater than the fictitious Lestrade, *and* that a historical Holmes would be greater than the fictitious Holmes, then we're switching the meaning of the word 'greater'. For, in precisely the sense in which a historical Holmes would be greater than the fictitious Holmes, the fictitious Holmes is not one eentsy bit greater than the fictitious Lestrade. And, in precisely the sense in which the fictitious Holmes is greater than the fictitious Lestrade, the real Holmes is not one smidgen greater than the fictitious Holmes. As a real-life detective who can solve real-life crimes, the fictitious Holmes is a hopeless failure, a nullity, a cipher. There's not an ounce of greatness in him.

What we have here is a confusion of two entirely different usages of 'greater'. When we first look at the Ontological Argument, we easily overlook the fact that the expression 'greater then' means something quite different in Premiss 1 than it means in Premiss 2. We tend to suppose that a nonexistent God would be quite great but an existent God would be even greater. But this is misleading, for, in the precise sense in which an existent God is greater than a nonexistent God, a nonexistent God is bereft of any particle of greatness.

In the history of discussions of the Ontological Argument, this weakness in the Argument has mainly been addressed in discussions of *whether existence is a property* (or whether existence is a predicate). Immanuel Kant was the first philosopher to claim (in opposition to the Ontological Argument as advanced by René Descartes) that 'existence is not a predicate'. Discussion of whether existence is a property has been of great use in clarifying some of the basic principles of logic. However, it's still not quite resolved by philosophers of logic whether existence can be a property. What we have seen above is that from the standpoint of criticizing the Ontological Argument, whether existence is a property is not the crux of the matter. Even if existence is a property, the Ontological Argument still fails.

The flaw in the Ontological Argument is more fundamental and more simple: the Argument contains a *fallacy of equivocation*. A fallacy of equivocation is a feature of an argument which is unsound because one of the terms switches its meaning in the course of the argument (and the conclusion depends on this switch of meaning). The fallacy of equivocation in the Ontological Argument occurs with the term 'greater than'. 'Greater than', in the sense in which God is held to be greater than (for instance) the greatest human being, means something entirely different from 'greater than', in the sense in which an existing God is held to be greater than a purely imaginary God.

The equivocation is difficult to spot because of the vaguely inclusive nature of the word 'great' (or in some versions of the Argument, 'perfect'), to refer to a rag-bag of different qualities. If only one quality were being referred to, the fallacy would be more obvious:

1. Think of the biggest elephant you can possibly think of.

2. An elephant that exists is bigger than an imaginary elephant.

3. Therefore the biggest elephant you can possibly think of must exist.

Could God Be the Greatest Conceivable Thing?

I've been using the phrase "greatest thing we can possibly think of." I'm now going to shorten that to 'greatest conceivable thing'.[33] However, God cannot be the greatest conceivable thing, because God plus his creation (all the things he has created) are together greater than God alone. (In other words, the metaverse must be greater than God, who is only part of the metaverse.) So God is not the greatest thing that exists.

Even if 'greatness' were to be confined to persons, and denied to unthinking rocks and stars, then this criticism still holds. God plus Robert Schumann is a lot greater than God without Robert Schumann. It just won't do, of course, to respond that anything done by Schumann is 'really' done by God. For several reasons, notably the Problem of Evil (which we'll look at in Chapters 14 and 15), classical theists are most anxious to insist that what individual persons (angels, jinns, or humans) other than God do is *not* done by God. They may even contend that God bears no responsibility for what these other persons do.

What could the proponent of the Ontological Argument say against the criticism that the entire metaverse must be greater than God? There are basically two answers he might have to it. One is to say that everything God has created is part of God. The other is to deny that God plus his creation is a thing. Let's look at each of these in turn.

In classical theism (in the orthodox theologies of Christianity, Judaism, and Islam), God's creation is not God, nor is it part of God, nor is any part of it God or part of God. Thus, for instance, you and I are not God, nor are we parts of God. The Devil is not God, nor is he part of God. The opposite view, that you and I are God, or parts of God, and that the Devil (if he exists) is God, or part of God, is called, in one form of the idea, pantheism, in another form, panentheism. So in taking this line, the theist gives up classical theism and embraces either pantheism or panentheism.

The other way of answering my criticism would be to say that the greatest conceivable thing has to be a single entity, and God plus his creation is not a single entity. This answer can only be sustained if the Ontological Argument automatically excludes collections of things and applies only to individual things. But if we reword the Ontological Argument so that it refers to 'the greatest conceivable thing or collection of things', it doesn't lose any of the sense or force it had when it referred to 'the greatest conceivable thing'. If 'greatness' is applicable to God, then 'greatness' is applicable to the metaverse, God plus his creation. For example, imagine God plus his creation and call this M. Now suppose that God had made his creation twice as great as in the case of M. Call this second possibility M2. Then M2 is greater than M.

Is the Greatest Conceivable Thing Conceivable?

My third ground for criticizing the Ontological Argument is to point to a difficulty with the very idea of the greatest conceivable thing. Since the greatest conceivable thing is a knowledgeable person (we're accepting this for the sake of argument), being the greatest conceivable thing implies knowing as much as we can conceive anyone knowing. However, some kinds of knowledge are such that they are inherently unlimited. What this means is that however much knowledge we can conceive of someone having, it's always possible to imagine someone having more.

Consider the series of positive integers (an integer is a whole number). It begins 1, 2, 3 . . . Now, what's the highest integer? The correct answer is: There can be no highest integer. Anyone who thinks there could be a highest integer has merely not understood the concept of 'integer'. You can always add 1 to any integer, however big. The series of integers goes on for ever.

You might ask God to name the highest integer, and an omniscient God just could not do this, because there is no highest integer to be named. To ask for the highest integer is as pointless as asking for a square circle. It is part of the definition of an integer that we can add 1 to any integer, so no integer can ever be the highest.

But what this means is that, if God knows any integers, the highest one he has ever specifically thought of must be a finite integer, and we can conceive of an imaginary God who has specifically thought of a higher integer than the real God has thought of. Let's consider a specific application.

> The decimal places of *pi* constitute an infinite series. Suppose God exists. If we ask God to name the last decimal place value of *pi* he has thought of, the answer can only be a finite number. However, for any finite number, we can always name a greater number. Therefore we can always conceive of a hypothetical nonexistent God who can name a later decimal place value of *pi*. 'Great' includes 'knowing a lot' and 'knowing more than' implies (other things being equal) 'being greater than'. Therefore, if God exists, we can always conceive of a nonexistent God who is greater than the real God. Therefore, God cannot be the greatest conceivable thing.

Pi is a number used in calculating the measurements of circles and spheres. It's approximately 3.14159265. For most practical purposes, we only need to know *pi* to a few decimal places. Mathematicians using computers have now calculated pi to many thousands of decimal places. Unlike, say, the decimal expression of one-thirteenth, which is 0.076923 . . ., with the '076923' repeating indefinitely, the decimal places of pi display no regular pattern. There is no short cut, having been given *pi* to a hundred decimal places, to quickly find what numeral occupies the two hundredth decimal place. You just have to keep on working out all the decimal places until you get as far as you want to go.

The decimal places of *pi* constitute an infinite series. There are many other such numbers, for instance the 'exponential number' known as *e*, which is roughly 2.71828183. Such numbers are called 'irrational numbers', and it has been proved that for all irrational numbers the decimal places will never repeat or terminate.

Infinity is not 'a big number'. Infinity means you can always add more and still not get there. No matter how big a number you have, you can still add 1 (or, for that matter, multiply by fifty trillion), and you are no nearer the end, because there is no end. It is, therefore, *impossible* for anyone to 'know' the whole of an infinite series like the decimal places of pi.

A theist might respond like this.

> God's thoughts are so much higher than our thoughts that he can dispense with our tools of thinking. Since God can directly perceive the precise ratios involved in circles and spheres, he doesn't need to

calculate any decimal places of *pi*. He doesn't have recourse to *pi* at all.

By analogy, we might consider a domestic dog's 'beliefs' about where its food comes from, as contrasted with its owner's beliefs. The owner's knowledge of where dog food comes from and how it gets into the dog's bowl is so much superior to the dog's that whatever 'concepts' the dog may have are just ridiculously inadequate, especially if the owner happens to be production manager at a dog food factory. Similarly, our mathematics, including our need for *pi*, and perhaps for any numbers, would appear just as ridiculously inadequate by comparison with God's way of thinking. God's way of thinking has no need for such mathematical devices as recurring decimal places and infinite series.

Accepting all that, it's still a part of God's knowledge how much he knows of the content of the theories devised by humans, just as it is part of our knowledge how much we know of the content of a dog's consciousness. To know everything that it's logically possible for anyone to know, God has to know what we know, and he also has to know those logical implications of our intellectual tools that are beyond us. He must know—what no human poker player can possibly know—all those precise circumstances in which it's correct to raise pre-flop with a pair of nines.

Consequently, since it remains necessarily true that any God must know a finite number of decimal places of *pi* (counting zero as a finite number), and since we can always conceive of a non-existent God who knows more decimal places of *pi* than any given God, there cannot be a God who knows the most conceivable decimal places of *pi*, and therefore there cannot be a God who is the most knowledgeable conceivable person, and therefore there cannot be a God who is the greatest conceivable thing.

Traditionally God has been depicted as possessing some proficiency in arithmetic. According to *Matthew*'s Jesus (10:30), "The very hairs of your head are numbered." Unfortunately for God's math skills, *1 Kings* 7:23 (repeated at *2 Chronicles* 4:2) strictly implies that *pi* is equal to 3. Oops.

God Containing an Infinite Collection of Items

In response to the above, a theist might simply claim that God is instantly aware of all the decimal places of *pi*. The theist could *say* that God's mind is infinite, and that he knows all the elements in an infinite series. Thus God knows every decimal place of *pi*, and he knows every integer. He doesn't have to look them up; he's instantly aware of each number in every series. It's true that God couldn't name the last decimal place of pi, because there is no such numeral, just as he couldn't name the highest integer, but he still knows all decimal places of *pi* (and all integers) because he is infinite. Augustine took essentially this position when he claimed that God knows the identity of every number, even though the number of numbers is infinite. I suspect the position is logically incoherent but I don't know how to prove that.

This may look like a satisfactory position for the theist to take. Haven't theists often said that God is infinite? However, it's a position few theists will want to take. Theists who have said that God is infinite have generally also said that God is simple. It is one thing to say that God is infinite and another thing to say that God contains an infinite collection of items.

Some theists have actually denied that an infinite collection of items can exist, even in God's mind. This is the basis for the Kalam Argument, favored by William Lane Craig. We can now see that the Ontological Argument is incompatible with the Kalam Argument. Anyone who does maintain that God, being infinite, can know all the numbers in an infinite series, cannot also accept the Kalam Argument (which we looked at in Chapter 6). It's essential to the Kalam Argument that the whole of an infinite series cannot have any actual existence outside mathematical theory. When someone objects to the Kalam Argument that if there is no actual infinite, God can't exist, since God is supposed to be infinite, the advocate of the Kalam Argument replies that although God is infinite, he is simple. He does not contain an infinite series of items.

Yet according to classical theism, God must contain at least one set of items: 'things God knows'. Or even, 'real numbers God has specifically thought of'. Is this set finite or infinite? If, for instance, God knows all the decimal places of *pi*, then there's an actual infinite collection of pieces of knowledge in God's mind, and this contradicts the Kalam Argument. A proponent of the Kalam Argument must accept that the number of pieces of knowledge in God's mind is finite. If God does not know all the decimal places of *pi*, he knows a finite number of decimal places of *pi*, and we can 'possibly think of' someone greater than God, a hypothetical imaginary God who knows one more decimal place of *pi* than the hypothetical actual God. Thus, the entity whose existence is claimed to be proved by the Kalam Argument cannot be the greatest (or most perfect) conceivable entity. Therefore, no one can accept both the Kalam Argument and the Ontological Argument.

The argument I have given here is simply one way to pin down a broader insight. For any quality that has no inherent limits, there cannot be any value for that quality which cannot imaginably be exceeded. Whatever value that quality has, one can always imagine that quality with a greater value.

Suppose that the universe had existed in every way just like it has, with one difference: Beethoven wrote twice as many symphonies (and wrote all his other actual pieces too). The almighty God of classical theism could have accomplished this entirely costlessly, by an effortless miraculous intervention, without withdrawing resources from any other project. And it won't work to say that God has already done this in a parallel universe—we'll just make it part of the supposition that in that parallel universe, in our hypothetical example, Beethoven wrote four times as many symphonies.

A God who created a universe in which Beethoven wrote twice as many symphonies would have to be greater than the God who actually exists (if he exists). Greatness is as greatness does. This example brings out, once again, that there can be no upper limit to the greatness of something 'possibly thought of'. The greatest being we can 'possibly think of' is just incoherent and threrefore absurd, like the highest integer or a square circle.

A theist might reply that God's greatness is only potential, not actual. He can do anything he likes, but it is no diminution of his greatness if he doesn't do everything he can. Yet if I were to say that I am a greater poet than Arthur Rimbaud, because, had I put my mind to it, I could have written poetry even better than his, some literary pedant might suggest that my usage of the word 'greater' was eccentric.

If it's true, as I believe, that the greatest conceivable thing cannot exist, then this disposes of the Ontological Argument. It doesn't show that God doesn't exist, for God might exist and not be the greatest conceivable thing. The list of God's ten qualities I gave in Chapter 1 does not include being the greatest conceivable thing. My conclusions, then, are: 1. that the Ontological

Argument fails to show that God exists, and 2. that if there were a God, we would be able to conceive of a greater God than that actual God—and this fact should not trouble the believer in God.

Every so often, some philosopher dusts out the Ontological Argument and gives it a new twist, hoping to find some version of it which is sound. This was done by neo-Hegelians around the end of the nineteenth century. It was done again by several philosophers, notably Norman Malcolm and Charles Hartshorne, in the mid-twentieth century. The neo-Hegelians were poor logicians whereas Malcolm and Hartshorne were highly expert logicians.

The arguments of Malcolm and Hartshorne both proceed by showing that if the greatest conceivable thing exists, then it exists necessarily, and if it does not exist then it necessarily does not exist. In other words, if it exists, it must exist, while if it doesn't exist, it can't possibly exist. They then claim that there is nothing to show that God logically can't exist, and so we're left with the alternative, that God must exist.

But there are several good arguments showing that God (let alone the greatest conceivable thing, which is a more ambitious concept than God) cannot possibly exist. I look at some of those arguments in Chapters 13–18 of this book.

8

Do We Get Our Morals from God?

Morality means judgments about right and wrong. There are two popular arguments linking God with morality:

1. The existence of morality is evidence for the existence of God.

2. Without belief in God, people would behave more immorally than they would with belief in God.

The second of these has nothing to do with whether belief in God is *true*, so it has no place here. I will look at it in Chapter 20.

The Divine Command Theory

One popular theory is that morality consists of God's commands. According to this theory, we know that it's wrong to murder people or to short-change our customers because God has issued commands to that effect. This seems straightforward enough, but it can be interpreted in two quite different ways:

1. God's commands inform us about what is right and wrong.

2. God's commands make some actions right and others wrong. (If God had decided to issue different commands, different actions would be right and different actions would be wrong.)

A few theists (William of Ockham was one) have maintained #2 but most theists have maintained #1.

There's a difficulty here for theists who favor the Divine Command Theory. Does God say that good actions are good and bad actions are bad because these judgments are correct—independently of what God thinks? Or are good actions good and bad actions bad just because God says so?

If 'good' and 'bad' are defined by God's say-so, then it's a very weak assertion to claim that God is good—like saying that everything Hitler did as Fuehrer, in accordance with his new National Socialist law, was perfectly legal. But that's a trivial point. The important point is that if God were to announce tomorrow morning that murder is right, and if we could somehow know that God had made this announcement, it would not cause us to think that murder is right. We would simply say, 'Well, God has gone bad—what a shame!—but murder's just as wrong as it was yesterday.'

The issue raised here is whether morality is independent of God's wishes or is determined by God's wishes. If someone says, 'God would never announce that murder is right, because God is good', she's acknowledging that morality is independent of God's wishes. She's asserting that God is a good person (by some standard independent of God's say-so) and a good person would never say that something wrong, like murder, is right.

What Are God's Commands?

The Divine Command Theory doesn't do much for the claim that morality comes from God. Yet there's a more elementary problem with it. Morality is above all practical; it guides our everyday actions. As a practical matter, if we think that morality comes from God's commands, we need to know what God's commands are. But where do we go to ascertain what God has commanded? The usual answer is: some religious tradition. Yet all religious traditions are shot through with ignorance and fallibility.

You often hear people say that the Ten Commandments are the basic essentials of morality, but most people who talk like this couldn't tell you what the Ten Commandments are. The Ten Commandments are given in two places in the *Torah* (*Exodus* 20:2–17; *Deuteronomy* 5:6–11) and these two versions differ somewhat. It takes a bit of work to reconcile the two versions, and to make the result come out to ten. And so there are different Jewish, Protestant, and Catholic versions of the Ten Commandments.

Most Americans think of the Protestant version, which includes the commandment not to make any graven images (absent from the Jewish and Catholic versions in their abbreviated forms), though American Protestants are not usually hostile to sculpture (as Jews and Muslims are). Both *Torah* sources of the Commandments have God declaring that he punishes children, grandchildren, and great-grandchildren for the sins of the first generation. Both *Torah* sources command us not to do any work on the seventh day of the week. One *Torah* source implies that wives are chattels and both imply that slaves are a legitimate form of property.

The Ten Commandments tell us not to "kill." Most Americans who say they revere the Ten Commandments can't see any con- nection between this and the U.S. military dropping bombs on innocent people in foreign countries. Some Christian and Jewish authorities inform us that "kill" should be read as "murder," though 'murder' means unlawful killing, and humans have fre- quently found it child's play to classify any killing they want to do as lawful. The scribes who lovingly preserved the Ten Commandments in the *Torah* also lovingly preserved the glowing accounts of mass murder, ethnic cleansing, and enslavement of captured young girls for recreational purposes, all directed and warmly approved by Yahweh himself.

The *Torah* contains many commandments purportedly from God, including the commandment not to boil a kid-goat in its mother's milk (*Exodus* 23:19; 34:26; *Deuteronomy* 23:19). The rabbis have run with this one and said that God's intended mean- ing is that meat may never be eaten with any dairy products, despite the report that Abraham once fed God himself with a meal of curds, milk, and veal, and the Big Guy happily ate it up (*Genesis* 18:8). Are the Ten Commandments then somehow elevated above the *Torah*'s numerous silly rules, so that we know that, in the case of the Ten Commandments, they really are from God, for all peo- ple, and for all time? This isn't clear: the Jesus of the gospels says that the two greatest commandments are to love God and to love one's neighbor, and neither of these is in the Ten Commandments. The rabbinic tradition is that the *Torah* has 613 commandments, and none of these is to be ranked above the others. Jews give less emphasis than Christians to the Ten Commandments, preferring to call them the Ten sayings or the Ten Words.

It would be possible to go on at length showing the ambiguity, the obscurity, the convenient flexibility, the silliness, and in some cases the moral unacceptability of the ethical teachings found in the *Tanakh*, the *New Testament*, and the *Quran*. Theistic authorities often have ways of interpreting their scriptures to produce something tolerable in the way of ethical principles. But what's happening here? No one actually gets their morality from God's commands. They get God's commands from their morality. What else could they do?

It might seem that there's no way to determine God's commands, but actually there is one way. Since God is all-benevolent toward humans, we can find out what system of morality is best for humans, and infer that this is what God commands. But that system of morality will be just the same as the one most atheists would come up with.

Is Morality Objective?

Many theists—and also many atheists—maintain that 'morality is objective', by which they apparently mean, not merely that there are correct and incorrect conclusions within the framework of morality, but that basic moral judgments (like 'murder is evil') are factual judgments (just like 'water is a compound of hydrogen and oxygen'). In my view this is a mistake, but since I can't see how it could take us any closer to the existence of God, I won't take up space to refute it here.[34] If anything, the view that 'morality is objective' seems to suggest that what is right or wrong can be ascertained by purely factual investigation, and that, if true, would imply that God is no help in determining what's right and what's wrong.

A theist, believing that morality is objective, might say that God both made the world and handed down the moral law. But does this mean that God could have made the world exactly as it is, only with a different moral law? In that case, the moral law would not follow from any non-moral facts of the world. But then, how would that be different from there being no objective moral law, and God capriciously decreeing an *arbitrary* moral law? Alternatively, if the moral law actually follows from non-moral facts about the world, then we don't need the God hypothesis to discover the moral law.

Theists who reason from morality to God's existence seem to suppose that God's authorship or endorsement of a moral code would settle what is right and wrong. That would be true if we knew that God was all-good by standards independent of God's say-so. But if we didn't know this, we might judge God's preferred moral law to be wrong and conclude that God is not all-good by such standards. Though it's generally prudent to flatter the mighty, it's only right to proclaim that even infinite might does not make right.

Morality Is a Natural Feature of Humans

Unlike grizzly bears, humans typically live in communities. Though often surprisingly stupid, humans are (at least in some narrow respects) less stupid than any other known animal. Many of them are capable, for example, of reading and understanding a book like this one, something which is way beyond any non-human animal that we know of.

Unlike many animals, humans are not strictly programmed to do specific things (such as build a nest); more than any other animal they are capable of learning, and what they learn is to a very large extent dependent on the conditions in which they find themselves. For instance, some groups of humans learn to be very aggressive and to kill other humans quite readily, while other groups learn to avoid physical conflict as far as they can. Humans have a fairly lengthy period of early dependency; in the years immediately following birth, they can't survive without the help of grown-ups. Humans use language to communicate.

Given all these elementary facts about humans, there's just no getting away from the emergence of some kind of morality. Human groups are characterized by a high degree of compliance with explicit rules, mixed with a varying but usually fairly limited amount of deviance from the rules. Punishments and rewards are features of every human group. Punishments and rewards, either actual or hypothetical, are often announced in words (sometimes, the punishments and rewards are nothing but the utterances of words).

I am certainly not here attempting to offer a 'theory of the origin of morality'. (For example, I am saying nothing about the extent to which the specific moral rules that arise are due to genetic influences.) I'm merely pointing out that the emergence of some sort of morality is not at all surprising in human populations. Given the elementary conditions of human life, it's what we would expect.

The Argument from Consciousness

Some people have claimed that the existence of consciousness among humans is evidence for the existence of God. Why would anyone think that?

These things exist: rocks, rainbows, stars, atoms, bolts of lightning, birds' nests, magnetic fields, oceanic tides. Call these 'physical'. These things also exist: thoughts, hopes, fears, imaginings, hunches, dreams, daydreams, recollections of past events, awareness of colors and smells, experience of pains and pleasures. Call these things 'mental'.

The relation between the physical and the mental has always given philosophers a lot of trouble. We know that something mental can cause something physical: my intention to write this book (something in my mind) caused the manufacture of the physical object you now hold in your hands. Something physical can cause something mental: the fact that some people hold this book in their hands will cause them to become atheists. We also know that there's a very intimate connection between mental events and physical events going on in people's brains.

One obvious and natural conclusion is that mental events just *are* physical events. Having a daydream or remembering an appointment simply *is* a number of events going on in your brain. Quite a lot of philosophers favor this theory, sometimes called 'mind-brain identity' and sometimes called 'materialism'. For several reasons I don't need to go into here, other philosophers find this difficult to accept. The most popular alternative is dualism: the mental and the physical are two different realms which somehow interact with or accompany each other. However, most people who favor dualism would say that the mental only emerges when certain physical conditions exist.

So all materialists and many dualists would agree with the following two statements:

1. If a certain kind of arrangement of matter comes about, then mental events occur.

2. If mental events occur, then a certain kind of arrangement of matter has come about.

In saying "a certain kind of arrangement of matter"[35] we are thinking of a brain, though we don't need to rule out other possibilities. Most philosophers today would accept both of these statements. Theists have to reject #2 (since God is a disembodied mind), but most theists would probably say that, except for spirit beings such as God and angels, #2 is correct, and probably most theists would accept #1. There is one strand of thinking among theists which says that a physical body is needed for human consciousness to exist—hence the need for a physical resurrection. Swinburne apparently takes the view that God miraculously intervenes to make #1 true in our world, and might conceivably have created another universe, with the same physical laws, in which #1 did not hold. But still, he does accept that #1 holds true in our universe (wherever non-human spirits are not involved).

The one thing that everyone accepts, including Swinburne, is that there is some kind of very close association between mental events and brain events. Yet on Swinburne's account this is something of a puzzle, since God could just have easily have given a population of evolved animals consciousness without those animals having any particular brain events, or even brains at all. In fact, God could have given all the human faculties, plus telepathy, to a Gannymedean slime mold, as Dick did in *Clans of the Alphane Moon*. Swinburne's theory is therefore messy and *ad hoc*—exactly what he says he doesn't like about some other theories. Since in fact, in everything we observe, we find states of consciousness only in the presence of highly developed brains, the simplest and most straightforward theories are: 1. that states of consciousness just are states of certain highly developed brains or 2. that states of consciousness, while not themselves identical with any physical arrangement of matter, somehow spring into existence when matter is arranged in a certain way.

If the brain gives rise to consciousness, we are a long way from knowing how it does that. But this doesn't mean that the theory that the brain produces consciousness is a bad theory. All the findings of brain science tend to show that consciousness is dependent on the existence of a brain that has not been seriously damaged. Nothing we observe suggests that some spirit independent of the brain is employing the brain as an instrument. It's therefore quite reasonable to say that consciousness is made possible by brain activity, even though we don't know how this works. It's possible that future observations might clash with the theory that the brain gives rise to consciousness, and brain science might have to change direction, introducing spirit activity to explain what is observed. But so far people working in brain science have seen no need for this.

The Dependence of Mind on Brain Doesn't Imply Physiological Determinism

Some people react to the suggestion that consciousness is caused by brain activity with incredulity. How can something as wonderful as a Beethoven string quartet or Einstein's theory of relativity be produced by mere matter? But we could just as well ask, how can these things be produced by mere spirit? We don't know very much about matter (except that it's much more subtle and complex than it looks) and we know nothing about spirit, so why assume that sublime productions of the human mind are more likely to come from spirit than from matter?

The theory that consciousness is a product of the brain can also give rise to serious misunderstandings. Some people conclude that the mental events are illusory, and that physical events are 'what's really going on'. Or they conclude that the mental events, while real, are nothing more than effects of non-mental physical processes in the brain. Neither of these conclusions follows, and in my judgment they're both utterly absurd. Caesar crossed the Rubicon because of certain thoughts going on in his mind. If these thoughts were identical with events in his brain, or if they were not identical with but were made possible by events in his brain, either way, this cannot mean that the events in his brain 'really' made him cross the Rubicon while the thoughts had no part to play. The theory that the brain gives rise to thoughts is compatible with the commonsense theory that thoughts help to determine the precise physical state of the brain, and help to determine our bodily behavior.[36]

An Argument from Reason

Some theists have maintained that if there are no spirits then we can't trust our own reasoning ability. C.S. Lewis repeated many times his assertion that if our thoughts are due to "chance atoms" then they cannot arrive at truth. Alvin Plantinga has put forward a more elaborate argument to this effect. Plantinga says that if Darwinian evolution and "metaphysical naturalism" (denial of the existence of spirits) are accepted, then we can't rely on our own intellects. He quotes Darwin, who wondered, in a pessimistic passage in a letter to a friend, whether anyone would trust in "the convictions of a monkey's mind."

Plantinga argues that natural selection would favor behavior conducive to survival and reproduction, and this would not confer an advantage to holding true beliefs. Against the obvious point that an animal with true beliefs would be more likely to survive and reproduce than an animal with false beliefs, Plantinga imagines circumstances where false beliefs would do just as well. For example, Plantinga supposes a man running away from a tiger. He might be doing this, says Plantinga, not because he believes the tiger is a danger, but because he believes the tiger is a cuddly pussycat, and he wants to pet it, and also believes that running away is the best way to pet it.[37]

Much of the criticism of Plantinga has argued that being able to arrive at true beliefs will be favored by natural selection. This is obviously true. Though one can construct rare instances where a conjunction of false beliefs would lead to the same behavior as much more accurate ones, or even cases where a highly inaccurate belief would by chance lead to success while a more accurate belief would lead to disaster, this will not be the case on the average and in the long run.

Plantinga's statement of his argument insinuates that beyond such instances of knowing the truth, we have to know something more: some general thesis about the reliability of our intellects. Can I do better than random at deciding whether or not it's true that I'm now being attacked by an elephant? Can I do better than random at deciding whether or not it's true that I now have a spear penetrating my abdomen? Can I do better than random at deciding whether or not it's true that I am now hungry? For practical purposes, all we have to do is make a lot of specific judgments of truth or falsity about particular circumstances. The reliability of our intellect is not something additional that we have to establish.

But these are all side issues. Plantinga assumes that naturalism and evolution mean that the mind can only do what it's been selected for. But this is no part of Darwinism: the human mind can compose fugues or solve sudoku, just as the human body can tap-dance or do handstands, and I suggest that finding out the truth is more like these things: it does not have to have been selected for to be a real human accomplishment.

The whole basis of the argument is faulty: if my mind has been constructed by an omnipotent spirit, why should I place any more reliance on it than if had been formed by millions of years of natural selection? No reason is given, or could be given. The *origin* of the mind has precisely nothing to do with its *reliability*—that would be an example of the Genetic Fallacy.

As for the monkey's judgment, if the monkey were deciding the truth or falsehood of whether that looming shape was another monkey or a leopard, whether that object in the water was a log or a crocodile, whether that branch six feet away could support a monkey's weight, I would place quite a bit of trust in the convictions of the monkey's mind.

9

Can We Know God Directly?

People who appeal to religious experience as indicating the existence of God will sometimes deny that this is an *argument*. They mean to imply that their experience is more persuasive than any argument, that they just know there is a God because they experience him, and that's that.

This claim does not hold water, for two reasons.

First, the theist who appeals to her own religious experience as evidence is usually talking to someone else who has not had any such experience. She is therefore offering her own experience as *evidence* of the existence of God, and this is nothing more nor less than an argument.

Second, while we can accept that someone who reports an experience has actually had that experience—we may assume that she is truthful and that her memory is good—the claim that the experience is an experience *of God*, a God who actually exists outside her imagination, is *a fallible intellectual conclusion on her part*.

Just as Monsieur Jourdain had been talking *prose* all his life without realizing it, the theist who appeals to her religious experience is offering an *argument*, whether she appreciates this fact or not.

Is Religious Experience a Form of Perception?

A standard argument for God goes like this:

Common-sense knowledge (there's a tree in the yard) and scientific knowledge (water is a compound of hydrogen and oxygen) both ultimately depend on the evidence of the five senses. Subject to certain precautions and conditions, we rely on the data we get by looking, listening, touching, and so forth. When people report that they have experienced God, they are similarly reporting their perceptions. So why shouldn't we grant the reliability of these perceptions?

As Swinburne puts it, "Just as you must trust your five ordinary senses, so it is equally rational to trust your religious sense" (1996, p. 132).

Nearly everyone can see the tree in the yard, and can see it whenever they want to just by going and looking, whereas many people never report having perceived God, and the overwhelming majority don't report that they can routinely perceive God. The theist's response to this is that some kinds of perception (such as correctly 'seeing' what is under a microscope) require training and practice. By such arguments, it's possible to show that there are parallels between perception of the physical world and 'perception' of the spirit world.

When we see a tree in the yard and conclude that there is, in fact, a tree in the yard, we are applying a *theory*, the theory that we are surrounded by physical objects. It may seem unfamiliar to call something we all take for granted a theory, but after all, we can reconsider what we have hitherto taken for granted, and in some cases, perhaps, reject it (as Neo does by popping the red pill in *The Matrix*).

In making sense of the experience of our senses, no other theory is a serious rival to the theory that there are physical objects. There is no need to belabor this point, as theists do not dispute it. When we turn to 'religious experience', however, the situation is different.

We can't help noticing that the objects of religious 'perception' are a lot less well defined and more culturally molded than anything in the realm of common-sense knowledge. Numerous people—perhaps not a majority but certainly at least a very substantial minority—have had experiences they may variously describe as experiences of God, experiences of Heaven, peak experiences, mystical experiences, experiences of oneness with the cosmos, or transcendental experiences. In this broad sense, 'religious experience' is a normal human attribute, like love of music or delight in competitive games.

It looks very much as though these same kinds of experiences are interpreted, by people in theistic cultures, as experiences of God, and are interpreted by people in nontheistic cultures as experiences of something other than God. (Alternatively, it's possible that the experiences may differ somewhat, and the quality of the experience is itself partly determined by the prior interpretation.)

Thus, Buddhists have such experiences, and many Buddhists systematically cultivate such experiences. There is a long history of Buddhist discussion of what happens in meditation and other 'altered states', but no Buddhist ever interprets such an experience as an experience of God, because Buddhism rejects belief in God and people raised in Buddhist cultures just don't think in terms of God. I have never heard of a case where some practitioner of Buddhist meditation says, 'Because of my recent experiences, I now see that Buddhism is in error: there is, after all, an almighty Creator God'.

My impression (which could be tested by quantitative research) is that, inasmuch as there is input from the raw experience itself, as opposed to cultural preconceptions, it is rather away from the God of classical theism and towards something more general and more diffuse. In Abrahamic cultures, mystics tend to be suspected of the heresy of pantheism.

Roman Catholics (as well as Orthodox Christians and Anglo-Catholics) routinely report religious experiences in which they perceive the Blessed Virgin, whereas Protestants, Jews, Muslims, and Zoroastrians never report anything remotely like that. There are people living in communities in which witchcraft is believed to be omnipresent, and in such communities (whether they also believe in God or not), individuals frequently report that they have directly felt the baleful influence of witches. In cultures where there is no such belief, there are no such reports. Everything that can be said in favor of people's reports that they have experienced God can equally well be said in favor of other people's reports that they have experienced abduction by space aliens, with its attendant surgical operations in space ships. Yet most believers in experiencing God are skeptical of reports of alien abductions.

If only a quarter of the world's population reported that they could see oak trees, while the other three-quarters just insisted there was just nothing there, this would be an amazing anomaly in the realm of sensory experience, of a kind which has never actually occurred. The analogy with ordinary sense experience is not, after all, very tight. But no doubt this could be accounted for somehow—it would be unreasonable to insist that religious perception be *exactly* like ordinary sense-perception. The theist could claim, for instance, that Buddhists never perceive God because when they meditate they are doing something analogous to 'not looking in the right place'.

Delusional Interpretations of Experiences

We have experiences which we classify as perception, and we have other experiences which we don't classify as perception. If we have the experience of seeing a tree, we usually accept that there is a tree there to be seen, whereas if we 'see stars' from receiving a bang on the head, we don't accept that those stars are there to be seen. The 'stars' are just products of our own internal make-up; they are not entities existing outside of us. The question arises, with religious experience, whether there is 'really something out there' or whether the experience is of something internal, without an external object.

By taking 'perceive' in a broad sense, any experience may be described as perception. If you feel cold, you may think the temperature of the air has dropped, but a thermometer may convince you that you're wrong. You may then say that you wrongly supposed that you were perceiving a lower atmospheric temperature. You were really perceiving a sickness of your body.

If I have a toothache and you have a toothache, this doesn't mean that we're perceiving the same thing. I am perceiving something wrong with one of my teeth, whereas you are perceiving something wrong with one of your teeth. The fact that the two experiences are similar does not mean that both relate to the same object. If there were some environmental features, say electrically charged rocks, which brought on toothache in people who went near them, then we might say that two people having toothaches were perceiving the same thing: electrically charged rocks. But since nothing like this actually occurs (as far as I know), we say that two people having toothaches are aware of something within themselves that just coincidentally happens to be similar.

There are science-fiction stories in which ordinary people encounter beings who can read their minds and talk to them tele-

pathically. Usually in such stories, the people picking up these telepathic messages are in no doubt that this is what they are doing—
the messages are so specific, concrete, detailed, and testable in
their implications, that there is no question about it. But suppose
someone starts to receive what are seemingly telepathic messages,
but has doubts about this. They begin to wonder: Are these messages what they seem, or is that a misinterpretation on my part; are
they really more like vivid dreams or hallucinations?

How would the person in this predicament decide? At first he
might be influenced by the intensity and vividness of the perceptions. But this is not reliable. We know from the experiences of
people who have swallowed drugs like LSD, or have had their
brains stimulated by the instruments of brain surgeons, that the
most powerful impression of 'reality' can be created artificially. We
also know that a minority of people (some of them diagnosed as
'psychotic') frequently have these experiences without artificial
aids.

In science-fiction stories where people start to receive telepathic
communications from alien beings (or, as in *The Chrysalids*, from
mutated humans) the question usually doesn't arise whether they
are deluded. The reason is clear: the messages cohere and provide
information that is sometimes independently confirmed. However,
outside fiction, whenever God speaks to devout believers, he
always talks exactly like a fortune cookie. He rarely says anything
specific enough to be tested, and when he does, what he says is
wrong approximately fifty percent of the time.

Of course, the experience itself *is* real. That's not in dispute.
What's in dispute is the interpretation the person has placed upon
the experience, the inferences he has made about entities existing
outside himself.

If the person's own conviction that he has perceived God, or
angels, or the Blessed Virgin, is not itself evidence that he has really
done so, what would count as evidence? The answer, of course,
is—we all know this already—independent corroboration.

Corroboration does not in itself directly substantiate a theory.
What is involved in corroboration is always (at least tacitly) a comparison of two or more theories. We compare the theory that religious experiences are forms of perception of external realities with
the theory that religious experiences are essentially private and
subjective, that is, they are primarily perceptions of internal reali-

ties, realities within oneself, probably associated with realities within one's brain. We fail to find a single piece of evidence that can most easily be explained on the theory that these experiences are perceptions of external realities, whereas we find many pieces of evidence that can most easily be explained by supposing that these experiences are internal.

A theist might claim that my request for corroboration merely shows my materialist bias. I ask for perceptions of a spirit world to be corroborated by observable indications within the physical world, but I do not ask for perceptions of the physical world to be corroborated by observable indications within the spirit world. Hence, I am not being fair to the spirit world.

However, theists began this discussion by claiming that religious experience is a form of perception, similar to ordinary perception of the physical world. Their argument fully acknowledges that everyday perception of material objects is the gold standard of 'perception'. The materialist bias is in the theist's argument from the beginning. Furthermore, on a practical level, if you and I disagree and try to resolve our differences, it's a good idea to start from those areas where we agree. In the Abrahamic world—the world of Judaism, Christianity, and Islam—there's virtually no disagreement that the realm of physical objects does exist, whereas there always are, and always have been, people who suspect that there is no spirit realm.

We might conceivably meet someone, perhaps an adherent of some kind of mystical sect, who maintained: 'The entire physical world is just one vast hallucination. It has no existence and all the evidence of our senses means nothing. But there is a real world of which we can become aware, a world of gods and other spirits.' This doesn't sound very promising. I would ask such a person: 'Why do you think that?' and take it from there.

Some advocates of the Religious Experience Argument seem to think that we accept the evidence of our senses because each act of physical perception is, so to speak, sharp, crisp, and compelling. As you may have guessed, I reject this. The vivid nature of an individual instance of perception, in my view, counts for next to nothing. However, to those entangled in this way of thinking, I point out that to liken the devout believer's experience of God to the ordinary person's experience of seeing a tree looks like a bit of a stretch.

We do have information about what religious experience is like. Former believers are able to testify to what the discourse about such experiences used to be like for them. Believers talk among themselves about such experiences, and their conversation never has any of the precision of a discussion of the buds opening on that tree in the yard or of the sadly wayward brass section in last night's performance of the Brahms *Requiem*. They also report on their arduous struggles to retain their 'faith'. No one who can see a tree in the yard talks about struggling mightily to keep his faith in the existence of the tree. We can form a fair notion of what the devout believer's 'experience of God' is like. It sounds, by turns, very much like wishing hard, or compulsively pretending, or claiming to experience something that it is felt to be meritorious to experience, or getting a thrill out of daringly affirming something evidently untrue ('Yes, Virginia, there is a Santa Claus'), or regressing to the mental state of the five-year-old who says he has a big, chatty, invisible companion.

Just suppose that someone who claims to have directly perceived God really has directly perceived something external to himself. There would still be the possibility that he has radically misconstrued what he has perceived. Sensory perception does not automatically come with an accurate analysis of the object perceived. When I see a tree, I see a machine for using sunlight to make sugar, but this information is not given to me directly in the act of seeing the tree. When someone perceives something they take to be God, they obviously cannot immediately perceive that this entity made the universe and knows everything.

The Lesson of Nunez

'The Country of the Blind' is one of H.G. Wells's most intriguing and memorable stories. Climbing in the Andes, a man named Nunez falls over a precipice and lands in an isolated valley inhabited by a population of humans, every one of whom is totally blind. Not only are they blind, but they have no notion of what it would be to see. When Nunez tries to explain to them that he can see, they take him to be insane, and eventually they propose that he must be operated on surgically, to remove his eyes, which are apparently the cause of his wild delusions. This story, written by an atheist, has been cited by theists as a good illustration of why we should credit the testimony of religious experience.[38]

But Nunez would easily be able to prove to these blind people that his ability to see was no delusion. 'Just stand over there, twenty feet away from me, and I'll tell you exactly what you're doing.' At first, such demonstrations might be seen as tricks. But they would be so reliable and consistent that given half an hour's experimentation there could be little doubt remaining. This person, it would be clear, has an ability that no one else has.

One brief attempt of this approximate sort is made in the Wells story, but Wells the adroit story-teller makes it come out that the demonstration is unconvincing. However this failed demonstration does occur, and both Nunez and the blind people readily understand what is being attempted—the corroboration of an apparently fantastic claim. Wells had to include some such incident, or the reader would think of it for himself, and dismiss the story as unconvincing. But a lot of narrative skill is needed to make the reader accept that the sighted man could not convince the blind people he can do something they can't.

Among other elements, Wells's story is helped along by the fact that the blind people's non-visual senses are prodigiously developed, and that they sleep by day and stay awake by night, when Nunez's vision is not so sharp, furthermore they have no windows on their buildings, so that the interiors are in darkness. But an even more fundamental premiss of the story is that no one in the blind population is a dissident thinker. Everyone is enthusiastically orthodox in rejecting, not only the possibility that Nunez can see, but also many other facts such as the possibility that there might be other humans outside the valley.

Now compare this with the theistic parallel. The conventional view in our world is, not that there is no spirit world, but that there is such a world. Millions of people are eager to believe in such a world, and seize upon everything that could, by the wildest stretch of the imagination, be construed as evidence for it. Transparent frauds like John Edward and Sonya Fitzpatrick easily win the loyalty of millions of TV viewers.

Just imagine, for comparison with Nunez, some religious entrepreneur proposing to a number of journalists, theologians, or other credulous types, that he could demonstrate the existence of supernatural phenomena only at dead of night, only under very strict and unusual condition s, and only if they will pay attention over a long period of time. They would be falling over themselves to witness and document this marvel, and to give him the benefit of any possible doubt. The dogmatism of the blind people in the Wells story is all in the wrong direction. In our world, people thirst mightily for some corroborative demonstration, but no corroborative demonstration has been produced. Further, the story would lose all plausibility without the feature that the blind people are greatly superior to Nunez in their senses of hearing and touch—do we want to say that people who have religious experiences are always deficient in their ordinary perceptions of the physical world?

And so the example of 'The Country of the Blind', properly considered, tells *against* the theistic interpretation of religious experience.

10

Faith Doesn't Have a Prayer

Theists often pray to God and think that God is listening. Sometimes they even attribute events, such as their child's recovery from an illness, to prayer, and this confirms their assumption that there is a God. Theists are eager to point out that *intercessory* prayer (asking God to do something) is only one form of prayer. Still, it's the only form of prayer we can test for its effectiveness.

In studies of intercessory prayer, sick people are divided into groups and the names of one group given to church activists who are asked to pray for them. Some studies with lax controls have found a positive effect of prayer, and theists often claim that the effectiveness of intercessory prayer has been demonstrated scientifically. But now major studies conducted with more rigor have found no effect. Most recently, STEP (Study of the Therapeutic Effects of Intercessory Prayer) was funded by the Templeton Foundation, which generally propagandizes for theism and presumably hoped to get experimental evidence that prayer works. Instead, the study clearly indicated that intercessory prayer does not work.

STEP was directed by Herbert Benson at Harvard, under rigorous conditions. 1,802 patients recovering from bypass surgery were divided into three groups, two of which "received prayer" (an expression meaning that active Christians had been given their names and were praying for them; to be strictly factual, they received nothing) and one of which was not prayed for. No effect of prayer on recovery could be found, though there was one rather odd outcome. Because researchers wanted to test for a possible effect on health of patients *believing* that they were being prayed for, members of one of the groups were prayed for and were informed that they were being prayed for. This group suffered *more* complications than the other two groups.[39] This shows that if you believe you're being prayed for, your health will worsen, so take care.

The usual theist account of intercessory prayer is that God listens to people praying and responds by intervening miraculously in the physical world, for instance by making a cancerous tumor disappear. Just how we should imagine the omniscient and omnipotent God, Creator of the Universe, reacting to being fed some names rather than others as part of a medical study is not entirely clear; I suspect that such a being would be incapable of humor and would therefore not be amused.

Some people who believe in the efficacy of prayer believe that it works directly, not by way of God (or by way of saints who then go and intercede with God). In other words, some unknown kind of force emanates from the mind of the praying person and affects the wellbeing of the person prayed for. Since the evidence we have to date indicates that intercessory prayer doesn't work at all, this theory is no better than the God theory. But it does illustrate that even if prayer did work, this would not necessarily show there was a God. The hypothesis of such a mental force is extravagant, but the God hypothesis is way more extravagant.

Arguments from Faith

Theists often appeal to 'faith'. But what is faith? Paul called it "the substance of things hoped for, the evidence of things not seen" (*Hebrews* 11:1). All Christians agree that faith plays a big part in their religion, but when it comes to specifying what faith is, they are all over the map.

A popular conception of faith has the following elements:

1. **Belief in God (or in some particular type of theistic doctrine) does not come easily. You have to work at it.**

2. **Belief in God is meritorious. Disbelief in God is less meritorious, or even blameworthy.**

3. **Belief in God cannot be attained by the same type of approach we use to settle the truth, or the likely truth, of**

other hypotheses (that there are kangaroos in Australia or that O.J. Simpson slew his ex-wife). A special approach, involving a willful act of commitment, or 'leap of faith' is required.

Isn't this all a bit suspicious? There are various contentious opinions I have arrived at after a great deal of investigation and argument, among them that Alger Hiss was a Soviet spy, that Lee Oswald and no one else shot John Kennedy, that there is no such thing as a Freudian repressed memory, and that currently fashionable alarms about global warming are hugely overblown. I have spent hundreds of hours arguing with opponents about each of these. I have never dreamt of suggesting that it is sinful to entertain a doubt about my opinion, or that some extraordinary leap of faith is necessary, and I have never met anyone taking the opposing view who has argued like that.

If the God hypothesis is a promising one, then we don't need to appeal to faith. If the God hypothesis doesn't sit well with the evidence we have, then we should reject it and it would be wrong to seek to cling to it by giving it some privileged exemption from criticism. Faith is always at war with truth, because if we try to make ourselves arrive at a predetermined conclusion, we run the risk of not dealing honestly with the evidence.

Some theists minimize the difference between faith in God and belief in other factual claims. Theists of this type maintain that we often resort to faith, and that what we're doing when we have faith in God is not at all unfamiliar or unreasonable. A favorite example of John Henry Newman's was the belief that Britain is an island.[40] Newman's primary audience was people residing in Britain. In Newman's day there were no satellite photographs showing Britain completely surrounded by water.

What Newman's example illustrates is that much of what an individual knows is not the outcome of personal observation by that individual but is picked up by that individual from the culture transmitted by other individuals. If personal observation is considered the most persuasive kind of evidence, then the view that Britain is an island can be made to sound quite suspicious. But, as Perry Mason never tired of pointing out (in the eighty-three original stories by Erle Stanley Gardner), circumstantial evidence is the best evidence we have, and eye-witness evidence is the worst.

If Britain is not an island, then it is joined to some continent, presumably Europe, by land. We don't have any reports that anyone has walked from Paris to London without crossing a major stretch of water. If such a report came our way, we could investigate it. We know that some people, such as William the Bastard and the Emperor Napoléon, had a strong incentive to find such a land passage. We do have many reports from people who have sailed along Britain's east coast and seen a lot of salt water to the east.

It would be unfair to give the impression that Newman jumps straight from this example to faith in God. However, my point is that believing Britain to be an island is most definitely not a case of believing something 'on insufficient evidence'. Nothing even remotely analogous to faith is involved here. The theory that Britain is an island is a good theory, and was a good theory in the nineteenth century, and nothing ever beats a good theory except a better theory.

I may cling to a theory in the teeth of some seemingly contradictory evidence, and I may be right to do so. On hearing that a friend of mine has been accused of a dastardly crime, I may take the view that I know him sufficiently well to be sure that he's innocent. I might express this by saying that I have faith in his innocence. If that were all that were meant by faith, I would have no objection, except to say that introducing the word 'faith' here can be misleading (given that theists have often employed it to signify something different). In this example, one category of evidence outweighs, in my judgment, another category of evidence. And in making such a judgment I *could* be mistaken. The evidence for my friend's guilt may pile up to the point where I have to abandon my belief in his innocence. There would be no merit in my saying: 'no matter what the evidence, I will always cling to the hypothesis of my friend's innocence.' That would not be meritorious; it would be foolish.

One possible source of confusion is that 'faith' may be applied to cases where the theory we adopt is not *justified* by the evidence—even by all the evidence, taken as a whole. If the theory's not being justified by the evidence means that the evidence does not render the theory certain—does not logically imply the theory—then that's frequently the case. But it may still be true that the theory is justified by the evidence in a different sense: that the theory beats all rival theories (that we can think of) in accounting for the evidence. Therefore the fact that a theory we feel we ought to accept outruns the evidence, in the sense that it goes further than can be deduced from the evidence, is never grounds for suggesting that the theory must be accepted on faith. All good theories outrun the evidence in that sense (as do most bad theories).

At the other extreme, there are theists who emphasize the unreasonableness of faith. They candidly proclaim that faith in God is utterly different from the approach we take to any other factual question. However, this view is much rarer than is generally supposed. It's often attributed to the fourth-century Christian Tertullian, who is notorious for having said 'I believe because it is absurd' or 'I believe because it's impossible'. In fact, these quotations are torn out of context, and Tertullian took almost exactly the opposite view. Tertullian very definitely defended the claim that Christianity is reasonable and not at all absurd.

Better candidates for people who might have held that we should have faith in God against all reason would be the seventeenth-century Catholic Blaise Pascal and the nineteenth-century Protestant Søren Kierkegaard. But even these would be controversial attributions. Let's just imagine some Christian admitting that Christianity defies all rational standards and should be accepted because of its very absurdity. One problem with this approach is that we have no way of choosing between two rival belief-systems both demanding to be 'accepted on faith', unless, perhaps, we are to choose the more absurd of the two. Christianity is indeed pretty absurd, but we could probably come up with something even more absurd if we put our minds to it.

Another problem with such an approach is that it tends to assume that belief can be a matter of choice. Yet we cannot believe whatever we choose to believe. Belief is involuntary. If you doubt this, try making yourself believe—even just for a few seconds—that there are no kangaroos in Australia. As you can see, it's quite impossible. Although we can never believe just what we choose to believe, we can choose to take actions which may have the unexpected effect of changing our beliefs. A person can refuse to read *Atheism Explained* because she feels that this might 'undermine her faith'. She might be right, but even making that choice shows a certain awareness that her faith is liable to be undermined by being exposed to critical arguments, and thus her belief cannot be so very solid to begin with. Someone who refuses to listen to counter-arguments because afraid that they would cause her to change her views already believes that her views are shaky. In what sense, then, are they really her views? Such a person may have quietly crossed the borderline between believing something and pretending to believe it.

Blaise's Bad Bet

Blaise Pascal's famous Wager is cast in terms of belief in God's existence,[41] but this must be a slip due to the unfinished form of Pascal's notes. Pascal is well aware that merely believing in God is no better than being a Jew, a Muslim, or a Protestant: you'll still get the eternal damnation you deserve. Only full adherence to the Catholic Church's creeds will save you: that involves believing much, much more than the mere existence of God. In the course of his discussion, Pascal does show he's assuming that commitment to all the rigmarole of Catholicism, not simple belief in God, is the subject of his Wager.

If the Roman sect of Christianity turns out to be right, adhering to it will get you infinite and eternal happiness, as opposed to infinite and eternal torment, whereas if Catholicism turns out to be false, you will have lost nothing, especially as following Catholicism (Pascal claims) will net you certain benefits in this life. This, says Pascal, makes believing in Catholicism a very good bet. There are various other arguments implied by Pascal. For instance, he assumes that you really want to believe, and that diligently following Catholicism will have the effect of causing you to come to believe. But let's leave these aside and just look at the Wager itself.

I've pointed out that this won't do as an argument for God's existence, but only as an argument for the whole Catholic package. Apart from that, the Wager fails to consider a number of possibilities. Perhaps there's a God, but it's not the Christian God. Perhaps God is especially incensed at being insulted by the blasphemy that is Christianity, and will send all Christians, and only Christians, to everlasting torment. Or perhaps God rewards people with Hell or Heaven according to how well they have used the intellectual gifts he gave them. Thus, people who do a good job of arriving at the truth go to Heaven, while those who accept theories on inadequate evidence go to Hell, with the worst torments of

Hell reserved for those who swallow patent absurdities like the Trinity or the Real Presence.

Or maybe people are sent to different gradations of Hell or Heaven, according to their behavior in relation to the other conscious beings they encounter. Or perhaps there's a God, but no afterlife. Or perhaps there's a God and an afterlife, yet God does not reward or punish people in the afterlife for what they do or don't do in this life.

None of the boys in Vegas would take a second look.

Is Belief in God Self-Evident?

Theists have often claimed that the existence of God is self-evident, but usually this is just a hyperbolic reference to the Design or Cosmological Arguments. However John O'Leary-Hawthorne seriously maintains that the existence of God is self-evident, just as $2 + 2 = 4$ is self-evident. He contends that knowledge of God is 'a priori knowledge'.[42]

O'Leary-Hawthorne points out that some people reject the self-evident truth of $2 + 2 = 4$ and likens these people to atheists. Someone who can't see that it's obvious that God exists is like someone who can't see that $2 + 2 = 4$, or that a red bus is a bus. O'Leary-Hawthorne likens the Christian, confronted by an atheist, with an atheist, confronted by some alien creature which professed itself unable to see that some of the things the atheist takes as self-evident are true. This alien creature would lack some essential cognitive ability, and the atheist too lacks an essential cognitive ability, given to some humans and not to others, which O'Leary-Hawthorne calls "the gift of faith."

O'Leary-Hawthorne acknowledges that most Christian philosophers do not accept that the existence of God is self-evident, which means that those Christians have not received the gift of faith. So, by his own account, many believers in theism, perhaps most, suffer from the same cognitive deficiency as all atheists.

O'Leary-Hawthorne identifies being self-evident with being obvious. He uses the term 'primitively compelling' to equate these two (p. 127). He leaves the impression that some people just know that $2 + 2 = 4$ and some other people just can't see it. Confronted by someone who can't see that $2 + 2 = 4$ or that God exists, O'Leary-Hawthorne can say nothing to help them.

Although we may sometimes use the word 'self-evident' to
mean 'obvious', what O'Leary-Hawthorne really wants is a
stronger sense of 'self-evident', tantamount to 'necessarily true'.
What appears obvious often turns out to be wrong. The sense of
self-evidence O'Leary-Hawthorne wants for God is the sense that
survives mature reflection. But awareness of this kind of self-evidence is learned; it is the result of intellectual training. It's not
something that just pops into some people's minds and not other
people's.

A child may learn that 2 + 2 = 4 and may soon come to regard
it as obvious. But still, the child has not learned that 2 + 2 = 4 is
self-evident in the strong sense referred to by O'Leary-
Hawthorne. The child may suppose, for example, that we know 2
+ 2 = 4 is true because we have found by experience that whenever
we put two objects with two objects, we generally then have four
objects.

An arithmetic teacher may be confronted by a pupil who
believes it is obvious that you can divide by zero. The teacher has
to get the pupil to accept that you cannot divide by zero. If the
pupil becomes familiar enough with this fact, he will eventually
consider it obvious. But still, he has more to learn if he is understand that it is self-evident (that it is an 'a priori truth'). To most
people it is not obvious that there is no highest prime number, but
to someone with a smattering of mathematical knowledge, this is
exactly as obvious as 2 + 2 = 4. But this is still not self-evident.
However, to a mathematician specializing in primes and therefore
conversant with the proof that there is no highest prime, the nonexistence of a highest prime is indeed seen as self-evident.

O'Leary-Hawthorne has confused the issue in precisely this
way. He envisions "a race of skeptics who cannot bring themselves
to believe in arithmetic or the laws of logic." However, any intelligent beings can be satisfied that arithmetic and the laws of logic
are useful methods of computation. They don't have to believe
these disciplines contain a priori truths in order to "believe in"
them.

By identifying self-evidence with obviousness, and both with
the primitively compelling, O'Leary-Hawthorne gives the impression that self-evidence is something naive, unaccountable, and
untreatable. In fact, if someone fails to see that something is self-
evident, there is always something we can do about it. We can help

them to see its self-evidence (or at least, why we judge it to be self-evident) by characterizing it in a certain way. If O'Leary-Hawthorne wants to claim that the existence of God is self-evident, then he should be able to explain why.

11

The *Holy Bible* Isn't
Wholly Reliable

Properly read, the Bible is the most potent force for atheism ever conceived.

—Isaac Asimov

Some folks tell us that they believe in God because they have been convinced by the story of Jesus given in the *New Testament*. And some say that they believe in God because they have been convinced that the *Quran* could have come only from a supernatural source. Let's take a look at the *New Testament* in this chapter and the *Quran* in the next. We've already seen in Chapter 3 that the *Old Testament* (the *Tanakh*) cannot be relied upon.

C.S. Lewis and other Christian writers appeal to the argument that the only possible way to explain the origin of Christianity is to accept that Jesus was the Son of God, and therefore that there is a God. And some who are not prepared to rest on this argument will still maintain that the *New Testament* reports of the life, death, and resurrection of Jesus are so difficult to explain without supposing God's intervention that the *New Testament* makes the hypothesis of God's existence seriously worth considering.

There are two atheist replies to this line of argument:

1. The historical evidence does not favor the theory that the four canonical gospels (*Matthew*, *Mark*, *Luke*, and *John*) could be even roughly accurate accounts of events that really occurred.

2. Even if these accounts were roughly accurate, they are not completely dependable, so it doesn't follow that there has to be a God.

The *Bible* tells us that there is a God, and tells us various things about his doings, his opinions on sundry matters, and his often erratic emotional states. If what the *Bible* says is invariably true, then there is a God.

Some Christians claim that the *Bible* is 'the Word of God' and totally without error. This view is called 'inerrantism'. It's practically equivalent to what is now usually called 'fundamentalism'. Christians who are not fundamentalists usually accept that there are errors in the Bible, but argue that parts of it are reliable as history, and that therefore we know that Jesus did exist, was born of a virgin, turned water into wine, and rose from the dead.

Inerrantism is still a major force within Protestant Christianity and within American culture. The prefaces to the most popular editions of the *Bible* contain statements by the translators that they accept inerrantism. Students at fundamentalist colleges such as Moody Bible Institute are obliged to sign a declaration to the effect that they accept every word of the Bible as truth.

Many people who are not biblical inerrantists over-rate the *New Testament*'s historical reliability, and many of the arguments I will now present against inerrantism are also good arguments against excessive reliance on the *New Testament* as a human product, an ordinary source of historical evidence. By arguing against the inerrantist view, I will sometimes also incidentally be arguing against the broader view that the *New Testament* gives us reliable historical information upon which we can build a case for Jesus being the son of God, and therefore, for the existence of God.

There's No Reason to Suppose the *Bible* Is Infallible

Why should we suppose that the *Bible* is completely without error? Some people quote the *Bible* to this effect. This is obviously circular. I could easily insert a statement in this book, announcing that everything stated in *Atheism Explained* is true. If everything in *Atheism Explained* were true, then that statement would be true. But if you're wondering whether everything in this book is true, it wouldn't help you to have that statement, because if any one thing stated in *Atheism Explained* is false, then that statement would also have to be false; it would be just one more false statement in this book. There's no reason to accept a book's own assertion that everything in it is true, unless you already accept that everything in the book is true, in which case you don't need that assertion.

Nonetheless, I've persuaded the publisher of this book to put an announcement on the copyright page, solemnly declaring that everything in this book is true.[43]

Nowhere in the *Bible* is there any assertion that everything stated in the *Bible* is true. This just has to be correct, for the simple reason that no one writing any part of the *Bible* was aware that eventually a collection of writings would be made by the church, called 'the Bible', and would include this person's contribution.

Even if we suppose that some *New Testament* writers were miraculously aware of the future, this does not mean that they would write about entities which had not yet come into existence. If there's one thing that's obvious to anyone familiar with the *New Testament*, it is that many parts of it were written in response to immediate and narrow circumstances, and were written within the framework of knowledge of the immediate readers. None of those readers knew of an entity corresponding to what we now call 'the *Bible*', which was compiled a couple of centuries after the latest portions of the *New Testament* had been written.

The text most often cited in this connection is *2 Timothy* 3:16: "All scripture is inspired by God and is profitable for teaching, for reproof, for correction, for training in righteousness." What did this writer mean by "scripture"? *2 Timothy* is one of the latest of *New Testament* books, but still, the writer was probably unaware of quite a number that would be included in the Christian *Bible* over two centuries later. When *2 Timothy* was written, the *Old Testament* canon had only very recently been determined by Jewish rabbis, but its definite authority was not immediately accepted by Jews or Christians; this would take some centuries. Early Christians did extend the notion of 'scripture' to recent Christian writings. But the author of *2 Timothy* might have counted many books as "scripture" which would eventually be excluded from the Christian *Bible* (including some that have been lost), and not counted many books that would be included. Early Christian writers (even counting only those later judged to be orthodox) sometimes deny the status of 'scripture' to documents that ended up being included, and ascribe this status to others that ended up excluded.

The issue of the *New Testament* canon has never really been resolved by Protestants. Luther and Zwingli (and Calvin, though he was a bit less committal) wanted to drop several books from the *New Testament*, but eventually Protestants came to accept, more or less by inertia, the same books as the Catholic *New Testament*. Today most Protestants are surprised to learn that this was an issue in the Reformation.

At any rate, the author of *2 Timothy* does not say that all scripture is guaranteed not to contain any error. He merely says that it is inspired by God and is profitable in several enumerated ways. Protestants have for centuries revered Bunyan's *Pilgrim's Progress*, and would certainly claim that it is inspired by God and profitable in just those enumerated ways, but they would be horrified at any suggestion that *Pilgrim's Progress* is guaranteed inerrant (or that it has the status of scripture). So the Christian *Bible* (unlike the *Quran* or the *Book of Mormon*) does *not* claim for itself that it is free of error.

Why do some Christians think the whole Bible is free of error? Here we come to an ironic oddity. Typically, the people who take this view are evangelical Protestants, who reject the authority of any human institution, including any visible church, and rely on 'the *Bible*'. However, the *New Testament* did not exist prior to the Christian church. The *New Testament* did not create the church; the church created the *New Testament*. The history is very complicated, but roughly, the *New Testament* was put together in the fourth century from a range of existing writings, by church councils and by the opinions of influential bishops. They selected according to consensus from among the most highly respected documents, but the selection would not have been the same if it had been done fifty years earlier or fifty years later. Nor would it have been the same if one of the other major sects of Christianity had obtained the patronage of the Emperor.

So the evangelical Protestant who upholds Biblical inerrantism has to face the question: were these early councils and bishops guaranteed to be free from error? If not, then they could have made mistakes. But if they were inerrant, then presumably all earlier church councils were inerrant. And in that case, the question arises: at what point in history did church councils cease to be inerrant? Protestant arguments against the infallibility of the Pope are weaker than they look, because Papal infallibility is, just like Biblical infallibility, something ultimately decided by church councils. They are both forms of *church* infallibility, since both Pope and scripture are ultimately accepted because they were once authorized by the church.

Did God Dictate the *Bible* Word for Word?

Muslims usually claim that the *Quran* was dictated to Muhammad, word for word, by Jibril, acting on God's orders. This cannot be true of the *Bible*, because we can easily see that the various authors of the books of the *Bible* have different personalities and different interests.

The different books of the *New Testament* vary in their prose styles: some display a more educated form of Greek than others, some have more 'semitisms' (Jewish-derived turns of phrase) than others. If all these *New Testament* books were dictated word for word by God, why would they be in different literary styles? And does anyone really think that (to pick just one example) God dictated to the writer of *2 Timothy* the words: "I have sent Tychicus to Ephesus. When you come, bring along the traveling cloak I left at Troas with Carpus . . ." (4:12–13). And would God himself, dictating word for word, quote from popular Greek stories and poems of the period?[44]

On that point, it would have been quite a jape for God to have quoted instead from, say, a Chinese novel written a hundred years later (that is, in the future). But nowhere in the *Bible* is there a single piece of factual information that might have been unknown to the purely human authors at the time of writing; no author of any part of the *Bible* had any idea that there existed such a place as China. There are innumerable facts of nature which the ancient Hebrews and the early Christians did not know, but which would have been of immense interest to them, sometimes even of practical use, and none of these is ever let slip in the *Bible*:

- **Plagues are often caused by fleas biting rats and then biting people.**

- **The alternation of day and night is caused by the Earth spinning.**

- There is a cold region to the south as well as one to the north.

- The tug of the Moon's attraction causes the tides.

- The heart is a pump which makes blood circulate around the body.

- Diseases like leprosy are caused by tiny living organisms too small to be seen.

- All the materials found on Earth were generated inside stars.

And hundreds of similar items. Not once does the *Bible* divulge any factual knowledge unknown to people in the communities where it was composed. The *Bible* is a very large and varied compilation, and if it really were dictated word for word by a well-informed supernatural being, this absence of a single item of superior factual knowledge would be in need of a special explanation.

For all these reasons, Christian theologians, even fundamentalist ones, don't usually claim that God dictated the *Bible* word for word. What they claim is that God protected the various authors of the assorted books of the *Bible* from error. (Catholics make a similar claim about the Pope's *ex cathedra* pronouncements.) These authors wrote in their own literary styles, expressing their own interests and personalities, and according to the limitations of their own knowledge, yet God, in the person of the Holy Spirit, intervened just enough to exclude anything that would be false. God modestly confined his own authorial role to that of Very Scrupulous Fact-Checker.

Puzzles about Inerrantism

Christians often argue *both* that the *New Testament* is inerrant *and* that the writers of the gospels were people who knew Jesus and were writing from personal experience. These Christians don't always realize that if the first claim is true, the second is largely irrelevant.

Many memoirs, even entirely sincere ones, are rife with inaccuracies, and even the most accurate accounts usually have a sprinkling of mistakes. The mistakes multiply the greater the lapse of time between the events described and writing them down, and the gospels were written at the very least thirty years after the events they describe. No historian would assume that Caesar's or Napoléon's memoirs are inerrant. If the gospels are inerrant, this absolutely requires miraculous intervention by God. As regards inerrancy, the gospels could have been written last week in Kazakhstan, and it would make no difference. It is thus pointless to try to show that the gospels are eye-witness accounts by participants, if what you actually want to conclude is that the gospels are inerrant.

This is especially true because the gospels describe many things which no one who might have written them could have witnessed. No human individual (except Mary) could have witnessed that Mary was a virgin, or (except Jesus) what Jesus said to Satan in the wilderness, and it's extraordinarily unlikely that any Aramaic-speaking companion of Jesus could have witnessed what Herod said to the wise men or what Pilate's wife communicated to Pilate.

There's another puzzle. If the gospels are guaranteed to be inerrant then the omniscient God read every word before publication and intervened to eliminate the mistakes which would naturally creep into any ordinary document. Why didn't he also eliminate all the worst sources of misunderstanding? God would have known that the major impact of these documents would be on millions of people living thousands of years after the immediate audience of the first and second centuries C.E. Surely then, he would have helpfully removed obscurities or ambiguities, let alone apparent contradictions and glaring omissions. If the concept of the Trinity, for example, is so important, then why is it never explicitly stated in the *New Testament*? From the simple fact that the *New Testament* documents are written within the intellectual horizons of their time and place of composition, and are filled with obscurities and ambiguities, we can reasonably deduce that they are not guaranteed by God to be inerrant.[45]

The standard Christian line is that the biblical authors adjusted what they were writing to the level of understanding of their immediate readership. This just won't do. Much of the missing information would have placed no unusual burden on the understanding of those first readers and would have been enormously helpful both to them and to later readers. There is exactly one simple and satisfying explanation: whoever was responsible for the contents of the *Bible* did not possess this information.

There Are No Independent Sources for the Story of Jesus

The claims of Christianity about Jesus arise entirely out of the traditions of the early church. The *New Testament* itself is a product, not the originating source, of those traditions. Without exception, all information about Jesus comes from those traditions and from later non-Christian accounts which were most likely derived from those traditions.

We know of Jesus only from what Christians, members of a small and insignificant religious cult, were saying about him some decades after the supposed date of his death—and what they were saying was not uniform and was continually evolving.

Popular Christian apologists often strive to give the contrary impression, by citing supposed early non-Christian references to Jesus. Here they are—all of them:

- In 112 C.E., Pliny the Younger, governor of the Roman province of Bithynia-Pontus, wrote a letter to the emperor Trajan, mentioning that there were Christians in his province who had been gathering before dawn to sing praises "to Christ as if to a god." Eighty years after the supposed date of the crucifixion, this is the earliest Roman reference to Christians, and it tells us nothing about the life of Jesus, not even whether Pliny had heard the name 'Jesus'.

- About the same time, or perhaps a few years later, the historian Tacitus, in his *Annals of Imperial Rome*, says that the emperor Nero had put the blame for the great fire in Rome onto "a class of men loathed for their views, whom the crowd termed Christians." Tacitus adds that "Christ" had been executed by Pontius Pilate. (Tacitus felt he had to explain to his readers what Christians were: he did not expect them to know this already.) Some Christians speculate that Tacitus might have checked this story of the origin of Christianity against Roman records, but this is not so. In Tacitus's day, as in that of the gospel writers, a governor like Pilate would have been referred to as "procurator," which is how the gospels and Tacitus refer to him. In fact, we now know that Pilate's actual title was the earlier one of "prefect." Tacitus was repeating the story of their origin told by Christians themselves, a story put together by Christians outside Palestine some years after the supposed date of the crucifixion of Jesus.[46]

- There are two references to Jesus in surviving copies of Josephus's *Antiquities of the Jews.* Josephus was a Romanized (and very pro-Roman) Jewish scholar. These two mentions both look like interpolations by later Christian scribes. One of them is clearly such: it could only have been written by an enthusiastic Christian, which we know that Josephus was not. This passage is missing from an early table of contents of the *Antiquities,* and does not begin to be cited by Christian writers until the fourth century.[47] At any rate, Josephus's *Antiquities* was most likely written in the 90s C.E. So it's too late to be an independent source: if Josephus had included references to Jesus, he could have gotten these from what Christians were saying. Josephus provides no independent testimony to the existence of Jesus, much less to any particulars about Jesus.

- There are references to Jesus in the *Talmud.* These are too late to constitute independent evidence. The earliest references to Jesus in the *Talmud* are early second-century at the earliest. The *Talmud* states that Jesus's father was a Roman soldier, but Christians shouldn't let this worry them, as the *Talmud* references to Jesus are just too late to have any historical significance, and are simply gossipy Jewish responses to the claims of the growing Christian movement.

Fundamentalist authors routinely cite several ancient writers as corroborating the gospel accounts of Jesus. But most of these writers are just too late. By around 70 C.E., some among the varied sects of Christians were claiming that Jesus had been crucified under Pilate around the early 30s C.E. As the Christian sects grew, non-Christians would hear this story, and would have no reason to question it, just as numerous Christians would later fail to question the main outlines of the legendary biography of Muhammad related by Muslims.

Some of the ancient writers appealed to do not provide any definite information about Jesus at all. For example, fundamentalist authors dealing with this topic routinely mention Thallus, a historian alleged to have written around C.E. 52, as testifying to the miraculous darkness at the time of the crucifixion (Strobel 1998, pp. 110–11). No writing of Thallus has survived, but we have a comment by the third-century Christian writer Julius Africanus, that Thallus was mistaken in attributing a period of darkness to an eclipse. There's no decisive indication that Thallus mentioned the crucifixion, or even mentioned Jesus at all, or had even heard of Jesus. Perhaps Africanus found a reference to an eclipse in Thallus, assumed it to be about the crucifixion darkness, and made his pious comment accordingly. Anyway, there's also no good evidence that Thallus wrote as early as 52 C.E.; he could have written as much as a century later.[48] If Thallus did mention Jesus, we cannot say that he wrote early enough not to have derived whatever he might have said from Christian sources.

How did educated Roman pagans react to the Christians' historical claims? At first the Christians were too few and too contemptible to merit any rebuttals, but when Christianity had grown to become conspicuous, educated Romans retorted that the Christian stories about Jesus were just made up.

We Don't Know Who Wrote the Gospels

It's commonly supposed, even by many non-fundamentalists, that two of the four canonical gospels were written by companions of Jesus.

We don't know who wrote the four New Testament gospels. They were originally anonymous. Their names were added by later church tradition. I'm going to refer to the gospels as *Matthew*, *Mark*, *Luke*, and *John*, and to their authors as 'Mathew, 'Mark', 'Luke', and 'John'. But we don't know their real names or anything about them except what we can deduce from the texts and from later church tradition. Even the developing tradition did not claim that *Mark* or *Luke* were written by eye-witnesses; the tradition claimed that 'Mark' had gotten his story from Peter.

At the very start of his gospel, 'Luke' explains how he came by the information contained in it. He states that "many" have written narratives, that the narratives originated with eye-witnesses, and that he has investigated these narratives. He does not claim that he witnessed any of the events himself, or that he had personally talked with any eye-witnesses, and he surely would have claimed either of these had they been true.

Matthew, Mark, and *Luke* contain many identical or near-identical phrases and sentences. For this reason they are called 'the synoptic gospels', 'synoptic' meaning 'seen together'. If you put passages from these three documents side by side, you can see that the wordings are too similar to be coincidental. This cannot be reconciled with testimony by three independent eye-witnesses (any court of law would conclude as much). Some Christians have suggested that the very similar wordings arose because the words of Jesus would have been especially revered and memorized, but this is incorrect: there are more verbal similarities in the narrative than in the words of Jesus, and the words of Jesus are *particularly prone* to be adapted by each writer in accordance with his own peculiar ideological outlook.

Independent eye-witnesses will often state details differently, while their stories more or less cohere. The similarities in *Matthew, Mark,* and *Luke* are not like this. They often differ on important essentials, while containing precisely the same, or only very slightly different, verbal formulas. These verbal similarities did not arise because the three writers got together and concocted their ·accounts in cahoots—for then they would have ironed out the embarrassing discrepancies.[49]

The similarities must have arisen either because one of them drew upon another, and then a third drew upon one or both of the first two, or because two of them were drawing independently upon one of them. There's considerable evidence to indicate—and the great majority of scholars, even fundamentalists, now believe—that *Mark* is the earliest and was used by 'Matthew' and 'Luke'. 'Matthew and 'Luke', working independently of each other, had *Mark* in front of them as they wrote. They also had another document, now lost, which scholars call 'Q'. Q can be partly reconstructed from the passages in both *Matthew* and *Luke* which are not in *Mark*.

'Mark' was ignorant of elementary facts about Palestine,[50] and it's doubtful that he had ever been there. He is writing for a predominantly gentile audience and seems to be a gentile himself.

Possibly all four gospels were written in Anatolia (Asia Minor, or what is now the non-European part of Turkey but was then Greek-speaking), though Rome and Alexandria are also possible. *Matthew, Luke,* and *John* were written after 70 C.E. (when Jerusalem was destroyed by the Romans). *Mark* may also have been written after the destruction of Jerusalem, though some scholars date it as early as 65 C.E.

Another piece of evidence against the 'companion of Jesus' theory is the way in which each of the gospel writers imposes his own doctrinal outlook upon the material. There are several examples of this, and I will here mention only the most striking: the Messianic Secret in *Mark.* In *Mark,* Jesus repeatedly instructs his disciples to keep his words secret. This is virtually an obsession of 'Mark', and of *Mark*'s Jesus. There's none of this secretiveness in the other three gospels, while several of their anecdotes contradict it. Associated with this, the incredibly slow-witted disciples in *Mark* never grasp who Jesus is, despite being told repeatedly, while in *John* the disciples always understand this instantly, without any trouble. Did Jesus continually urge secrecy upon his uncomprehending disciples or did he not? It's plainly ridiculous to suppose that he did and yet 'Matthew' and 'John' never thought it worth a mention, if 'Matthew' and 'John' had been personally close to the events they describe. And in that case, 'Mark', the earliest gospel-writer, must have described an entire theme of Jesus's ministry which had no factual basis.

If 'Matthew' had been among the twelve closest followers of Jesus, then why would he have so closely reproduced passages from *Mark,* whose author, everyone agrees, was not one of the twelve? If you are an eye-witness, do you give an account of what you have witnessed by copying out, with occasional elaborations and additions, parts of an account by a non-eyewitness?

As we read *Mark,* we notice that it is largely a string of brief anecdotes, in which the transition from one anecdote to the next is made by way of a similar phrase in both anecdotes, often a phrase not crucial to the substance, like the segues between the separate sketches in *Monty Python's Flying Circus.* Biblical scholars have called these transitions 'catchword connections'. From a close study of *Mark,* we can infer that 'Mark' was stringing together what were originally separate anecdotes, which must have circulated by word of mouth.

Attempts to Harmonize the Gospels with History

Luke tells us that Jesus was born when Herod was king and when Quirinius was governor of Syria. Yet historical evidence tells us that Herod was never king at the same time that Quirinius was governor of Syria. Quirinius became governor of Syria some time after Herod's death in 4 B.C.E. A trival point, certainly, but still, one of numerous little problems for those who think that the *New Testament* is inerrant.

We can respond to this discrepancy in at least three ways. The most straightforward is that 'Luke' made a mistake, but this contradicts inerrancy. Another is that the remark about Quirinius was not by 'Luke' at all, but was added by a scribe. This is possible but unhelpful. Any sentence in the *Bible* might have originated as a scribal insertion. We just don't have the originals.

We can simply assume that our version of *Luke* is correct and try to reconcile the historical evidence with the literal words of 'Luke'. This means that we have decided to treat *Luke* entirely differently from how we would normally treat a historical source. How might it be done? Christian scholars have come up with various solutions, including the theory that Quirinius was also governor of Syria earlier, though no record of this has survived (except for the remark in *Luke*). Fundamentalist Christian scholars are experts at this kind of job, which they have to perform hundreds of times over, because they feel they need to cling to the inerrancy of the Bible.

Isaac Asimov pointed out a parallel from the world of Sherlock Holmes devotees.[51] Some enthusiastic Sherlockians try to excavate 'the real facts' about Sherlock Holmes by puzzling over every little clue in the writings of Conan Doyle—their 'canon', or as they call it, 'the Conan'. (This is just an amusing pastime, of course.) The first name of Holmes's companion and memorialist Dr. Watson is clearly given several times as 'John'. Yet there is one passage where his wife refers to him as "James." A contradiction? Perhaps the Conan made a mistake?

A Sherlockian scholar reconciled the seeming discrepancy in the following way. Watson's name is given as John H. Watson. H. could stand for 'Hamish', which is the Scottish Gaelic form of

'James'. So the inerrancy of the Conan is preserved—at the cost of the outrageous implausibility that Watson's wife might be disposed to address him by his middle name translated out of the Gaelic (when the originally Gaelic form is domesticated in English and is never customarily translated into English).

Gospel Events which Never Happened

The New Testament gospels contain assertions of fact which are contrary to the historical evidence.

Matthew (2:16–18) claims that King Herod, hearing from the Wise Men that a 'king of the Jews' had been born, had all baby boys under two years old in and around Bethlehem killed. If such an event had happened, it would have been recorded. Josephus, who did not conceal his distaste for Herod, listed his atrocities, some of them much milder than this one. There's absolutely no historical trace of such an occurrence (except for the report in *Matthew*). Anyone who knows the *Bible* might guess that this yarn was suggested by *Exodus* 1:15–22, the tale of Pharoah's slaughter of baby boys, hoping to kill the infant Moses.

There's a story in *Luke* 2:1 that Augustus Caesar ordered a census of the entire Roman empire. Because of this imperial decree, Jesus's parents had to go to Bethlehem. This story may have arisen because there was a tradition linking Jesus with Nazareth, but if Jesus was to be identified as the Messiah, it would be more appropriate for him to have been born in Bethlehem, birthplace of the legendary King David.

There's no evidence of any imperial census at the appropriate date. A Roman census did not mean that residents of a town had to leave and travel to another town where their ancestors had supposedly lived. This would have caused a catastrophic upheaval in economic life every time there was a census, and such an upheaval would have been mentioned in documents. And there could have been no Roman census in Herod's kingdom, which was not yet a directly-governed part of the empire. Attempts by some Christian scholars to reconcile Luke's account with historical reality are criticized by Father Raymond Brown in his outstanding study of the birth of Jesus.[52]

A More Skeptical View

The bulk of what I have said above would be accepted by the great majority of *New Testament* scholars—and remember that these are mostly theologians by background and training, with a strong commitment to Christianity (or at least, the warm afterglow of such a commitment). However, in my view we should be even more skeptical of the *New Testament* story than these scholars typically are.

Bart Ehrman voices the consensus view when he claims that despite all the uncertainties and legendary elements in the *New Testament*, we can be sure of a number of basic facts about Jesus: that he did exist historically, that he was crucified, that he had siblings, and so forth. Ehrman's argument is that we should accept *New Testament* claims about Jesus when these are stated in the earliest documents, and when they run counter to the interests of the people who recorded them.

However, for its first century or two the Christian movement was a small, obscure, passionately motivated religious grouping— what journalists would now call 'a dangerous and manipulative cult'. It was also a movement divided into factions or sects with some beliefs that were opposed and incompatible. Its members had visionary or mystical experiences which were accepted as reliable sources of factual knowledge, and some of which became incorporated into the evolving doctrines of the movement.

The possibility that there might be historically unfounded stories in circulation among the members of such a religious movement becomes greater when we take into account the total destruction of Jerusalem by the Romans in C.E. 70. After that date, Christianity grew mainly outside Palestine and quickly recruited Greek-speaking gentiles who had no first-hand knowledge of events in Palestine. The earliest Christian groups in Palestine itself were quite likely wiped out or scattered. We do not know how they would have reacted if they had been able to read *Mark*; perhaps they would have dismissed this document as an astounding farrago of nonsense.

These are all rather general considerations. But there's one startling fact which should make us cautious about assuming that the gospels give much in the way of reliable information about the life of Jesus: most of the key claims about the events of Jesus's life are missing from the earliest Christian documents.

The genuine letters of Paul, and other letters not by Paul but almost equally early,[53] describe a Christ who was crucified and resurrected at some indeterminate historical time, which does not appear to have been recent. According to Paul, Jesus was a supernatural being, more than human but not claimed by Paul to be God, who took on human form and lived a totally obscure life. There is no mention of: a miraculous birth, Christ preaching (anything at all), Christ working miracles, Christ being in Jerusalem, or associated in any way with Pilate or Herod, Christ being Galilean, or associated with Nazareth or Bethlehem. Paul's obscure Jesus is difficult to reconcile with the gospel figure who performed spectacular miracles and had a popular following. And Paul never attributes any statements to Jesus, despite the fact that he is involved in controversies with other Christians where such quotations would have been very relevant, if he had known them. For example, Paul argues that it's no longer necessary to follow the Jewish law, but doesn't cite Jesus's defense of sabbath-breaking or his declaration that all foods are clean. It seems most likely that Paul did not know that there was a report of Jesus making these remarks, which were later to turn up in the gospels, or if he did know of them, considered them a new and false invention by a rival and spurious sect.

The Evidence for Jesus and Socrates

Confronted by the historical unreliability of the *New Testament*, fundamentalist Christians often respond with the following argument:[54]

> The period between the time of Socrates and Plato and our oldest copies of written accounts of them is thirteen hundred years. The period between the life of Jesus and our oldest copies of written accounts is less than one hundred years (or three hundred, if we mean complete documents rather than fragments). Yet no historian doubts the reality of Socrates and Plato!

The implication is that we can place more credence on what is written in the canonical gospels than we can in the accounts of Socrates and Plato. This argument is at best confused and misleading. If we're thinking about the dating of ancient documents and their copies, there are two distinct time periods to consider:

1. The period between the events described and the composition of the originals of the documents;

2. The period between the composition of the original documents and the oldest copies which have survived.

The fundamentalist argument talks about #2, whereas what matters most is #1.

The dating of the *original composition* of a document can be estimated by a number of methods, one of which is various clues the words in the document may give about the circumstances in which it was written, another is the dates at which other writers show that they know about the document. The dating of *the earliest surviving copies* can also be estimated by various methods, one being the style of calligraphy used by scribes.

The value of documents as historical evidence can be enhanced if documents by different people with different axes to grind agree on certain facts. The earliest documents referring to the life of Jesus are by Paul and others in the 50s C.E., about twenty years after alleged events in the life of Jesus described later in the gospels. However these letters say amazingly little about Jesus's life and they do not give the impression of recalling historical events within living memory.[55] The fuller accounts in the gospels are somewhere between fifteen and forty years later (thirty-five to sixty years after the events described), and now some very detailed stories appear. This follows the usual pattern documented by folklorists: legends become more elaborate and detailed, more concrete and specific, over time. First there's a legend, then it acquires names, dates, and places.

The accounts of Socrates were written by different people with different outlooks. Socrates is described in one way by Plato, in another way by Aristophanes, and in yet another by Xenophon. All three of these were people who lived in Athens at the time when Socrates was teaching. All of these people also wrote much that had nothing to do with Socrates and has been independently corroborated. Several other eye-witness accounts of Socrates have not survived but are quoted by later writers. Aristotle arrived in Athens a few years after Socrates's death and had conversations with people who had known him.

Think how different it would be if Athens had been destroyed within forty years of Socrates's death, and if all the first accounts of

Socrates had appeared thirty years after that, by people outside Attica, writing in a language other than Greek.[56] Also think how different it would be if a Church of Socrates had existed, struggling over the 'correct' view of Socrates, which they continually improvised as the spirit moved them, and striving to stamp out statements of deviant views.

There is much about Socrates which remains obscure and controversial. Plato puts elaborate arguments into Socrates's mouth. Whether Socrates ever said anything close to these, or whether Plato used Socrates as a convenient mouthpiece for his own quite different ideas, is still something on which scholars do not quite agree, though they tend more to the latter view. Aristophanes presents Socrates as an atheist, whereas Plato presents him as a believer in some kind of deity.

The period between the original composition of a document and the earliest surviving copies (Period #2.) is generally much less important than the period between the events described and the original composition (Period #1).

For example, everyone agrees that the books of the *Tanakh* (the *Old Testament*) were written centuries before the books of the *New Testament*, yet the earliest copies we have of some *New Testament* books are earlier than the earliest copies we have of some *Old Testament* books. This was true of *all* the books of the *Old Testament* prior to the discovery of the *Dead Sea Scrolls*, which began to be unearthed in 1947. A copy of the book of *Isaiah* found among the *Dead Sea Scrolls* is *a thousand years earlier* than the earliest copy available prior to the 1950s!

We can see, then, that:

1. The historical existence of Jesus is not as well supported by documentary evidence as the historical existence of Socrates.

2. Details of the actual life and opinions of Socrates are extremely uncertain.

3. Details of the actual life and opinions of Jesus are even more uncertain than details of the life and opinions of Socrates.

What If the Gospels Were Roughly Accurate?

Let's now suppose, contrary to a mass of detailed evidence, that the four canonical gospels were written by people who were close to the events they report. Let's grant for the sake of argument what we know to be untrue: that these gospels are generally reliable in broad outline. We would still have to correct them where they contradict each other or where they contradict well-attested historical facts, but then certain reported events which now seem not worth troubling with would appear to have some appreciable probability of having actually happened.

For comparison, suppose that we had no contemporary accounts of the sinking of the *Titanic* in 1912, but that in the 1930s (twenty years after the date of the sinking), a few brief reports appeared mentioning the bare fact that the Titanic had sunk, without specifying the date or the location, with a couple of other facts, such as the collision with an iceberg. Then, fifteen to twenty more years on, around 1950, four accounts were penned by purported *Titanic* survivors, each with a different point of view, but agreeing on a number of specific claims.

I generously take the case of an actual historical event, and with even more abundant generosity, I grant that, unlike the case of the gospels, these four accounts themselves claimed to be by eye-witnesses and, again unlike the gospels, we had no good reasons for discounting any such possibility. By our supposition, no other accounts of the *Titanic* survived, and all subsequent accounts were based on the ones just mentioned. No physical or other evidence, apart from these accounts just mentioned, ever came to light that the *Titanic* had even so much as been built in the first place.

Now if, for example, all four of these accounts stated that the ship broke in two before it sank, we would not judge it to be conclusively proved that the ship did break in two before it sank, but we would certainly judge this to be quite likely true, if not contradicted by physical or other evidence. On the other hand, if all four of them stated that before the ship sank, the heavens opened and a great booming voice from the sky said that everyone on board was going to heaven, we would be no more inclined to accept this than we are to accept the reality of the Angels of Mons.[57] To accept it as fact would be irresponsible sloppiness, despite the existence of four eye-witness statements to that effect.

If, then, the *New Testament* gospels were written by individuals close to the events described, this would not by any means be proof that any particular thing claimed by all four of them were true. But it would strengthen the case for viewing any such thing as very likely true.

Thus, in these hypothetical circumstances, we should no doubt view it as very likely that there was a man called Jesus (Yeshua) who hailed from Galilee, who was known as an itinerant preacher and miracle worker, who said some things approximating some of the sayings reported of him, who was received with acclamation by crowds in the street when he arrived in Jerusalem, who was executed by crucifixion, and whose followers, some years after his death, began to put about stories that he had risen from the dead. I can't accept any of this as likely on the evidence we actually have, but all of it would be accepted as quite likely under the hypothetical circumstances mentioned.

This evidence would not lead us to believe that this Jesus was God, or that he had any true and definite connection with God. The miracles reported of Jesus are exactly of the type reported of other miracle workers of the time, even down to minor details.[58] Being fathered by a god was attributed to notables in the ancient world, and our appraisal of this tale would not be heightened by our knowledge that it is based on a mistranslation of a text in *Isaiah*. Pronouncements attributed to Jesus never suggest more than mediocre percipience. The notion that he actually came back from the dead is less well corroborated and less likely than that Elvis Presley showed up in supermarkets and laundromats some time after his officially certified death in 1977.

Furthermore, these four documents indicate that Jesus made statements denying any possibility of his equality with God and affirming his status as completely subordinate to God. Other statements, which do indicate his divinity, we would conjecture to be later confabulations by our four witnesses, who would have had thirty to sixty years for their memories to become reshaped by their ongoing religious preoccupations.

Popular and Feeble Arguments from the New Testament Evidence

Here are some terribly weak arguments still regularly voiced by Christians:

1. All arguments about the 'empty tomb', such as those in Frank Morison's *Who Moved the Stone?*

We do not know that there was ever any tomb, occupied or empty. We do not know that there was a stone rolled in front of the tomb. We do not know, for instance, that there was ever any such person as Joseph of Arimathea. These are all legends, first reported in surviving documents at least fifty years later than the alleged events (Paul and the other earliest Christian writers say nothing about the circumstances of Jesus's burial, and the resurrection passages in *Mark* are not in the earliest versions of *Mark*, but were added later, as footnotes in most bibles will now tell you). These accounts are good evidence of what a group of Greek-speaking, predominantly gentile cult members outside Palestine believed some time between C.E. 70 and C.E. 100. They are rather thin evidence of anything that actually happened in Jerusalem around C.E. 33.

2. Arguments to the effect that something must have inspired the early Christians, and this could only have been eye-witness evidence of the life, death, and re-appearance of Jesus.

This line of argument under-rates the power of religious commitment. What inspired the Christian martyrs in Communist Russia and China? It was not that they were eye-witnesses to the events of Jesus's career. Someone told them stories, which they swallowed. Exactly the same could be true of the very first Christian martyrs. As it happens, even the *New Testament* tells us that the first recorded martyr was Stephen, a recent convert who had not witnessed Jesus in the flesh.

Apologists sometimes say, as though it were historical fact, that people who knew Jesus were prepared to die for the faith. There is no good evidence for any such claim. For example, we may take it as well established that there was an individual called Cephas (Peter), a Christian leader who clashed with Paul over such matters as circumcision, in the 50s.[59] That this Cephas had earlier personally known Jesus, or that he later went to Rome, became the first pope, and was martyred, is all uncorroborated and dubious legend.

3. Arguments which amount to pointing out that there are highly distinctive features of Christianity.

Of course there are, as there are of other religious movements. Only Scientology, for example (as far as I know), claims that every human soul is potentially near-omnipotent, and only Buddhism (as far as I know) denies the existence of the individual self or soul. The notion that 'all religions are really saying the same thing' is popular in New Age quarters, but is difficult to reconcile with any actual knowledge of specific religious doctrines.

Nonetheless, we do not lack for parallels with elements of Christian doctrine. The dying and resurrected god-king and the man born of a virgin mother are both commonplaces of pagan mythology.

4. The argument that if Jesus had not really risen from the dead, the authorities would have produced the body to scotch such rumors.

For at least a century, Christianity was so little known that hardly anyone paid it any attention. Romans knew less about Christianity than you know about the Branch Davidians. The gospels depict a Jesus who had a popular following, but earlier Christian writings such as the letters of Paul depict a Jesus who was totally obscure and died without notice. The gospels' account of a Jesus hailed by the crowd is probably a legendary elaboration, but even if it were true, the notion that the Roman authorities would go out of their way to rebut the wild claims of a bunch of fringe crackpots is ludicrous. Did the authorities produce the body of Elvis Presley when Elvis was sighted alive after his death? Furthermore, we do not know that anyone was publicly claiming that Jesus had risen from the dead until some years after the supposed date of the crucifixion. Palestine was soon seething with anti-Roman insurrection unrelated to Jesus, and this would have held the authorities' attention.

5. Arguments that Jesus was either the Son of God or an outrageous imposter (the assumption being that we will not want to call him an outrageous imposter).

In the first place, there are individuals who combine great charisma with willingness to be deceptive, so there's no reason to rule out Jesus's possibly being an unscrupulous mountebank. Joseph Smith, the founder of Mormonism, was one such rogue. However, second, we do not know anything with great confidence about the life of Jesus, so the factual evidence just doesn't exist to say that he had to be one thing or another. We have only the haziest notion of what the real Jesus said or did. The Jesus of the *New Testament* gospels is a composite figure, formed of layers of legend. Naturally, some of it might be true, just as some of the claims about Robin Hood or King Arthur might be true, but we can't be sure if this is the case, and if so, which are the true bits.

6. Arguments that the time elapsed between the events and the accounts of the events is too short to permit of the accounts being false.

Hume cites examples of recent Catholic miracles attested to by numerous credible witnesses, far better attested than anything in the gospels.[60] Yet these are miracles which no Protestant in Hume's day, and probably no educated Catholic today, would seriously maintain actually occurred. Today we have numerous new legends being created all the time, for example about the Bermuda Triangle, alien abductions, Area 51, hauntings such as the 'Amityville Horror', or about nonexistent Satanic cults,[61] or the complicity of the Bush administration in 9/11. The process of formation of these legends is the same as the formation of the *New Testament* stories.

Grossly false legends can spring into existence in the twinkling of an eye, and such stories may then be embellished and even transformed as they are passed along over the years.[62]

Biblical Prophecy Is Always Getting Left Behind

Some Christians, especially Pentecostals and Seventh-Day Adventists, claim that the fulfillment of Biblical prophecy demonstrates the amazing reliability of the Bible. This claim comes in two types: prophecies described in the Bible as having been fulfilled, and Biblical prophecies of events now current or future.

The reported fulfillment of prophecies in the Bible is suspect, because in some cases the prophecies were actually written after the events reportedly prophesied, and in other cases, the events were reshaped to fit the prophecies. The detailed prediction of future events given in *Daniel*, which presents itself as a prophecy written in the sixth century B.C.E., was actually (according to all but fundamentalist scholars) penned in the second century B.C.E.

The most ludicrous example of a reported event reshaped to fit the supposed prophecy is the Virgin Birth of Jesus. The early Christians outside Palestine were acquainted with the Greek translation of the Hebrew scriptures, and were not acquainted with these sources in the original Hebrew or in Aramaic. The Hebrew word 'almah' (young woman) was mistranslated as 'parthenos' (virgin). Not only is this a mistranslation, but the original text of *Isaiah* 7:14 is definitely *not* concerned with any miraculous birth (you can read it for yourself) so that even if the original word had been 'bethulah' (virgin), the intended meaning would be clear: 'a virgin will conceive' would have to mean 'a woman who is now a virgin will conceive', much as we might say 'One of these MIT undergraduates will one day win the Nobel prize', without implying that this person will still be an undergraduate when they meet the King of Sweden.

Over the centuries, various Christian groups have made definite predictions, derived from their interpretations of the Bible, of imminent events, most often the return of Jesus. These predictions fall into three categories (non-exclusive categories, for some predictions belong to more than one of them): 1. they are untestable—usually because no time limit is given (for instance: there will be a great end-of-the world battle called Armageddon); 2. they are events which might be predicted on the basis of common sense plus a knowledge of the present; 3. they have turned out to be wrong.

Many times over, the end of the world or the return of Jesus as an Earthly ruler have been predicted for a specified date, and have failed to occur by that date. If we are concerned with events in our own future, any derivation of predictions from the Bible is bound to be tricky and controversial. The European Community was formed by treaty in 1957, with six member nations. In 1981, it expanded to ten members, often referred to as 'the Ten'. Numerous Christian groups confidently identified this ten-member confederacy with 'the beast having ten horns' in *Revelation* 13 (and *Daniel* 7:7). The Community later acquired several new members, and currently has twenty-seven. Today, Christian prophecy groups say less about the beast with ten horns, and when they do mention it, try to find new groups of nations which number ten. This kind of thing, interminably repeated, is what Christian prophecy literature amounts to: drawing connections between what is going on now and what is said in the Bible, connections which are then forgotten as the world changes and new connections are made.

The Late Great Planet Earth, by Hal Lindsey, appeared in 1970 and quickly sold tens of millions of copies. It prepared the way for the 'Left Behind' literature, fiction and non-fiction books which in aggregate have sold hundreds of millions. Chapter 1 of *The Late*

Great Planet Earth gives examples of the fallibility of non-Evangelical fortune tellers. Chapter 2 repeatedly rams home the message that the way to tell a false prophet from a genuine one is that the genuine prophet's predictions are fulfilled with absolute accuracy in every detail.

The concerns and expectations of *The Late Great Planet Earth* are those of 1970. Communism is the great enemy which will grow in power until Armageddon. Russia will invade Israel by sea and China will invade Israel by land. Black Africa will go Communist and help Egypt to attack Israel. Overpopulation will probably— Lindsey hedges slightly on this—lead to terrible famines. The United States will cease to play any important part in world affairs. Its role as leader of the West will be taken by a restored Roman empire (the European Community), and "if the U.S. is still around at that time, it will not be the power it now is" (p. 96).

Lindsey modestly asserts that he is no prophet and that what he is saying is merely taking the Bible at its word. The thing to remember here is that whenever anyone tells you what God is saying, he is telling you what he, according to a theory he has, claims that God is saying. So what sounds like humility is really colossal self-conceit. Lindsey maintain that when Jesus speaks about the fig tree putting out its new leaves (*Matthew* 24:32), this means the establishment of the State of Israel in 1948. The generation which witnessed that event will live to see the Rapture and the return of Christ as King of Israel. A generation, in biblical terms, Lindsey assures us, means around forty years. Quite a number of Evangelical Christians, apparently influenced by Lindsey, expected the Rapture in 1988.

In 1980 Lindsey produced *The 1980s: Countdown to Armageddon*. Armageddon is now depicted as just a few years away. Although this book sold well, it was allowed to go out of print, presumably because its failed predictions were so embarrassing, and Lindsey was churning out new prophetic books all the time. He soon decided that a biblical generation was not forty years after all, but one hundred years. Among the events that have to happen before the return of Christ is the building of a third Temple on the site of what is now the Dome of the Rock, and the re-institution of a Jewish priesthood, along with regular animal sacrifices. While stranger things have happened in human history, I would offer high odds against this happening by 2048.

Lindsey's successive books always make adjustments to keep up with world events, but he has never candidly laid out his numerous failures, much less apologized for them. However Timothy La Haye, co-author of the *Left Behind* books, has apologized for his prediction that the expected Y2K disaster would provoke the collapse of American society. All these popular exponents of biblical prophecy now make much of militant Islam, which they barely noticed thirty years ago.

You might think that the repeated re-adjustments of prophecy would discourage anyone from trying their hand at it, but I will now make a prediction of my own. Whatever happens in international relations over the next fifty, or one hundred, or one thousand, years, the exponents of biblical prophecy won't see it coming.

12

Did God Compose the *Quran*?

Muslims often assert that the only good explanation for the *Quran* is that it had a Divine origin, and this claim is made in the *Quran* itself. Mormons make a similar argument about the *Book of Mormon*. The existence of the *Quran* is claimed to be proof of the existence of God. Three specific claims are:

1. That if the angel of God did not dictate the *Quran* to Muhammad, then Muhammad must have composed it himself, but Muhammed could not have composed the *Quran* since he was illiterate.

2. That the *Quran* itself is too sublime to be a human product. It is too beautiful and wise to have been formulated by humans.

3. That the *Quran* anticipates many later scientific findings and never contradicts any such findings.

There is a traditional story about Muhammad and the origin of the *Quran*. I don't believe it, but here it is. Muhammad was born in 570 or 571 C.E. into a well-to-do merchant family in Mecca, a trading town and a center for religious pilgrimage. His parents died early and he was raised by his uncle. Muhammad often went into a cave outside Mecca for contemplation. In 610 C.E., when he was about forty, he was visited by the angel Jibril (identified with the Hebrew archangel Gabriel) who commanded him to recite verses sent by God. These verses continued to be revealed to Muhammad over a period of about twenty-three years, up to his death. He recited these verses to others, who in some cases learned them by heart and in other cases wrote them down.

Muhammad became a prophet and a preacher, advocating strict monotheism and warning of a coming day of judgment. He recognized truth in Judaism and Christianity, but claimed that he had been sent by God to correct the misinterpretations that had developed in these teachings. Opposition to Muhammad grew among the Meccans, and in 622 he was forced to leave Mecca. He and his followers settled in Medina. The Meccans attacked Medina repeatedly, but were always defeated. After several years of these attacks, the Muslims, under Muhammad, attacked Mecca and occupied it. Most of the Meccans accepted the new religion of Islam, and their idols were destroyed. Muhammad died on 8th June, 632.

God or Muhammad?

Let's first assume that the standard account of Muhammad's life and the origins of the *Quran* is at least roughly correct. Anyone who accepts this story and is not a Muslim is likely to suppose that Muhammad himself composed the *Quran*, perhaps deluded into believing that the angel of God was dictating it to him.

Muslims contend that the *Quran* could not have been composed by a mere man. They therefore cite the *Quran* itself as proof of God's intervention, and therefore of God's existence. They usually maintain that Muhammad himself was illiterate and therefore could not have composed such a work.

This argument is worthless. First, there is the minor point that other aspects of the standard biography of Muhammad make it seem possible that he was literate. According to the story, he was hired by an older woman to manage her business. He later married her and continued to manage her business. Perhaps such a person would know how to read and write, and might later slyly deny it to add credence to his 'recitations'.

Yet this whole issue is a red herring, as no one claims that Muhammad wrote down the *Quran*. It's a fact accepted by everyone, including all the most traditional Muslim clerics, that the *Quran* was not written down as a whole until many years after Muhammad's death. It was preserved, the story goes, in the memories of those who learned it from Muhammad and recited it aloud

(Scholars guess that 'qu'rān' meant 'recitation'), and also as isolated written fragments.

In a culture where most people are illiterate and where there is a thriving folk oral tradition, it's not impossible for one person to compose and memorize a long work in his head. (It's not very likely either, and I don't believe it in this case. But at this point we're comparing only two theories: that the author was Muhammad and that the author was God by way of Jibril.) But even this hypothesis is not required. If we assume that the standard story is correct, we still have no proof that Muhammad ever knew the entire *Quran* by heart. He could have recited parts to some people, then forgotten them, and recited new parts to other people. Even the most traditional Muslim interpreters accept that the original order of the various suras (chapters) has been lost, and that the order we have in the present *Quran* does not derive from Muhammad. Tradition claims that the actual order in which the chapters were given to Muhammad was roughly the reverse of the order in which they now appear, but nothing would be lost by shuffling the chapters randomly. The *Quran* lacks the organic unity we find in great works of literature like the *Iliad* or the *Divine Comedy*. So, if Muhammad were illiterate, this fact alone does not argue against him being the all-too-human inventor of the recitations later assembled as the *Quran*.

The *Quran* and Science

Muslim propagandists continually assert that the *Quran* contains no factual errors, and amazingly anticipates the subsequent findings of science, thus proving its divine authorship. Maurice Bucaille gives detailed lists of the factual inaccuracies in the *Tanakh* and the *New Testament*, and contrasts this comedy of errors with the astoundingly accurate *Quran*.

Bucaille continually reiterates that the *Bible* is mistaken where the *Quran* is accurate. Typically, Bucaille asserts that passages in the *Quran* have generally been mistranslated, while the *Quran* offers less information than the *Bible* (and therefore doesn't repeat some of the errors in the *Bible*). Thus, Bucaille faults *Genesis* for its account of creation in six days, while claiming that in the *Quran* the word "day" should be understood as "period." (So Arabic 'yaum' can easily be read as 'period', whereas Hebrew 'yom' cannot possibly be read as 'period', a twin claim I will leave to experts in ancient Semitic languages.) This incidentally enables Bucaille to evade the seeming contradiction, where the *Quran* says the creation took eight days and in another place, six days, and in yet another place, two days, because there is not necessarily a contradiction between saying that something took eight periods and that it took six periods and two periods. Bucaille points out that the *Genesis* account of Noah's Flood cannot be true, because there was no disastrous break in the Egyptian and Babylonian civilizations at the time, whereas the *Quran*'s account gives no indication of the date and Bucaille implies that the Flood destroyed only a small portion of humankind—which seems to lose the whole point of the story of Noah taking pairs of all animals onto the Ark.

As a typical example of Bucaille's method, consider his own translation of *Quran* 55:33:

> O Assembly of Jinns and Men, if you can penetrate regions of the heavens and the earth, then penetrate them! You will not penetrate them save with a Power. (Bucaille, p. 168; the "Jinns" are the genies or fire-spirits living on Earth though invisible to us.)

Bucaille comments:

> There can be no doubt that this verse indicates the possibility men will one day achieve what we today call (perhaps rather improperly) 'the conquest of space'.

There can be some doubt, especially as the conquerors of space were all non-Muslims, and no trace has yet been found of the presence of jinns on Mars or the Moon. But Bucaille confidently chalks up the prediction of space travel to the *Quran*. In another example, Bucaille quotes God, referring to the unbelieving Meccans of Muhammad's day:

> Even if we opened unto them a gate to Heaven . . . they would say: our sight is confused as in drunkenness. (*Quran* 15:14–15; Bucaille, p. 169)

Bucaille takes the *Quran* to be referring here to the way the Earth appears to astronauts, as an "unexpected spectacle." For example, the sky appears black instead of blue. Bucaille comments:

> Here again, it is difficult not to be impressed, when comparing the
> text of the Qu'ran to the data of modern science, by statements that
> simply cannot be ascribed to the thought of a man who lived more
> than fourteen centuries ago. (p. 169)

Again, it's quite easy not to be impressed. If the *Quran* had
said: from a vantage point in the heavens, the sky looks black and
not blue, I would be mildly impressed. And if the *Quran* gave us
a couple of dozen facts like this I would be strongly impressed. But
the truth is that, contrary to the interminable claims of Muslim
propagandists, the *Quran*, just like the *Tanakh* and the *New
Testament*, does not contain even a single item of knowledge in
advance of its time.

At every step of Bucaille's exposition, if we bear in mind that
he's trying to prove that the *Quran* could only have been composed by God, what is striking is what the *Quran* does *not* say.
Bucaille mentions that the *Quran* refers favorably to bees, and
adds that we now know that bees communicate information by
means of dances. Someone reading Bucaille hastily might suppose
that the *Quran* refers to the bees' dances. If the *Quran* had stated
that bees communicate in this way, that would be remarkable
(though not strong evidence of God's authorship), but of course,
the *Quran* does no such thing. This is one of thousands of pieces
of information which would have been known to a God but were
not known to the composers of the *Quran*. The *Quran*'s limited
knowledge is illustrated by the statement that honey comes from
bees' abdomens (16:69).

Bucaille not only fancifully extends the meaning of Quranic
verses to associate them with later scientific discoveries, he also
decides how to interpret the meaning of what the *Quran* says by
ruling that it has to accord with modern science. Whereas no
Muslim is permitted to question the God-given authority of a single line of the *Quran*, the ascription of meaning to Quranic verses
is often wildly indeterminate. That this is Bucaille's procedure is
revealed, for instance, in his discussion of *Quran* 16:66, dealing
with the production of milk in the bodies of cattle. Bucaille, a surgeon by training, says that any physiologist would find this verse,
as translated by some "highly eminent Arabists" to be "extremely
obscure" (p. 195). That's to say, what the *Quran* says here, as
translated by experts in Quranic Arabic, is, from the standpoint of

physiology, ignorant nonsense. He provides his own translation, observing that it takes a scientific expert to correctly translate scientific statements. Even so, he has to add more than a page of commentary, stretching the sense of his own translation to make it connect with the facts of physiology.

He refers to the discovery of circulation of the blood by Harvey a thousand years after the time of Muhammad, and opines that reference to "these concepts" in the *Quran* "can have no human explanation." The reader might almost suppose that whoever wrote the *Quran* was aware of the circulation of blood, but there is no evidence of this, even in Bucaille's scientifically informed translation of 16:66.

Whoever composed the *Quran* did not know that blood circulates around the body, did not know that bees communicate by dancing, did not know the relationship between nectar and honey, and did not know what the Earth looks like from space. Similarly, they did not know that the stars existed before the Earth (41:10–12), that the stars are much further away than the Sun and Moon (37:6; 41:12), that continents continually move and mountains are continually created by this movement (16:15), or that the Earth orbits the Sun (18:86; 36:40).

The claim that the *Quran* anticipates modern science is now frantically preached by Muslims, many of them citing Bucaille. The most prominent Muslim missionary in the West today is Shabir Ally, who gives a long list of such 'scientific' arguments on one of his websites. Ally admits that the *Quran* doesn't exactly say that the Earth is spherical, but maintains that it easily allows that interpretation. Because of this, Muslims were able to accept that the Earth is spherical long before Europeans, who went through the Dark Ages supposing it to be flat.[63]

The truth is that Europeans went through the Dark Ages knowing full well that the Earth is spherical. This knowledge was developed by the Pythagoreans, 1,400 years before the Quran, and was elaborated in a highly sophisticated scientific theory by Ptolemy, 450 years before the *Quran*. (Eratosthenes had even calculated the Earth's circumference quite accurately, about 850 years before the *Quran*.) The early Christian church embraced Ptolemy's theory. Early Christian proponents of a flat Earth were few and marginal. But it does appear that whoever composed the *Quran* supposed the Earth to be flat (18:47; 20:53; 71:19).

Aside from this kind of carelessness, most of Ally's 'scientific' examples are like Bucaille's, in that they twist and contort some verse in the *Quran* to make it compatible with some aspect of modern scientific theory, then proclaim that the *Quran* anticipated that bit of science and therefore could only have been composed by God.

Muslims claim that as the *Quran* reveals superior knowledge, it must have come from God. As we have seen, this is false. The scientific knowledge in the *Quran* is backward compared with that of seventh-century Europe. Muslim scholars did rescue some of the ancient pagan knowledge, such as Aristotle and Archimedes, far superior intellectually to early Christianity or early Islam, which Christendom left to itself would probably have destroyed. But that came later.

Yet isn't there something odd about this way of trying to prove the *Quran*'s Divine authorship? Muslims, like Christians, believe that we're surrounded by teeming hordes of supernatural entities: angels, demons, jinns, and whatnot. From what Muslims and Christians tell us about these undetectable personages, it appears that some of them would know a lot of things unknown to ordinary humans and would have the capability to interfere in human affairs. In that case, you would expect some of them, in pursuit of who knows what demonic skullduggery, to have planted books among humans, containing information unknown to humans, thus giving these books tremendous credibility.

If the *Quran* had contained information unknown to humans fourteen hundred years ago, it would therefore not follow that the author was God; it could be some less exalted spirit being with less benign motives. However, the fact that nothing of this kind has ever occurred—that no book ever written contains information which could not have been acquired by mundane methods at the time of writing—corroborates the theory that there are no such spirit beings.

The Origin of the *Quran*

The *Quran* is just not good enough, as literature, as science, or as philosophy, to have been composed by an omniscient God, or even an outstanding human thinker. Indeed, any intelligent person reading the *Quran* with an open mind would conclude that it could not have had a single author, unless that author was afflicted by a serious thinking disorder. It gives the appearance of highly uneven, ill-assorted fragments gathered from different sources, overlaid with some incomplete later attempts at harmonization.

Everything about the *Quran*, like the *New Testament* and the *Tanakh*, reeks of a purely human, fallible, and ignorant origin, hemmed in by the cultural horizons of time, place, and prejudice. Like the *New Testament*, the *Quran* is uneven. It has some fine passages, as we expect from the accumulated and winnowed results of oral tradition. At its worst it is incoherent, contradictory, undistinguished, and just plain silly.

By the way, I have referred to what I have read in the *Quran*, though I have relied on English translations (for each text I have compared numerous translations). According to Muslim tradition, only the original Arabic *Quran* is truly the *Quran*. However, let's bear in mind there are over a billion Muslims in the world, and the great majority of them do not know even modern Arabic. Furthermore, an Arabic-speaking Muslim today is no better able to understand the *Quran* in the original than a twenty-first-century citizen of Detroit is able to understand the *Canterbury Tales*.

But it's worse, because Quranic Arabic is a long dead language, and there is little available in this language other than the *Quran* and writings derived from the *Quran*. Far less is known about the Arabic of the seventh century C.E. than, for example, the Greek of the first century. The language of the *Quran* is packed with obscurities, words and phrases which it is impossible for anyone to render precisely into any modern language (including Arabic) with any confidence. One scholar has stated:

> The Koran claims for itself that it is 'mubeen', or 'clear'. But if you look at it, you will notice that every fifth sentence or so simply doesn't make sense. Many Muslims—and Orientalists—will tell you otherwise, of course, but the fact is that a fifth of the Koranic text is *just incomprehensible*. (Gerd-R. Puin, quoted in Lester 2002, p. 121)

Puin is not denying, of course, that traditional interpretations of the *Quran* have imposed clear meanings on many Quranic verses. But, as one of the handful of the world's leading experts on Quranic language, Puin is able to make this judgment on the *Quran* in the original.

Silliness in the *Quran*

The *Quran* repeatedly challenges readers to produce verses of equal quality (2:23; 10:38; 17:88). Since much of the *Quran* is quite puerile, this is very easy, but when it has been done, the authors of these verses have met with death threats. However, people keep doing it—see http://suralikeit.com, evidently put out by Arabic-speaking Christians. Some passages in the *Quran* are undeniably silly. Muslims employ a lot of ingenuity to give these verses a respectable interpretation but in some cases this is difficult.

According to the *Quran* (72:1–15), some jinns (genies or fire-spirits) once flew up into Heaven to eavesdrop on the reading of the *Quran* taking place there (the *Quran* is supposed to be an exact copy of a book kept in Heaven). Meteorites (shooting stars) are flaming darts thrown by angels at jinns to keep them out of Heaven. These jinns overheard the message that Allah is one and has no wife or children. They were so bowled over by this news that they immediately converted to Islam. So some jinns have become good Muslims. Other jinns, however (presumably including those unfortunate enough not to have tried to illicitly eavesdrop on the doings in Heaven), will be used as fuel for the fires of Hell.

The *Quran* tells us that Solomon could understand the speech of birds and ants. He had an army of men, jinns, and birds. He used birds to drop clay bricks on opposing armies (105:3–4). When Solomon's army came to a valley of ants, Solomon overheard one of the ants saying to the others: "Go home, before Solomon's soldiers trample you." Solomon took a roll call of the birds in his army and found that the Hoopoe bird was missing. Solomon threatened to punish the Hoopoe, but then the Hoopoe showed up and told Solomon about a woman ruler (27:1–23). (The chapter then goes into a garbled version of the story of Solomon and Sheba.) The *Tanakh* also has incredible folk tales about talking animals: the snake in *Genesis* 3:1–5 and the donkey in *Numbers* 22: 27–28).

The composers of the *Quran* take many stories from Jewish and Christian sources, and restate them, usually with significant differences. Many *Old Testament* stories re-appear in the *Quran*, such as the story of Noah's ark. The *Quran* states that Jesus (whom Muslims call 'Isa') was a prophet of Islam, was born of a virgin

(3:47), and even that the birth of his mother Mary was miraculous. Given that so many Christians no longer believe in the virgin birth, probably more Muslims than Christians now believe in it. According to the *Quran*, it was made to appear that Jesus had been executed by crucifixion, but in reality he was rescued (4:157).

If there's a discrepancy between the *Quran* and the Jewish or Christian story which it reshapes, Muslims will claim that the *Quran*, being authored by God, has the story right, whereas the Jewish or Christian versions, though appearing earlier historically, must be incorrect if they diverge from the *Quran* (much as fundamentalist Jews and Christians deny that the yarn about Noah's Ark was adapted from the earlier Sumerian version of the Flood). However, if you compare the different versions, it often becomes clear that the *Quran* is giving a garbled version of an earlier Jewish or Christian story.

Is the Standard Story True?

Many western writers, including Christians, Jews, and atheists, have accepted the standard story of the life of Muhammad as historical fact. It has been repeatedly stated that whereas the origins of Christianity are murky, those of Islam are historically attested.

A typical example is Karen Armstrong, in her popular narrative account of the development of the idea of God, *The History of God.* Armstrong skates over the life of Jesus with expressions of misgiving. Though she apparently believes more of the gospels than I do, she does not bother to summarize what they say, but emphasizes— quite correctly—how very little is really known about the life of Jesus. But when she comes to Muhammad, she tells the story of his life, with affection and gusto, citing numerous detailed incidents as unqualified fact. Perhaps this might be justified because most of her readers are more familiar with the traditional life of Jesus than with the traditional life of Muhammad. But the innocent reader might be forgiven for assuming that there is some contemporary corroboration for this tale, that, for instance, there are written records from Mecca or Medina from the time of Muhammad, or at least within a few generations. But there's absolutely none.

Whereas the New Testament gives us an accurate, if spotty and selective, picture of what some groups of Christians believed from between twenty and one hundred years after the traditional date for the death of Christ, we can only speculate as to what Muslims believed twenty or a hundred years after the traditional date for the death of Muhammad. One significant difference between the origins of Christianity and those of Islam is that the Christian canon was substantially developed before Christianity attained state power, whereas the Islamic canon was developed after Islam had attained state power. We must therefore expect it to be more ruthlessly shaped in the interests of a ruling class.

The earliest surviving account of the life of Muhammad is by Ibn Hisham, who died in 834 C.E., 202 years after the standard date for the death of Muhammad. Ibn Hisham's biography incorporates edited material from an earlier biography, now lost, by Ibn Ishaq, written around 750. So we may charitably say we have access to an account of Muhammad's life from 118 years after the date given by legend for his death. None of the dates of events in Muhammad's life were given by Ibn Ishaq—they are all later elaborations.

Prior to modern times, it was customary to associate traditional sayings with an outstanding teacher or leader of the past. All kinds of sayings would be ascribed to some great figure, because this was the conventional way of thinking. At some point, a scribe would commit these sayings to writing, and this would reinforce the impression that there was a document 'written' by such and such an illustrious personage. The same applies to large-scale works, put together by the successive efforts of long-forgotten scribes. The *Torah* (the first five books of the *Tanakh*) was attributed to Moses—even though it includes an account of the death of Moses and of events that happened later. The *Analects* attributed to Confucius is now thought by scholars to be a product of successive accretions over centuries, not the work of a single author.[64] The *Daodejing*, the fundamental scripture of Daoism, was for long attributed to the individual Laozi, but is now known to have been built up by additions over centuries—it has been called an 'ancient hypertext'.[65] The *Old Testament* book of *Psalms* became attributed to the legendary King David, though these songs were most likely written much later, during the Babylonian exile, by several different poets. Another example is *Mark*, which bears the marks of its origin as a collection of sayings, probably originating from several different sources.

Even in our day, when printed and electronic records abound, it's very common to ascribe traditional sayings to famous figures who were not in fact responsible for them. Every few years some writer makes a splash by producing an article, or even a book, 'revealing' what scholars already know: that familiar quotations frequently imputed to famous people were not in fact uttered by those people.[66]

Muslim tradition depicts the *Quran* as something that was set on the death of Muhammad. Only its writing down and placing in a specific order came later. But this seems to be incorrect. Variant readings survived for centuries, though Muslims often had the conscious aim of trying to achieve a single canon. It's possible that what became the *Quran* was standardized only centuries after the supposed time of Muhammad, and the life of Muhammad was also assembled centuries later, from the sira, or scraps of tradition about Muhammad. Scholarly opinions differ on whether the sira were largely generated to explain the *Quran*, or whether they genuinely do give us independent information about Muhammad.

The most radical critic of the *Quran* was the brilliant scholar John Wansbrough, who argued that the *Quran* did not exist as a stable canon for at least two centuries after the death of Muhammad, and that the sources for the *Quran* came not from Arabia but from Syria and Iraq. The writings of Michael Cook and Patricia Crone are not quite as radical as Wansbrough's, but similarly give us an Arab military expansion which concocted Islam instead of resulting from it. In opposition to these theories, an important recent book by Fred M. Donner takes the arguments of Wansbrough, Crone, and Cook seriously, but argues for an early dating of the material which became embodied in the *Quran*.

The scholarly debate over the next few decades may make some progress in resolving these issues. Atheists shouldn't assume that the most radical theories of origin are always best. Eighteenth- and nineteenth-century critics of Christianity often tended to suppose that the *New Testament* consists largely of fourth-century forgeries. We now know that parts of it were written as early as the 50s C.E., while most of it is either very late first-century or early second-century. Quranic criticism may possibly take a similar course, though in this case there are far fewer relevant documents to be found, so there may always be greater uncertainty.

III

The Arguments Against God

If infinitely good, why fear him? If infinitely wise, why interest ourselves about our fate? If omniscient, why tell him of our wants or fatigue him with our prayers? If everywhere, why erect temples to him? If master of all, why make him sacrifices and offerings? If just, whence has arisen the belief that he will punish man, whom he has created weak and feeble? If reasonable, why would he be angry with a blind creature like man? If immutable, why do we pretend to change his decrees? And if inconceivable, why presume to form any idea of him?

—Paul-Henri Thiry, Baron d'Holbach,
   The System of Nature (1770)

13

How to Prove a Negative

I've heard numerous folks, atheists as well as theists, declare that we can never prove there's no God because it's impossible to prove a negative.

We can indeed prove negatives, and we do so all the time. In fact, if we couldn't prove a negative, we couldn't prove a positive either, since every positive statement implies negative statements (an infinite number of them, actually). If I prove that 'all the marbles in this box are white', I automatically also prove that 'none of the marbles in this box are blue', 'none of the marbles in this box are transparent', and so on.

What I think people are getting at when they come out with the claim that we can't prove a negative is that given a limited number of observations, we often can't demonstrate that something doesn't exist, because an exhaustive search is impracticable. We can't prove that there are no fairies, because although reports of fairies have been convincingly explained on the supposition that there are no fairies, and no credible observation of a fairy has been documented, still, we can't rule out the possibility that fairies might be very shy and very good at hiding, perhaps confined to a few remote locales and also able to turn invisible at will, and therefore, the possibility remains that some fairies have eluded all observation.

Yet does anyone really doubt that mammoths became extinct a long time ago? If they had survived, they would have been seen, and since they have not been seen, they have not survived. If you want a logical proof, here it is:

1. If mammoths were alive today, they would have been seen ($m \rightarrow s$).

2. No mammoths have been seen alive in the past ten thousand years ($\sim s$).

3. Therefore, there are no mammoths alive today ($\sim m$).

It's true that you can raise a doubt about statement 1. or statement 2. But you can always question the premises of any proof—that has nothing to do with any special difficulty in proving a negative.

Observation is not the only way to prove the non-existence of some entity. We can prove that a square circle does not exist because it is logically impossible: it is self-contradictory. We can prove that a perpetual motion machine does not and cannot exist, because its existence would contravene the laws of physics. In cases like these, proving a negative may be a lot easier than proving a positive: if there is no self-contradiction or contradiction of natural laws, this doesn't show that the entity exists, whereas if there is a contradiction, the entity does not exist.

We all know what a Pegasus looks like, we have seen pictures, and we have a definition of a Pegasus: it is a horse with wings, and its wings enable it to fly. Can a Pegasus exist? No, we can prove that this is impossible. Wings of that length could never provide enough uplift to enable something as heavy as a horse's body to be carried through the air.

In H.G. Wells's story, *The Food of the Gods*, a substance is discovered which, when fed to any animal, enables that animal to grow to a gigantic size. The story features, among other things, a giant wasp, able to fly and buzz and sting just like a normal-sized wasp, only much more terrifying because so much bigger. Such an organism could not exist, for a number of reasons. I will just mention two of them.

With any animal that relies on the motion of its wings for flight, an increase in scale will eventually cause it to be unable to fly. This is because the wings increase by area, while the mass of the body increases by volume. A very large-scale flying insect could not fly. Second, the way insects breathe cannot be simply scaled up. Insects breathe through a special kind of tube which just won't work on a larger scale (unless the proportion of oxygen in the air were to be increased). This is one reason why, despite the fact that there are far more species of insect than of any other type of animal, there are no giant insects. Wells's giant wasp would immediately suffocate. Therefore, a living giant flying wasp (assuming it's simply a scaled-up version of an ordinary wasp, with no other anatomical changes) cannot exist.

So we can prove that some things don't exist. However, there are ways to protect something from being proved not to exist. One way is to be so vague about the non-existent entity that it eludes any attempt to make deductions from its defined qualities. Another way is to make *ad hoc* adjustments to the qualities of the nonexistent thing. For instance, we might say that a Pegasus can fly because its body merely looks like a horse: it is really a fiberglass model of a horse, or because the Pegasus's wings are just for show: it actually flies because it contains an antigravity motor. Or perhaps the Pegasus exists and is able to fly, on a world with a denser atmosphere or lower gravity than ours.

Or we can deny the premises of the proof. We can, for example, deny the accepted laws of nature, saying that aeronautical engineers are mistaken about the mechanics of flight or biologists about the breathing equipment of insects.

The conclusions of any proof can always be avoided. This has nothing to do with proving a negative: we can do just the same with proving a positive. Does this mean that the whole exercise of proving something is pointless?

Not necessarily. Every proof is an argument and every argument can be presented as a proof. By framing an argument we put the defender of the nonexistent object in a position he may not have expected. He now has to defend claims he may not have realized earlier that he had to defend. Upon reflection, he may decide he doesn't wish to defend them. Alternatively other people, listening to his arguments, may find them less persuasive now they see what other assertions have to be made to rescue those arguments. The advocate of a perpetual motion machine commits himself to denying the first and second laws of thermodynamics. The process of debate exposes what is really entailed in defending a particular position, and this may be very different from what was seen at first glance.

When a defender of the Pegasus tells us that the Pegasus's body is made of hollow fiberglass, we may raise our eyebrows. When a

defender of the all-loving, all-powerful God tells us that earthquakes and epidemic diseases are engineered by fallen angels,
whom God could not keep in line because he 'just had to' guarantee their free will, we may raise our eyebrows even higher.

It's always possible to rescue God's existence from refutation by
redefining 'God'. Proving the nonexistence of God is always proving the nonexistence of God defined in a specific way, and it is
therefore surprisingly similar to theological debates on 'God's
nature'. If it ever turns out that there is, after all, a God, then atheists will have contributed to the accurate description of God's
nature. If, as I think, there is no God, then capable theistic
philosophers like Augustine, Aquinas, Ockham, Descartes, and
Swinburne have inadvertently contributed to demonstrating God's
nonexistence.

Why Does God Pretend Not to Exist?

How long, God? Will you hide your face forever?

—Psalm 89:46

One of the most basic and obvious facts about God is that he is
never observed by ordinary people in their everyday lives, nor by
scientists seeking to get at the truth about reality by empirical
observation. Although the *Torah* has numerous reports of humans
seeing various parts of God's anatomy (*Genesis* 32:30; *Exodus*
33:23), these are now always taken metaphorically. Theists now
agree with 'John' that "No man has seen God at any time" (*John*
1:18).

God cannot be discerned by sight, smell, sound, or touch. Nor
can any activities demonstrably God's be detected by the most sensitive of scientific instruments. We have already (in Chapter 9)
looked at the suggestion that people have other ways of perceiving
God, ways not dependent on the evidence of their five bodily
senses, and we have seen that this is a mistake.

Among devout believers in God, bouts of 'loss of faith' are as
commonplace as influenza. Believers are always liable to be
haunted by the terrifying specter of Doubt. They often report that
there have been times when they have felt they should believe, but
can't.[67] The fringes of Christian communities are inhabited by
individuals who want desperately to believe but can never manage

to summon up the 'faith'. There's no counterpart of this phenomenon in any other area of human knowledge. The closest thing I know is Winston Smith's frantic attempt under torture, in *Nineteen Eighty-Four*, to convince himself that two plus two equals five.

We can imagine a world in which no one, or hardly anyone, would seriously doubt that there was a God, because his existence would frequently be corroborated by experience.

> Suppose . . . that an articulate voice were heard in the clouds, much louder and more melodious than any which human art could ever reach: Suppose, that this voice were extended in the same instant over all nations, and spoke to each nation in its own language and dialect: Suppose, that the words delivered not only contain a just sense and meaning, but convey some instruction altogether worthy of a benevolent being, superior to mankind: could you possibly hesitate a moment concerning the cause of this voice? and must you not instantly ascribe to it some design or purpose? (Hume, *Dialogues*, p. 213)[68]

There are many other ways in which the existence of God could be made plainly manifest to everyone.

If someone thought God regularly spoke to her, say, in a voice heard inside her head, we'd be inclined to suppose this a kind of hallucination. But if the purported utterances by God were genuinely informative, imparting much detailed information that the recipient of these messages had not been able to find out independently, we would become convinced that some rather remarkable entity was indeed communicating with her by this method. And if everyone, or just some people, received such messages from this apparent entity as a matter of course, and the different messages all fit together nicely, and all imparted genuine information, then we would all be convinced there really was some such entity. Other information might convince us this entity had more of the attributes of a god.

Alternatively, God might simply appear to people. God could manifest himself in human form, just as he is often described in *Genesis*. It would be quite easy for the human form to say and do things which made it clear that it was the embodiment of God. Or God could take a non-human form, such as a gleaming cylinder topped by a halo, available for conversation with humans and full of fascinating and sometimes helpful information. Or God could dictate a book to someone, not filled with the human ignorance of the *Bible* or the *Quran* but containing ample information which only an entity vastly more knowledgeable than any human could have set down.

The fact that God is not observable does not in itself indicate that there's no God. We all accept the existence of entities which we have not perceived. I accept the existence of quarks and magnetic fields. Currently most physicists accept the existence of 'dark matter', and actually believe that dark matter makes up most of the matter in the universe. Yet no one has yet observed any dark matter, either visually or with the aid of special instruments. Physicists accept that there's a whole lot of dark matter out there, because this supposition makes sense of many of their other observations.

God, however, sheds no light on our factual knowledge. We don't understand algebra, economics, gardening, or electronics any better by supposing there's a God, whereas we would, for instance, understand gardening better if we had a knowledge of biochemistry or plant biology. We can make just as good sense of the world on the supposition that there's no God as on the contrary hypothesis.

It can be tricky to determine whether some entity not directly observable exists, as people found out when Louis Pasteur began to argue that bacteria exist. But God is an intelligent mind who, we are often informed, wants humans to believe he exists. He is also all-powerful, and therefore could easily make his existence clear to humans. So here we have a contradiction.

This thought gives rise to an argument, or family of related arguments, known historically as the Argument from Silence, the Argument from Divine Hiddenness, or the Argument from Nonbelief.

1. God could easily have shown strong evidence of his existence to humans—strong in just the same way that the evidence of the existence of trees, stars, and other people is strong.

2. God wants humans to believe that he exists.

3. Therefore God must have given strong evidence of his existence to humans.

4. Humans have no strong evidence that God exists.

5. Therefore God has not shown humans strong evidence of his existence.

6. Therefore, God does not exist.

In a slightly different form, the Argument goes like this:

1. God could easily have arranged things so that everyone would believe that he exists.

2. God wants humans to believe that he exists.

3. Therefore God must have arranged things so that everyone would believe that he exists.

4. Many humans do not believe that God exists.

5. Therefore God has not arranged things so that everyone believes that he exists.

6. Therefore, God does not exist.

One common theist response is 'How dare you make demands of the Almighty?' This misses the point. The atheist is not asking God to do anything. The atheist is merely scrutinizing the claims of the theists, to see what they're worth. If I ask a believer in the Loch Ness Monster about Nessie's food supply, I don't expect to be asked 'How dare you make demands of Nessie?' In either case, we're just concerned with the possible truth of some claim, so naturally we have to test that claim by looking at what the claim would imply if it were true.

Furthermore, if God is omnipotent, then every logically possible state of affairs is just as easy for God to bring about as every other. Omnipotence implies, not just that God can do anything, but that he can do any one thing just as easily as anything else. So another, more jocular comment on this theist response would be: 'Precisely because he is Almighty, what we are demanding of him amounts to nothing'.

Since God could easily have ensured that his existence was as obvious to humans as the existence of trees or stars, the fact that this is far from being the case demonstrates that God, if he exists, has made a conscious decision to pretend not to exist, yet theists nearly always claim that God wants humans to believe in his existence:

Craig may appear to dispute this. He says:

> Although I've found that atheists have a hard time grasping this, it is a fact that in the Christian view it is a matter of relative indifference to God whether people (merely) believe that he exists or not. For what God is interested in is building a love relationship with you, not just getting you to believe that he exists. (Craig and Sinnott-Armstrong, p. 109)

What Craig says here is not in the least hard to grasp, but it is highly idiosyncratic to Craig. If they think God doesn't care much about humans believing in his existence, why did the Christians spend thirteen hundred years torturing to death anyone who disputed it?

All flippancy aside, Craig's view here is shared by at best a tiny minority of Christians, most of them late-twentieth-century Americans. If we look at what the *New Testament* says about conversion to Christianity, we find that belief is often mentioned, while a love relationship is rarely so much as hinted at. "He who has believed and has been baptized shall be saved, but he who has disbelieved shall be condemned" (*Mark* 16:16).

At any rate, you can't enjoy a love relationship with an individual of whose existence you're unaware, so belief in God's existence is a prerequisite of any such love relationship. Craig himself has spent much of his life trying to convince people that God exists, so he presumably really does suppose this is a belief God prefers to have disseminated.

The Moral Freedom Defense

A popular theist reply to the atheist Argument from Hiddenness is to say that if God's existence were palpable, this would unduly coerce people, taking away their moral freedom. I'll call this the Moral Freedom Defense. Variants of this argument are advanced by Swinburne, Van Inwagen, and Michael J. Murray.[69] The common element is that a person who was absolutely convinced of

God's existence would fear God's retribution for wrongdoing, and would therefore choose to behave well out of simple fear of this retribution. In this connection, Van Inwagen makes much of Hell, and Murray too mentions eternal punishment.

To me, this argument is quite startling, for a number of reasons:

- 1. The Moral Freedom Defense presupposes that we have no good evidence that God exists. If we did have such evidence, then it would be pointless to come up with an explanation of why we don't have it. I suppose it might be claimed that we have *some* good evidence, but not enough to be conclusive, but that balancing act would be ungainly.

- 2. If belief in God's existence makes you believe in eternal punishment for wrongdoing and thus gives you an incentive to behave better, and that means you can't be properly tested for your moral rectitude, then those who do now believe in God's existence can't be properly tested for their moral rectitude. The good behavior of those who believe in God must be devalued compared with the good behavior of those who disbelieve in God (with presumably those who merely suspect there might be a God given an intermediate rating). This means that the good behavior of atheists is worth more than the good behavior of theists, which would be gratifying.

- 3. Proponents of the Moral Freedom Defense in fact spend part of their time arguing that God's existence is a reasonable conclusion on the facts, and then, when asked about the Argument from Hiddenness, they tacitly concede that God's existence is not a reasonable conclusion on the facts. It follows that these proponents, when they try to persuade others that God exists, are undermining God's purpose in pretending not to exist.

- 4. To pretend not to exist, God must arrange things so that all the arguments available to us for his existence are unsound. Therefore, the arguments for God's existence proposed by the theists are all unsound, which is just what we suspected. But if these arguments are all unsound, then the best theory is, not that God is pretending not to exist, but that God (with total sincerity) just doesn't exist.

- 5. The argument presupposes that if you believe in God, you will automatically conclude that God has arranged punishment for sin in an afterlife. But many people, like the authors of the *Torah*, have believed in God without believing in an afterlife. If someone were to be convinced of the existence of God and an afterlife, but never heard Christianity or Islam preached, that person would not suspect that there was punishment for wrongdoing in the afterlife. The notion of eternal punishment for wrongs committed in this life would strike anyone who was not already familiar with it, but had somehow come to believe in the God of classical theism, as simply preposterous. (I'm not concerned here to comment on the merits of eternal punishment; I'm just pointing out that belief in God or an afterlife does not automatically lead to belief in retribution in the afterlife.)

- 6. The three authors mentioned are all in the Protestant tradition. If original Protestantism meant one thing above all others, it meant that you cannot, by your good works or your belief in the existence of God, escape the fires of Hell. You can only do that by having faith in Christ. Evidently, these three authors are liberal rather than evangelical Protestants, and believe (as Muslims do) that people's fate in the afterlife will be largely governed by their good or bad behavior in this life. But the mere fact that the founders of their tradition thought otherwise helps to bring out the arbitrary quality of the present authors' reasoning, their assumption that if you come to believe in God you will automatically be intimidated into behaving more morally.

- 7. For two thousand years Christians have been preaching that all who do not accept their preaching will roast for ever in Hell, and precisely for this prudential reason had darn well better accept it. The Jesus of the gospels preached that we should fear God because he can send us to Hell (*Matthew* 10:28; *Luke* 12:5). Until well into the twentieth century, 'brands plucked from the burning' was the cliché, in Protestant countries, to characterize baptisms by foreign missionaries. For a vivid account of a typical instance of fear of Hell in a Catholic culture, take a look at Joyce's *Portrait of the Artist as a Young Man*, Chapter 3. Until about eighty years ago, one of the nicest things you could say about someone was that he was 'God-fearing'.

But now we're told that God would rather have people disbelieve in him than believe in him for fear of Hellfire. I don't want to nail the theists to the cross of their historical errors, but if they're now going to abandon a key element of what they have been preaching for two thousand years, they ought to explain how theism got it so seriously wrong for so long.

- 8. Theists often maintain that belief in God is desirable because it is conducive to morally good behavior. But a proponent of the Moral Freedom Defense cannot consistently offer any such argument.

- 9. Morally good behavior is held to be unworthy, or at least suspect, if influenced by belief in God. The Defense therefore seems to hint at some correct motive for moral behavior, untainted by belief in God. Rigorously followed through, it would lead to the view that many motivations for moral behavior are undesirable. For instance, a Hindu who disbelieves in the God of classical theism but believes that if he behaves badly he may be reincarnated as a praying mantis would also be compromised, in having an extraneous incentive to behave correctly. It would certainly be interesting to hear the correct motive for moral behavior, the one God would prefer us all to have. Evidently it would have to be intrinsically atheistic.

Aside from these difficulties, how plausible is it that the optimal choice of an almighty and all-knowing God's would be to select souls for eternal segregation according to their behavior in this Vale of Tears, for which purpose it is necessary to deceive them into supposing that there is no God? How could omniscience feel the need to run quality checks on human souls, quality checks which will only work if the owners of these souls are deluded?

The notion that such a God would grade human souls according to their moral choices is itself barely coherent. Either the crucial moral choices stem from some fundamental aspect of the individual soul, in which case God could foresee the choices without having them actually played out, and could therefore pre-empt that train of events by creating only those souls pre-designed to make the right choices, or the crucial moral choices share in the indeterminacy associated with free will, in which case they are the type of choices which you might make differently if you could live your life several times over. But in that case, it would be unjust for an omniscient authority to punish people eternally for making the choices they just happened to make in the one earthly life allotted to them.

The Appeal to Unintelligibility

Theists sometimes respond to criticisms of their claims by saying that God is far beyond our understanding. The claim that God is unintelligible may take the form of claiming that God has an unknown purpose in pretending not to exist. The claim is, not merely that God has a purpose that we don't know about, but additionally that God cannot divulge that purpose to us. If we knew what God's purpose was in pretending not to exist, then this might easily incline us to believe that he exists.

This is a kind of ultimate deterrent: it annihilates any argument. Yet like other ultimate deterrents, it annihilates assets on both sides equally. Everything the theist tells us about God, and every possible case he can make for the existence of God, appeals to our understanding of God and of his motives, character, and qualities. The theist tells us that there is a God, and that God is this way and that way. If we cannot begin to understand God's purposes, then all the theist's assertions about God are in vain. Theism requires that God be comprehensible in broad outline, if not in perfect detail.

14

Vast Evil Shows There Is No God

How can there be a benevolent God when there is so much evil in the world? This question occurs to anyone who has watched a loved one die a slow, agonizing, and undignified death, and it occurs to many as they contemplate some of the horrible events reported in history or on the daily news.

As an argument against a benevolent God, this was stated crisply by Epicurus, around 300 B.C.E. Within Judaism, Christianity, and Islam, it has often troubled thoughtful believers, and has become known as the Problem of Evil.

The Problem of Evil arises because God is held to be all-powerful, all-knowing, and all-good. God's being all-good is usually taken to mean that he is all-benevolent towards humans, or at least, to the group of humans of which the believer in God happens to be a member. This assumption is satirized in Fitzgerald's *Rubaiyat of Omar Khayam*, where some of the clay pots argue that since the Potter has made them, he is bound to be solicitous of their welfare, and would never permit them to be broken or tossed out with the trash.

Personally, I would not judge a tremendously powerful (but not strictly omnipotent, omniscient, or all-loving) creator too harshly for being somewhat indifferent to the plight of all the conscious entities he had brought into being in the course of his checkered career. But I will not pursue that line here, since it so happens that almost all theists (Peter Geach and Brian Davies are possible exceptions) insist that God wishes us well and is, just like our political leaders, ceaselessly preoccupied with the true welfare of all his mortal subjects.

According to the standard theism of Christianity or Islam, God is almighty, and therefore anything he might do is not in the least difficult for him. For God, everything is effortless. He could instantly stop any child's pain. If he's so good, why doesn't he?

It seems to follow from God's being all-good and all-powerful that he would be bound to act to prevent evil. If God can do anything he wishes, and is bound to do good, then it cannot be the case that he does not do good every chance he gets. And yet he conspicuously does not do good on many occasions, when he could, quite effortlessly, prevent monstrous evils from occurring.

Before we look at the Argument from Evil, we should notice that it has two distinct forms:

A. How can God allow evil in general, any amount of evil?

B. How can God allow every bit of actual evil?

Question A. is quite subtle and philosophically interesting, and has puzzled Christians since Augustine (354–430 C.E.), and earlier puzzled the pagan philosophers Plato and Plotinus, whose general metaphysical outlook was taken over by the intellectual leaders of the early Christian church. But most atheists don't consider it a strong argument against the existence of God. Atheists are more likely to press Question B. A lot of discussion by theologians addresses Question A while ignoring Question B.

The defender of the hypothesis of an omnipotent, omniscient, all-loving God not only has to explain how such a God could allow 'evil'—some unspecified amount of evil—but how such a God could allow every single evil event that happens. God is all-powerful, and this means that he could stop any single piece of evil. He would not have to exert himself in the slightest. It would be *just as easy* for him to stop any single piece of evil as it would be for him to permit it to go ahead—that follows from God's omnipotence.

If ninety percent of actual evil could somehow be reconciled with an all-powerful, all-knowing, all-loving God, this would not really answer the Argument from Evil. The other ten percent of evil which did not fall under the terms of that reconciliation would show that God as defined cannot exist. All actual evil, every last bit of it, has to be shown to be strictly necessary, or we must reasonably conclude that there is no God as classically defined (though there could be a more limited or less benevolent god).

This doesn't mean that the theist would have to produce a special argument for each concrete example of evil. A satisfactory theist defense could be general and abstract. But it would have to convincingly apply to every individual case of evil. Such a defense fails if it applies to some instances of evil but not to others, and it fails especially decisively if we can identify whole classes of evil to which it is inapplicable.

The atheist case, then, is that there exists at least one actual evil which an omnipotent God could have abolished or reduced, without thereby generating a greater evil. The theist claim has to be that there exists not a single actual evil which an omnipotent God could have abolished or reduced, without thereby generating a greater evil.

Evil Is an Illusion

One reply to the Argument from Evil is that there really is no evil. It's an illusion. This is the view taken by the religious sect known as Christian Science, and by some Hindu thinkers. But it is not widely popular with theists.

What's wrong with this approach is that the illusion of evil is an evil. Therefore, if there is an illusion of evil, there is real evil. The evil may be misunderstood, but as evil it's real.

One conspicuous form of evil is suffering, and suffering cannot be an illusion. While one can experience the hallucination that one is seeing an object which is not really there, one cannot experience the hallucination of having a toothache which is not really there. Imaginably, one might have a toothache when there is nothing wrong with one's teeth, but a toothache is defined by the actual subjective experience of pain. If pain could be created by "nerve induction," as with the gom jabbar in Chapter 1 of *Dune*, it would still be pain. The same is true for suffering in general. 'The illusion of suffering' is therefore incoherent. Even if we could make all suffering vanish by a quick mental exercise, we have not been informed of the trick for doing that.

The Greater Good

Once the reality of suffering and other forms of evil is admitted, there is essentially only one possible reply to the Argument from

Evil, though it takes several different forms: By permitting some evil to occur, God makes possible a greater good than would otherwise be possible. Therefore, he acts to achieve a greater good, by permitting some evil, and if he were to intervene to prevent evil, the outcome in its totality would be worse. And so, by preventing evil, God would be committing evil, and by permitting evil he is acting for the best. We can call this the Greater Good Defense.[70]

Now this evaluates God's behavior according to its consequences; it applies the ethical doctrine known as consequentialism to let God off the hook for his failure to prevent preventable evils. Yet theists are often opposed to consequentialism—doing evil that good may result (*Romans* 3:8)—at least as it applies to humans. This must be a case of 'Licet jovi, non licet bovi' (What's permitted to Jove is not permitted to an ox).

A theist might object that doing evil is not quite the same thing as permitting evil to occur. However, if God is omnipotent and omniscient, then these are indeed the same thing. An omnipotent and omniscient God is morally responsible for any event that occurs. If God is omnipotent and omniscient, then everything that happens is something God does.[71] And furthermore, even though, in the context of human frailty, we draw an important distinction between making a bad thing happen and allowing something bad to happen, we do not always hold the latter to be blameless.

The Greater Good Defense takes one of four forms:

1. The Defense from Ignorance. There could be some reason, altogether unknown to us, why God had to permit a whole lot of evil, in order to bring about a greater good. We can't say what this reason is, but, since we don't know everything, neither can we prove it doesn't exist.

2. The Counterpart Defense. Good cannot exist without its counterpart, evil. The existence of evil is essential to the existence of good. Or (a related contention, but not quite the same thing): We cannot conceive of good without conceiving of evil.

3. The Opportunity for Good Defense. The existence of evil provides the opportunity for good, for example when a person's suffering provides the opportunity for another person to act compassionately or for that person to act courageously.

4. The Free Will Defense. God could achieve certain good objectives only by giving people free will, and if people have free will, God cannot stop them doing things which bring about evil outcomes.

1. The Defense from Ignorance

The Defense from Ignorance easily slips into the Appeal to Unintelligibility, which I rejected in the previous chapter. In trying to determine whether there is a God or not, as in trying to settle any other factual issue, we have to use whatever brains and imagination we have. The assertion, 'There may be something you haven't thought of which will lead to the opposite conclusion', is always true but rarely helpful. At best, it's a reminder of the truism that all of our judgments are fallible. It does not provide us with a warrant to reverse any one of our judgments, once we have done the best we can with the evidence at our disposal.

2. The Counterpart Defense

The Counterpart Defense is not important for atheism, since it is an answer to Question A only, and offers no reply to Question B. If we were to accept that there has to be some evil to make the existence of the good possible or conceivable, then a tiny, token amount of evil would do the trick. God could greatly reduce the amount of actual evil without endangering the conceivability or the existence of good.

Even so, the Counterpart Defense is mistaken. A quality may hold for every existing thing, and its absence or opposite might hold for nothing at all. For a possible example, consider the fact that everything we have any knowledge of exists in time. Humans have no experience of anything that does not occur in time. For all we know, there's nothing outside of time. Yet for thousands of years thinkers have speculated about the possibility of timelessness, or of entities outside time. Many human minds have been acutely aware of time, and have asked questions like 'Why does time seem to have just one direction?' and 'Could anyone travel in time?' even though they have never witnessed absence of time, travel in time, or anything that would contradict a single, all-enveloping flow of time.

Awareness of time, measurement of time, discussion of time's attributes—all these are entirely feasible without there being anything timeless. And further, even if no one had ever thought of these things, it could still be true that everything in the universe occurs in time, and there is no need for there to be any timelessness for temporal phenomena to be universal.

What goes for 'time' goes for 'goodness'. There could conceivably be a universe without evil, and in such a universe, intelligent minds could become aware of the non-evilness of everything, and could even discuss the hypothetical possibility of evil. This awareness would have to be non-evil, of course, but it might well be non-evil, or even good, as it would help those folks to appreciate how lucky they were to live in a universe without evil. It's also imaginable that the universe might have been wholly good, or at least wholly non-evil, without anyone thinking of the notion of evil. There is no conceptual problem about a universe lacking in actual evil, whether or not we suppose that in such a universe anyone comes up with an idea of evil.

Someone might question this line of argument by suggesting that evil—roughly, 'bad things'—has to exist before consciousness and intelligence could evolve. I think this is correct. However, only an atheist (or at least someone who rejects the God of classical theism) is permitted to think this! A theist must accept that God existed prior to any Darwinian struggle for survival, and most theists would also accept that hosts of angels did too. No orthodox theist can deny that there could be a universe without evil, in which intelligent minds could become aware of the possibility of evil, since that is just what they claim did prevail before the defection of Lucifer, and will again prevail, "world without end.".

There is a special sense in which evil may be a necessary counterpart of good. It's essential to the evolution of acting, purposive animals that they prefer some outcomes to others. The categories 'more preferred' and 'less preferred' are inescapable for any population of purposively acting beings. If we now equate 'less preferred' with 'bad' and 'more preferred' with good', we can say that good and bad are inescapable categories of purposive action.

However this fact doesn't rescue the Counterpart Defense. If you're playing tennis, you would prefer not to hit the ball into the net, but would you describe such an event as 'evil'? Someone could have an idyllically happy life, free of all disease and mental agony, every day a delight, and such a person would continually be looking at more preferred and less preferred outcomes. Either we can define these less preferred outcomes as below the threshold of what counts as 'evil', or we can say that this is evil of an extremely minute kind, and its necessity does nothing to justify the existence of truly terrible evil.

3. THE OPPORTUNITY FOR GOOD DEFENSE

Theists point out that evil makes possible good which would otherwise not arise. If there is suffering, which is bad, this may stimulate compassion, which is good. It may also help to teach the sufferer to bear suffering calmly, which is also good—though whether this would be equally good if suffering were far rarer is not so clear. But our human standards of good and evil are already adapted to a world where bad events are commonplace.

Is the amount of evil sufficiently paid for by the noble actions it evokes? Does the perfectly benevolent God perceive a moral profit on the deal? Are the Holocaust or natural disasters fully paid for by the heroic efforts of resisters and rescuers?

Even theists will usually say no. If the answer were yes, this would suggest that acting to bring evil into being, even extreme and appalling evil, would be not such a bad thing.

While bad events sometimes bring out the best in people, they far more often bring out the worst. In the medieval Black Death, for instance, appallingly callous and cruel behavior far outweighed benevolent and helpful behavior. Parents generally abandoned their children and spouses abandoned their partners if they showed signs of plague. Robbery and other forms of violence are generally more common in lower-income than in higher-income communities. Suffering is a school for vice more often than for virtue.

15

Can Human Free Will Explain Why God Allows Vast Evil?

The most popular defense to the Argument from Evil is that God wanted to create intelligent beings who would possess free will. Having free will is an enormous good, and yet it means being able to commit evil. Therefore, God had to allow the possibility that humans might commit evil if he endowed them with free will.

The Free Will Defense runs into some obvious objections:

1. *Natural Evils.* Much evil is not under the control of humans and does not result from any decisions by humans.

2. *Evil Outcomes from Non-Evil Decisions.* The way the Free Will Defense is nearly always stated implies that human decisions with evil consequences are morally evil decisions. But this is not true. Evil outcomes may come from human decisions which are morally unobjectionable (either morally good or morally neutral).

3. *Free Will and a Guarantee of Goodness.* God could have given people free will and at the same time guaranteed that their choices would always be good. (Or, God could have given people free will and at the same time guaranteed that their choices would be good more often than they in fact are.)

4. *Different Characters.* Given persons with free will, what they will probably decide to do is influenced by their characters, and God could have made these characters different.

5. *Different Circumstances.* Given persons with free will, what they will probably decide to do is influenced by their circumstances, and God could have made these circumstances different.

6. *Persuasive Intervention by God.* There are many ways to influence a person's behavior that do not involve coercion or manipulation, and God could have employed these ways to change people's behavior, without taking away their their free will.

7. *Coercive Intervention by God.* Contrary to first impressions, God's use of coercion or manipulation would be compatible with human free will.

8. *Collectivizing Humans.* A morally perfect God would not treat his created persons as collectivities but as individuals. Such a God would at least see to it that the evil consequences of an action by individual X would predominantly fall on X and not predominantly on other persons.

We'll look at each of these objections a bit more closely. But before we do, we have to quickly consider the idea of free will, why it's controversial among philosophers, and what it implies for the God hypothesis.

Some philosophers argue that there is no free will: the existence of free will is a delusion. If there's no such thing as free will, there's no Free Will Defense to the Argument from Evil, and therefore there's no God as defined by classical theism. The vast majority of today's theists believe in free will—and it's not just that they happen to believe in free will. They have to believe in free will to save their theism, because without free will they would realize that they have no answer to the Argument from Evil.

But is the Free Will Defense really an answer? Let's see.

Sidebar: Free Will and Determinism

Let's take a look at some philosophical ideas on free will and determinism. I will reveal my own views on the subject, but I will not seriously try to persuade you of these views, for two reasons. First, on the main points my view of free will is similar to that of most theists and dissimilar to that of many atheists. Second, I claim that whichever view of free will is taken, it cannot rescue the Free Will Defense to the Argument from Evil. So I do not hang my criticism of the Free Will Defense on any particular theory of free will.

The philosophical issue of free will and determinism arises because some people believe that whatever someone chooses to do, that person was bound to choose to do. The reason for thinking this is that the world we observe seems to be pervaded by laws of cause and effect. In similar circumstances, we usually get similar outcomes, and when we seem not to, we often find upon closer examination that there was really some crucial difference in the circumstances that we had overlooked. If we embark upon any process of production, such as brewing beer, we assume that if we repeat the conditions, the product will be the same as before. If the product turns out different, we look for a difference in the conditions of its production.

These observations give rise to the conjecture that everything that happens is the only possible result of the immediately preceding circumstances. Provided these circumstances are specified exactly enough, what happens is the only thing that could have happened. Now, if this is true of every individual event or outcome, then it is true for all events. And what this implies is that everything that's happening right now—the total state of the universe right now—is the only possible result of everything that was happening a moment earlier—the total state of the universe a moment ago. And since this also applies to what was happening a moment ago in relation to what was happening a moment before that, it follows that everything that is happening now was fixed billions of years ago.

Look around the room where you're now sitting. Take note of some of the subtle details—that barely detectable scuffing of the carpet, that slight indentation in the lampshade—and also of yourself—that ache in your left foot, that sudden, unaccountable recollection of a dear friend's smile. All of these, down to the last minute nuance, were fixed shortly after the Big Bang, more than fourteen billion years ago, before the stars had formed, when the universe was nothing but hydrogen gas in space. If you believe this, you're a determinist. If you disbelieve it, you're not a determinist.

Let's suppose that human beings are not exempt from the laws of cause and effect. They are part of nature, and everything that happens within human beings is, just like everything else in the universe, the only thing that could have happened given the immediately preceding circumstances.

It follows that whatever a human chooses to do, she was bound to choose to do. It's the only thing she could have chosen to do, given all the immediately preceding circumstances, which include circumstances relating to her brain and her mind (we can leave open at this point what the relation between the brain and the mind is). The determinist does not deny the distinction between being locked up in a cell and being free to wander around, so in that sense the determinist does not dispute that our actions can be free or unfree. But the determinist insists that our 'free' actions are the inevitable results of all the circumstances that preceded them.

By the way, a common error is to say that determinism implies that we can explain or predict what a person will do on the basis of that person's character, genes, early environment, or personality traits. This is mistaken, as a simple example will illustrate. Suppose that someone is making up her mind on a matter that is rather finely balanced—she could easily pick either of two alternatives; it's a close thing. Now suppose that, at the moment of decision, a cosmic ray passes through a particular part of that person's brain (as such rays are doing all the time) and suppose that this particular passage of a cosmic ray makes it the case that she chooses option A rather than option B.

The cosmic ray could have resulted from an exploding star a billion light years away—it was generated by an event a long way away and a billion years in the past. Still, this hypothetical occurrence is fully compatible with determinism. But it is *not* compatible with the claim that the person's choices are determined by her character, genes, early environment, or personality traits.

It works in reverse too. It might conceivably be the case that people always do what their character, genes, culture, or the like determine, but that there is indeterminism in physical processes, including perhaps the physical processes that lead to a person's character, genes, culture, and so forth. Determinism in the full, cosmic and metaphysical, sense is therefore completely independent of psychological, social, cultural, or genetic determinism.

Does determinism rule out free will? One theory, called Compatibilism, says that determinism and free will do not conflict. The Compatibilist says that when you make a choice and act on it, then provided what you do really is the outcome of your mental process of decision-making, you have free will in the only sense that counts—and it just doesn't matter at all that the outcome of your mental process of decision-making was also the only possible outcome of a preceding state of the universe.

Those who cannot accept compatibilism, and feel that free will is both real and vitally important, have usually argued that determinism applies to physical events but not to mental events. They therefore have to argue that mental events are not physical events in the brain. They also have to go further, and argue that mental events do not *correspond* to physical events in the brain. And they have to go further than that, and say that mental events are not subject to laws of cause and effect. Human decisions are exempt from the strict causality that governs atoms and energy fields. While determinism rules absolutely in physics and even biology, it does not rule, or perhaps it rules with occasional lapses, in human psychology.

If there is determinism, there can be no free will defense to the Argument from Evil. This applies whether the determinist holds that there is no free will, or whether he holds that free will and determinism are compatible. The reason for this is that if there is both free will *and* determinism, then an omniscient, omnipotent God could have created people endowed with free will and still predicted exactly how they would exercise their free will. There would therefore be no contradiction, and therefore (taking God's omnipotence seriously) not the slightest difficulty, in God endowing humans with free will and also guaranteeing that they would not do anything with evil outcomes. (Notice that I'm not conceding here that God would not be able to foresee what people would do, and therefore ensure that no free-willed person did anything to cause evil, even if there were no determinism. This isn't self-evident. But it's a less straightforward matter than in the case of determinism.)

For the last hundred years or so, the entire context of these discussions has changed, because physics now tells us quite emphatically that determinism is false. The view that physical processes are deterministic was common among scientists and philosophers until the end of the nineteenth century. In 1905 quantum theory began. As it was later developed, this theory showed that all the most fundamental processes are not deterministic at all. They are subject to chance.

The results of experiments have now convinced physicists that there is nothing 'behind' the chance outcomes. Chance is fundamental. Randomness is an objective fact about the universe, and is *not* due to the limitations of our knowledge. Even many of the laws of nature we think we have discovered are nothing more than statistical generalizations of random behavior. Physics tells us that things are happening all the time *without any cause*.

This doesn't mean that, in a given set of circumstances, *anything* could happen. It merely means that a range of things, at least two alternative things, could happen, and which of those alternative things actually happens is not fixed beforehand but may happen with a certain probability. So quantum indeterminism does not deny that what happens is largely governed by what happens earlier. But this influence of what has happened on what happens next is loose and approximate.

According to physics, what happens is not the only thing that could have happened given the immediately preceding circumstances. And therefore, the universe precisely as it is right now is not the inevitable, only-possible outcome of the universe precisely as it was a billion or a million, or a thousand years ago, or one second ago. How does quantum physics, and the scientific consensus that events very frequently happen without any cause, affect the issue of free will and determinism? Actually, less than you might suppose.

Long before quantum physics, philosophers had entertained the notion that events might sometimes happen without a cause. But they had reasoned as follows: 'If there are events without causes, then this doesn't give us a kind of free will that escapes from what we see as distasteful about determinism. It's true that if events can happen without a cause, then a person deciding to act in one way can truly say they could have acted differently. But then, an uncaused event in the person's mind is what made that person decide the way they did. So it wasn't the person's choice that made it happen that they did what they did, but that uncaused event in their mind. But this is no better than determinism, because something not under that person's control—the uncaused event—determined the outcome. Far from human choice having a way to escape the web of cause and effect, any escape from the web of cause and effect means that there is no choice.'

My own view (a very unpopular one) is that this objection is empty. It sees the 'uncaused mental event' as a seizure interrupting a deterministic process, whereas I see all processes, physical and mental, as probabilistic, not deterministic.[72] We thus have two facts, 1. human actions are the outcome of human choices,[73] and 2. the choice made is not the inevitable result of earlier states of affairs. Perhaps something more is needed for free will, but if so, I'm not sure what.

Now let's get back to the objections to the Free Will Defense.

Objection #1:
Natural Evils

Many evils are not due to human free will, as they are not the results of human actions. Earthquakes, tsunamis, infectious diseases, hereditary diseases, venomous snakes and tapeworms, . . . there's a large class of serious evils which don't appear to be covered by the Free Will Defense.

In addition to the natural evils which afflict humans, there are natural evils which afflict non-human animals. The animal kingdom is an interminable cycle of pain and frustration.

It's doubtful if most non-human animals experience suffering in anything like the same way as humans, or even that many of them experience suffering at all. But with some animals, especially the more intelligent mammals, there surely is something quite closely analogous. Long before humans walked the Earth, predator was ripping apart prey, and in the case of some predators like cats, keeping their prey alive and toying with it, and parasites were worming their way painfully into the bodies of hosts.

I've seen three attempts to answer this objection and thus keep the Free Will Defense alive:

1. Natural evils are caused by evil spirits, such as fallen angels, who, like humans, became evil because they were granted free will and made the wrong choices.

2. Today's natural evils result from the actions of early humans exercising their free will.

3. Persons with free will can only inhabit a world governed by physical laws, and it is not logically possible for God to have made a physical world with any fewer natural evils than the one we have.

1. NATURAL EVILS ARE CAUSED BY EVIL SPIRITS

Alvin Plantinga, one of the most distinguished philosophical advocates of theism of our day, advances the possibility that natural evils can be blamed on fallen angels. He asks:

> Do we have evidence for the proposition that the Lisbon earthquake was not caused by the activity of some disaffected fallen angels? I certainly do not know of any such evidence. (Plantinga 1967, p. 155)

Plantinga doesn't count it as 'evidence against' that we have a satisfactory natural explanation that does not appeal to undetectable entities. Plantinga does not offer any criticism of the theory of the causation of earthquakes by movements in the Earth's crust. He evidently doesn't accept the view I hold, that evidence for or against any theory is always a matter of comparing that theory with its rivals. He would presumably have to say that if his car won't go and he finds that the fuel tank is empty, he then refills the tank whereupon the car runs again, he has no evidence against the theory that the car had stopped running because of a hex cast by a vindictive leprechaun.

If the activities of fallen angels were somehow required to make sense of our observations of the world, we might entertain this hypothesis. But it appears to be entirely redundant.

Furthermore, God would be acting unfairly, and would therefore not be all-good, if he failed to protect humans from the evils caused by fallen angels.

2. Natural Evils Are Caused by the Bad Decisions of Our Ancestors

The traditional Jewish and Christian view (though rejected by Muslims) is that of the Fall of Humankind and Original Sin. Taken literally as a historical account, this story is contradicted by the findings of paleontology and archeology. There was never a time in the lives of humans or their hominid ancestors when disease, injury, and violent death were not commonplace. There's no trace of a prehistoric decline from a superior way of life, either materially or morally.

If God decreed suffering for millions of humans because of choices by their ancestors, then God would be morally odious. But the evidence clearly indicates that this tale is untrue. Humans could not have come into existence without predation and killing as an everyday necessity. In this metaphorical sense it's perfectly true that humankind was 'conceived in iniquity'.

Van Inwagen proposes that we may attribute the destruction caused by earthquakes to "an aboriginal abuse of free will"—the bad choices made by members of a small population of primates thousands of years ago (2006, p. 90). He supposes that when they were morally upright, these primates were miraculously protected from natural evils like earthquakes. When they abused their free will, this protection was withdrawn. It's not clear whether the deactivation of immunity from earthquakes resulted naturally from the bad choices of those primates, or whether God made a special intervention to punish their descendants for those bad choices. Geology clearly tells us that earthquakes, volcanic eruptions, floods, asteroid strikes, and other disasters have been continuous on the Earth for billions of years. Wherever we look at fossils of early humans and pre-humans, we find evidence of disease and injury, affecting children as well as grown-ups. Human life was brutal and tragic from the getgo.

Although there was in fact no Fall, the concept of the Fall is also not consistent with God's goodness. If humans were constituted so that sins by two individuals would make it practically impossible for all their descendants to behave morally, and this would ineluctably lead to vast amounts of suffering, then that could only have been due to a decision by God to make humans that way. That decision couldn't be characterized as compatible with God's goodness.

3. Natural Evils Are Required by Natural Laws

Bruce Reichenbach claims that God could not have put his creatures into a universe without at least the level of natural evils in our universe.[74] His basic idea is that the universe had to be physical and had to be governed by natural laws, and the operation of natural laws is bound to lead to nasty problems for physical creatures. Against the atheist claim that we can imagine a world with fewer evils, Reichenbach retorts that we may think we can do this, but we can't imagine such a world in all its precise detail, therefore we can't know that removing one evil won't indirectly lead to equally bad or worse evils.

God wanted to make a world in which moral agents—persons with free will—could live. The world, says Reichenbach, is either entirely miraculous, or entirely governed by natural law, or some mixture of the two. If it's entirely miraculous, there can be no moral agents, because there can't be cause and effect. If the world is a mixture of the two, this would alter "rational predictability" on which we rely, and therefore is also out of the question. So God had no option but to make a wholly physical world subject to invariable natural laws. Reichenbach goes on to point out that there are hidden consequences to any changes one might make in such a world, and it is practically impossible for us to trace out all the ramifications of any change. If, for example, there is nothing which kills people, then overpopulation may result. Since we don't know all the repercussions of any change, we can't be sure that any

change would lead to a better outcome than what we have. Only
God could know that. (Notice that Reichenbach is bound to
oppose the common theist view that God has on some occasions
miraculously intervened.)

To keep it brief, let's suppose that God had to create a universe
with exactly the physical laws of our universe. Why couldn't God
have intervened occasionally to delete some of the worst evils afflicting humankind? Why couldn't he, thousands of years ago, have got
rid of the smallpox bacillus or changed the structure of the Earth's
crust so that there would be no more earthquakes or tsunamis? This
falls under Reichenbach's category of a mixture of natural law and
miraculous intervention, but it would not "make rational prediction
and rational action impossible." Rational prediction and rational
action would be exactly as possible as they are today.

I suppose Reichenbach might respond that, thousands of years
in the future, human science might conceivably develop to the
point where scientists could know that the Earth's crust 'should
have' been such as to generate earthquakes and tsunamis, or could
determine how many and what type of malignant micro-organisms
'should have' been thrown up by evolution. This might then provoke a kind of ideological crisis of confidence in natural laws. But
nothing disastrous would come of this. People would be able to
handle it. They might conjecture that God had been helping us
out, and they would be right.

We can't help noticing that what Reichenbach declares to be
impossible for God to do is precisely the kind of thing that the vast
majority of theists assume that God has actually done. So the chief
difference between our universe and the hypothetical one is that in
the hypothetical universe, when theists tell us that God is looking
out for us, they would be telling the truth.

Reichenbach evidently accepts the current scientific consensus
on cosmology and evolution. He therefore accepts that the world
we now have is essentially the outcome of the Big Bang, followed
by billions of years of events governed by physical laws, without
any divine intervention (p. 113). He seems to assume that God
had to rely on the blind undirected processes of physical nature to
bring about the origin of life and consciousness. Here, as so often
with modern theistic arguments, we keep on tripping over the tacit
abandonment of God's omnipotence.

Objection #2:
Evil Outcomes from Non-Evil Decisions

Advocates of the Free Will Defense often fall into the habit of talking as if human choices leading to evil outcomes are morally wrong choices, and if all humans behaved morally perfectly, these evil outcomes would not happen. Because people have free will, they can make good or evil choices: they choose to make evil choices, and evil results.

Yes, there are many cases where people commit evil actions, with evil consequences. If this were not frequently the case, we would have to reconsider our classification of actions as good or evil. But is it always true that evil results of human actions are results of morally wrong human actions?[75] I will mention two kinds of instances where behavior that is not morally wrong leads to evil outcomes.

Many human evils are the outcome of actions arising from mistakes due to acceptance of false theories because of limited knowledge. People cannot rightly be held morally culpable for acting for the best according to their limited knowledge. For example, a recurring major evil in human cultures is the persecution, often the killing, of minorities perceived as 'different'. While no doubt some people take part in these pogroms and witch-hunts from evil motives, other people may participate from non-evil motives combined with a false theory of the world.

The culture which produced the moral imperative to kill all those believed to be witches had to be a culture steeped in ignorance. But given that ignorance, for which individuals in that culture cannot personally be blamed, a person might honestly be alarmed at the threat posed by witches, and conclude that harsh measures are necessary to protect the community from witches. If illnesses and accidents are largely due to the malevolent magical practices of a few individuals, if the individuals responsible can be identified, and if there is no way to dissuade them from their malign behavior, then there would be a good case for catching and killing them. Some people might therefore have supported the killing of witches from morally impeccable motives combined with false beliefs.

I suppose the theist might retort that limited knowledge is 'an evil', and that therefore actions guided by mistaken theories are 'evil', and so this is no exception to the rule that evil outcomes can be traced back to evil acts. But this would be to confuse two distinct issues. If mistaken beliefs can be characterized as 'evil', this does not gainsay the elementary principle that actions motivated by wholly good intentions in conjunction with erroneous beliefs are morally blameless. What is often taken for granted by proponents of the Free Will Defense is precisely that human acts leading to evil outcomes are morally wrong acts, that if everyone behaved perfectly morally, evil outcomes would evaporate. And this is not true, because people can act morally, though mistakenly, with appalling results. Although there is something bad about limited knowledge, virtuously motivated action guided by a false but sincerely held theory, which is the best available to a person in a given situation (including that person's limited intellect), cannot be morally wrong.

My second type of evil outcomes from morally unobjectionable actions is situations where persons are so circumstanced that any of the alternative courses of action they select will lead to evil outcomes. In such cases, though an evil outcome can be traced back to human actions, it would be the case that there existed no alternative actions which would have not given rise to an evil outcome.

To illustrate this possibility, I will first mention a simple imaginary example which I don't claim to be typical. Suppose that a community of one hundred individuals is placed in a situation where no more than half of them can survive, but if the attempt is made for all to survive, they will all starve to death. Then, whatever decision is made, its making will involve free will and will lead to a very bad outcome. Looking at the particular decision and the outcome, we may be able to trace the evil outcome back to that decision. And yet, it could be the case that any alternative decision would have led to equally bad or worse outcomes—that the decision taken was the single possible option that led to the least evil of all feasible outcomes.

That is an unlikely example, chosen as a simple illustration, but it seems obvious to me that the same principle applies many times over, in far more complex examples where it is practically impossible to identify all the specific options and the outcomes which would have ensued.

One of the great evils in human history is war. Wars arise because whole communities, or the leaders of these communities, have differences which they decide to settle by fighting. It is an aspect of human nature that individuals tend to identify with their own group and readily have suspicions of other groups.

Now, it may be said, if everyone were perfectly moral, no one would go to war. But is this plausible? It implies that the only moral course is to be a total pacifist, and possibly an anarchist too. This line has not been generally popular with theists, but still, the tiny minority of theists who have taken such a position (some Mennonites and Quakers, perhaps) could be right. If so, however, this emphasizes an associated point: that knowing the right course of action may be almost impossibly difficult, and someone acting for the best according to his lights may be tragically mistaken. War is an evil, but in some circumstances reluctance to go to war can lead to worse outcomes than readiness to go to war.

Someone might claim that right is always on only one side in any war. All that is necessary, then, to avoid all war, is for no one to take up arms in an unjust war. But if right is always on one side, it is asking too much of people that they are always able to know which side is in the right. The issues in many wars are complex, and it is a natural fact about humans that individuals tend to identify with their own group, to be suspicious of other groups, and to see things from the point of view of their own community's culture. This fact derives from more fundamental facts: the necessity to conduct policy discussions in simplified, symbolic terms, which in turn arises from the need to economize by making decisions on the basis of incomplete information.

You should easily be able to construct other examples, for instance human practices arising from the genetic endowment mandating sexual appetite, sexual attachment, sexual jealousy, desire for sexual novelty, and sexual rivalry.

Objection #3:
Free Will and a Guarantee of Goodness

If God's omnipotent, couldn't he have given people free will and at the same time guaranteed that they would in fact always make the 'right' choices?

Theists will generally deny that this is possible. But how can it be impossible? According to classical theism, God himself cannot possibly do anything evil. Theists also claim that God has free will.

If God combines free will with a guarantee against ever committing evil, then it cannot be impossible to combine free will with a guarantee against ever committing evil.

God, if he decided to create other beings with free will, would also create them, in his own image, with a guarantee against their ever committing evil. The theist who says that God has free will (and they nearly all do) cannot claim that free will and a guarantee against committing evil are metaphysically incompatible, and will therefore find it hard to deny that God could have created humans with a guarantee against their ever committing evil.

A theist might respond to this that humans are not God, but something less. Still, the 'something less' is not possession of free will, so human free will doesn't explain why humans couldn't have been made in such a fashion that they never made a morally wrong choice. What is the quality that God possesses, making it unthinkable for him to do any evil, that could not have been conferred on humans when God created them? Whatever it may be, it is not free will.

Theists often claim that it is God's *nature* that rules out the possibility of his doing anything wrong.[76] In that case, God should have created humans with a nature that ruled out the possibility of their doing anything wrong. If the reply is that they were so created, but that then they succumbed to temptation, and their nature turned evil because of this 'fall', then one day God might succumb to temptation and develop an evil nature, or perhaps this happened long ago (and God defined as necessarily all-good no longer exists). But if God could not possibly succumb to temptation, then humans (or some other type of intelligent creatures— nothing is gained by quibbling about the zoological category 'human') could have been made so that they could not possibly succumb to temptation. I see no escape from the conclusion that if there were some quality of humans which made it impossible for them not to be guaranteed against making evil choices, that quality had to be something other than free will. Therefore, whatever reason God might have had for making humans in such a way that they would be likely to cause a lot of evil, it was certainly *not* that he wanted to let them have free will.

Leaving aside the counter-example of God himself, it has seemed obvious to many thinkers, both theists and atheists, that there is no problem about God giving his creatures free will *and* ensuring that they make only right choices. This position is suggested by compatibilism (which I explained above). It's also suggested by the view that God knows the future, foreseeing all outcomes from the beginning. The view that God foreknows everything that will happen may go along with determinism or with indeterminism.

The idea that God might give people free will *and* ensure that they always made right choices does not involve God giving anyone an irresistible psychological compulsion, as Van Inwagen strangely seems to suppose. Everyone's decisions between good and evil could be finely balanced, spontaneous, even whimsical, and absolutely lacking in any compulsiveness. But God who, in making the universe, sees every single event in its entire history, in all its detail, as one vast (though to God's eye not especially vast) tapestry, taken in at one glance, would just will into existence *that* universe—that one there, so to speak (if we imagine God consulting an infinitely long list of every possible universe)—one precisely specified universe in which it happens to turn out that no one chooses evil.

If determinism is correct, then there is no Free Will Defense. This holds if there is no such thing as free will, and it also holds if there is free will *and* determinism. If both human free will and metaphysical determinism are true, then God could both give people free will *and* set things up so that they always make 'good' choices. Therefore, anyone advancing the Free Will Defense has to reject compatibilism—the view that both free will and determinism are true. A proponent of the Free Will Defense has to accept free will and reject determinism.

But even if there is no determinism, if God foresees everything then there is still no Free Will Defense. The view that God is outside time (or outside 'our' time), and sees the whole spacetime world as a simultaneous block with time as akin to one spatial dimension, would entail that God, in making the world, intends every detail of it, including those that are not deterministically related to other details.[77]

Objection #4: Different Characters

Free will implies 1. that people have genuine choices, and 2. that the results of their choices are not the inevitable outcomes of earlier circumstances. I'm going to assume here that these two conditions are all that it takes to give us free will.[78]

Free will does not, then, mean that anyone is likely to do just *anything*. A little thought shows that free will *could not* mean this, if free will really exists, because it's an observable fact that people vary in their dispositions. The existence of free will does not imply that someone who hates the taste of fish is just as likely as anyone else to order sashimi.

For simplicity, I'm going to call everything in a person's makeup that influences the probability of how that person will behave that person's 'character'. We know that people's characters are very largely influenced by their genes: whether someone is shy or outgoing, aggressive or submissive, stable or excitable, good or bad at math or music, is largely a matter of genetics. There are also character-forming influences from upbringing, from the broader culture, and from accidents of a person's life history.

If people have free will, then people of widely varying inherited dispositions have free will. Some people become sadistic killers, and whether someone becomes a sadistic killer involves that person's free will. But not all individuals are equally likely to become sadistic killers. Many people simply never find anything appealing in such a course. Genetic variability ensures that some individuals are more prone to become sadistic killers than others. For instance, men are more likely to become sadistic killers than women, and men with some specific genes are more likely to become sadistic killers than other men.

Whatever determines people's characters influences the kinds of actions that people carry out, and this fact is fully compatible with free will. It follows that in deciding to create humans with specific characters, God has a big influence on the range of likely human actions.

We should not be distracted by considerations alien to omnipotence and omniscience. For example, someone might point out that the genes of an individual especially prone to become a sadistic killer are a recombination of genes that, in other permutations, would be highly beneficial to the population. This is true. But God did not have to use natural selection, he did not have to use genes, he did not even have to give his free-willed creatures physical bodies. And assuming he had decided on genes, he could still have intervened piecemeal to modify the outcome. And even if he had intervened on billions of occasions, this would have been just as easy for him as not intervening—that follows from his omnipotence.

Objection #5:
Different Circumstances

The probability that someone of a given character, with free will, will choose one option rather than another is influenced by the circumstances in which that person finds herself.

Take a person A, with wants of a certain kind, these wants being influenced by her character. Whether A can get something she wants by harming person B is a matter of A's circumstances. For example, among some animals, rape never occurs, because it's impossible for a male to overpower a female, or because the male sexual appetite is only switched on by a signal of female receptivity.

Combining Objections 5 and 6, we can say that a person with free will is still probabilistically influenced by his character and circumstances. Given human history, it appears that the characters and circumstances of humans, for which God (if there be a God) bears responsibility, have been conducive to acts with evil consequences.

Here we must be aware of a possible equivocation. We all know fine people, people of admirable virtue. It is not outlandish, given God's omnipotence, to imagine that all humans could have been raised to that level. But according to one strand of Christian thinking, derived from Paul, all humans with the sole exception of Christ are totally depraved and fully deserve to roast in endless Hellfire. If theists claim that universal moral excellence by ordinary standards would still mean universal total depravity and thus horrendously evil outcomes, then, first, this does not look like a persuasive factual claim, and second, it would be wrong of God to make impossibly severe demands on beings he has created. On such a hypothesis, God would be morally contemptible and therefore not the God of classical theism.

Objection #6:
Persuasive Intervention by God

There are various ways in which person A can interact with person B, and influence B's behavior without taking away B's free will. Most notably, A can supply information, A can persuade, and A can advise. It does not matter here whether A is God or someone else.

Suppose I shout to someone 'That's a bad idea', they reconsider what they were about to do, change their minds, and don't do it. Surely that person's free will is intact, yet I have prevented some amount of evil (on the supposition that my judgment of the intended action was correct). The God of classical theism is a person who could talk to people, either literally, or telepathically, or by more indirect means. In talking to them, God could make his identity and his advice quite unambiguous, just as one human can, when offering advice to another. This would not cancel people's free will. There might be people who would hear the advice and still go against it, but surely very few. At any rate, it's a palpable fact that God does not generally talk to people in this way. Although I have been speaking of 'advice', often the mere provision of information would be sufficient—and then God wouldn't even have to disclose his identity.

Here the theist might say that God does advise us, for example through the Ten Commandments. Yet, first, we must not make the mistake of supposing that the evil which results from people's actions results only when they break the moral rules of some religious tradition or other, and never results when they comply with those moral rules. The ancient Hebrews did not see any contradiction between the Ten Commandments and stoning witches to death or slaughtering Canaanite babies. Was this a mistake on their part? If so, it was a mistake shared by the authors of the *Torah*, who were indispensable in transmitting the Ten Commandments. And, second, God could advise people more directly and more convincingly.

On the first point, great plagues which have killed millions of people and caused millions to suffer horrible agonies, would not have been curtailed by everyone obeying the Ten Commandments, or the entire *Torah*, but could have been curtailed if people had been given reliable information about transmission of infection, along with appropriate public health measures. (They could have also been prevented if God had not created infectious viruses and bacteria in the first place, or not permitted fallen angels to create these micro-organisms, but that was covered under Objection 1. At this point we're confining our discussion to evil resulting from human behavior.)

If for some reason having God talk to people is unacceptable, God could have planted a prestigious book in a human culture, containing helpful practical advice. Instead of *Leviticus*, crammed with pointless idiotic restrictions on what to eat and how to behave, there could have been a book filled with insights into bacteriology and other factual matters, along with rules of thumb for healthy living.

Consider the great reductions in human suffering that have been made possible by the invention of anesthetics. Is there any reason why God could not have imparted some of the technology of anesthesia to people thousands of years before they were able to develop this knowledge for themselves, without any help from the Almighty? This would not have hurt free will, and would have been easy for God to accomplish (because of omnipotence, it would have been exactly as easy for him to accomplish it as to refrain from accomplishing it).

It would not have been any abrogation of people's free will to inform them of the facts, and stop, or reduce, the killing of witches. The same applies to the killing of the Jews down the centuries in Europe. If God had imparted to the Christians of Europe a few key facts, for example that the gospel accounts of the railroading of Christ by Jewish leaders are purely legendary, and that the activities of the Jews as merchants and moneylenders did not deduct from, but added to, the real incomes of Christians,[79] then the recurring massacres of Jews, like the recurring massacres of supposed witches, would not have occurred, or would have occurred on a lesser scale.

Objection #7:
Coercive Intervention by God

Proponents of the Free Will Defense say that almighty God wanted to give humankind free will, and therefore 'had to' accept that humans would use their free will to cause horrendous evils. I have argued that there were many things the hypothetical God could have done, non-coercively and person-to-person, to reduce the amount of evil, without taking away anyone's free will.

But surely, you may think, I must accept that if God wanted to let humans keep their free will, he had to refrain from coercively intervening to prevent evil, either by directly modifying people's thinking, or by sabotaging their evil plans. I accept nothing of the kind.

If a bank security guard says to a robber, engaged in robbing a bank: 'Drop that gun or I will shoot you' (or a more pungent expression carrying this essential message), is the security guard taking away the bank robber's free will? (And if so, one might be tempted to jocularly add, is the guard expanding the free wills of the other people in the bank at the time, as well as the free wills of all the bank's depositors and stockholders?) If you think that security guards may stop bank robberies without abolishing human free will, why would you suppose that God cannot conduct analogous coercive operations?

If we're to think about the whole notion of what it might mean to deny people free will or to take away their free will, we need to look at three different aspects of free will: the *exercise* of free will, the *scope* for free will, and the *capacity* for free will. When people speak of 'taking away someone's free will', it is often unclear which of these is meant. And the Free Will Defense trades on this unclarity.

The *exercise* of free will is executing a chosen course of action. If on one occasion someone forcibly prevents me doing what I want to do, then I am prevented from exercising my free will in a specific way. My capacity for free will remains intact.

A person's capacity for free will is only of value because of exercises of free will, but preventing a particular exercise of free will does not detract from a person's capacity for free will. That is, a person prevented from doing a particular thing still 'has free will', just as much as if they were not prevented. Scope for free will refers to the general conditions which make it possible to contemplate various courses of action. If I am locked up in a cell, my scope for free will is much less than if I am at large, but my capacity for free will is no less. If I die before the age of ten, as most children did throughout all of human history up to the industrial revolution, then my scope for free will is restricted in a different way.

It is a fact of life that specific exercises of our free will are continually being blocked off by circumstances, including the actions of other people. If God made the world, then God has arranged things this way. If it's a question of God 'taking away our free will' in the sense that circumstances for which the omnipotent God must be responsible prevent us from doing certain things we would like to do, then God is taking away our free will every second of every day.

Yet this normal human condition, in which we find our scope for free will narrowly restricted and our conceivable exercises of free will blocked off at almost every turn, is spoken of by the proponent of the Free Will Defense as one in which we retain all our free will. It seems, then, that by saying that God leaves us with our free will, the proponent of the Free Will Defense must mean that we retain our *capacity* for free will. But as we have seen, nobody is suggesting that God should take away our capacity for free will, rather it is suggested that God continue to do what he is doing—preventing us doing what we want to do on innumerable occasions every day—but do this a bit differently, so that we are prevented from doing certain things which lead to a huge amount of appalling evil (and perhaps stop being prevented from doing certain things which would lead to good).

Many of the occasions where God might act to prevent an exercise of free will by one human would incidentally facilitate exercises of free will by other humans. The whole notion that God cannot intervene coercively because this would take away people's free will is therefore nothing more than a dreadful muddle.

Objection #8:
Collectivizing Humans

Although proponents of the Free Will Defense speak of God's desire to leave us with our free will, it's clear from an examination of what they say that they are actually thinking of something rather different.

The real principle to which they appeal is that if some free-willed person created by God harms another free-willed person created by God, then God washes his hands of the matter. God is not going to assume the responsibility of protecting any free-willed creature (or any animal) from the harm done by another free-willed creature. Victims have to suffer at the hands of aggressors.

This is not compatible with God's benevolence towards humans and his omnipotence and omniscience.

Are Atheists Sissies?

Suffering is evil, or alternatively (depending on precisely how we define 'suffering' and 'evil') excessive suffering is evil. But theists sometimes insinuate that atheists are sissies. They are too sensitive to suffering and should be tougher. Aren't there other kinds of evil? (See Swinburne 1996, p. 102.)

I agree that suffering is not the only evil. I go further and assert that departures from happiness are not the only evil. There are departures from happiness that do not amount to evil, and there are evils other than departures from happiness (Steele 2005b). Given the way things actually are, it's even worth purchasing some good things by an increase in the amount of suffering. All this applies to the world as it actually is, not to the immensely better world you or I would have created if we had been omnipotent and omniscient.

Yet suffering or excessive suffering is an evil, and it is one that is clear-cut. One evil other than suffering is unfulfilled potential, the kind of tragic outcome described in *Jude the Obscure*. I could recast everything I have said here about suffering in terms of unful-filled potential. But the identification of unfulfilled potential is generally more subtle and more controversial than the identification of suffering. It's therefore easier to talk about suffering as standing for evil in general. To raise the question of evils other than suffering cannot save the Free Will Defense, since these other evils are just as rife in the world, and could equally well have been avoided or greatly reduced by God, if there were a God.

Theists sometimes say that the existence of extreme pain is jus-tified by its role in preserving and protecting life. No doubt this is true from the standpoint of natural selection alone, but omnipo-tence and omniscience must answer to a higher standard. It could not be beyond the wit of an omnipotent, omniscient creator to devise a way to have organisms seek their survival and health with-out suffering. For instance, it could be that when certain kinds of injury or threat of injury appear, the normal brain functions would be over-ridden by a sort of irresistible compulsion, akin to post-hypnotic suggestion, only stronger. This over-ride would make the organism behave in some way most appropriate to its wellbeing. Of course, this would work only roughly and probabilistically—but just the same is true of pain.

As against this, some recent work by philosophers suggests that emotion may be a precondition of conscious thought. This might imply that some suffering must accompany any intensely effective awareness of injury. I think an omnipotent God would be able to get around that, but rather than pursue a lengthy examination of this issue, I will merely point out that it would be possible to have an over-ride of the kind mentioned *in at least some cases*. In fact, if any design were involved, it would be a simple matter to retain pain in some circumstances but eliminate pain in the many occasions (the majority, perhaps) where pain is perfectly useless.

One response to this might be that God could have done it, but could not have arranged for it to evolve by natural selection. That may be true, but there is no imperative for God to confine his creative role to setting up the natural laws which would cause life to evolve by an undirected process. Any outcome reachable by natural selection over millions of years could have been attained in an instant, by the divine equivalent of a snap of the fingers. Furthermore, God could have arranged for evolution by natural selection and also miraculously intervened piecemeal from time to time—precisely what many theists (when they are speaking in other contexts) insist that he has done.

The Biology of Evil

If we accept classical theism, we have to go to extraordinary lengths to explain why there is so much evil. And the explanations are inconclusive, as they can be paralleled by similar arguments defending the existence of a perfectly evil God. A perfectly evil God would want to keep humans alive so that they could endure as much suffering as possible, he would want to keep their hopes up so that he could cruelly dash them, he would want them to have free will, knowing that they would commit atrocities, and he would want some paragons of virtue, so that they could be tormented by the wicked (Russell 1945, p. 590).

If we suppose that there is neither a good God nor an evil God, but just no God (or a God indifferent to human welfare) then there's no difficulty about explaining the existence of evil and the amount of evil that exists. The Problem of Evil is only a problem for the theist. The evil we observe is pretty much what we might expect on the hypothesis that we have come about by an undesigned process of evolution and if the universe were indifferent to our fate. Instead of stipulating a benevolent and omnipotent God, and then trying to come up with reasons why the omnipotent God is in practice impotent, we can account for the existence of bad things, including very bad things, by pointing to natural facts.

Consider the example of sickle-cell anemia in humans. Humans are susceptible to malaria. For every gene that you and I carry, we carry two versions, known as alleles. We get one of each from each of our parents. If one of those alleles is a sickle-cell allele, it puts some sickle cells into our blood, giving us some very slight health problems but also a lot of immunity to malaria. But if both of the alleles that an individual inherits are sickle-cell alleles, then that person has sickle-cell anemia. Sickle-cell anemia causes bouts of pain and other suffering, and a shorter life. If there is no malaria, sickle-cell anemia gradually disappears (over thousands of years) as it is now gradually disappearing among African Americans. But if malaria is rife, sickle-cell anemia spreads in the population until it reaches a high level (but not one hundred percent, as the person with the best chance of survival is the person who carries only one sickle-cell allele).

If some benevolent and very clever designer were designing people, and wanted to give them some protection against malaria, because he had their welfare at heart, he would not come up with a crazy scheme like this, which purchases some protection against the horrors of malaria by horribly tormenting one child in every four born to parents who both carry the 'protective' allele. But this is just the kind of thing that is liable to emerge from the blind, undesigned process of natural selection. This is one extreme version of a tragedy that's very common: a gene spreads in the population because it gives a reproductive advantage to people who have it as one allele, while it causes serious health problems for the smaller number of people who inherit it as both alleles. Other problems are caused by the genetic mechanisms known as 'linkage' and 'pleiotropy'. Genetic diseases may be favored by natural selection because the genes responsible for them also have beneficial results.

The Free Will Defense Contradicts Religious Orthodoxy

I've been looking at the Free Will Defense purely as it relates to the existence of God, without considering other beliefs commonly held by theists. But if we introduce some of the other beliefs to which most theists are committed, we find additional difficulties.

The *Bible* has many stories of God intervening in human affairs, and if we believe even a tenth of them, then we must conclude that God does not refrain from interfering in human affairs because 'he wants to leave humans with their free will'. Nothing could be further from his thoughts!

We read that God drowned the Pharoah's army by miraculously parting the waters of the Red Sea (*Exodus* 14:27–28). However, before this occurred, God had repeatedly intervened to harden the Pharoah's heart so that he would refuse to allow the Hebrews to leave Egypt (*Exodus* 10:1–2, 20, 27; 11:9–10). In other words, *Exodus* reports that the Pharaoh, left to his own free choice, would have let the Hebrews go, but God miraculously intervened to bend the Pharaoh's mind, against his prior will, to refuse to let the Hebrews go. God's motive (*Exodus* makes clear) was to show off, by drowning the Pharaoh's armies. The motive of the scribes who concocted this tale (or the fireside raconteurs who gave it to the scribes) was presumably to emphasize God's untrammeled and fearsome despotism. In *Job*, we are told that God, because of a bet by Satan (with whom God is on fairly cordial terms) inflicts numerous sufferings upon Job, including the deaths of his wife and children. And don't forget that a little bit earlier, God had deliberately slaughtered the entire population of the world except for eight people.

It follows that even if the Free Will Defense worked (and we have seen that it does not), it is not available to believers in the inerrancy of the *Bible*, or of the approximate reliability of the *Bible*, for several stories in the *Bible* are quite incompatible with God strictly abstaining from interference in human affairs.

Another difficulty stemming from theological convictions arises from belief in Heaven. Christians and Muslims, and most Jews, believe in an eternal afterlife of perfect happiness for at least some sizeable number of humans (usually that group of humans whose opinions conform most closely to those of whichever theologian is speaking).

Now, if some humans are to enjoy eternal bliss, then it cannot be the case that God 'has to' allow the possibility of enormous evils to fall upon humans (Mackie 1982, p. 162). The usual Christian or Muslim view of Heaven is that human souls in Heaven will continue to possess free will, but will never encounter any evil, for 'all eternity'—for gazillions of years to come. So how could it be that, for a few million years, God 'had to' allow all sorts of evils to befall humans and other mammals?

Swinburne apparently notices this problem, and suggests that souls in Heaven will be limited in some ways, lacking the fullness of opportunity available to humans today.[80] Swinburne's proposal presumably means that other persons such as angels, who also once had the kind of free will that God felt he had better not constrain, permitting the rebellion led by Lucifer, will also eventually have permanently limited capacities if they are not to be destroyed.

But this does not answer the objection I have raised here (nor does Swinburne explicitly offer it as an answer to this objection). Why is appalling suffering something God 'has to' fail to prevent for a few million years if he is then going to prevent it for all conscious beings, including humans, for uncountable eons upon eons? How can it be the case *both* that terrible suffering is the price God *had* to pay for generating a population of souls endowed with free will *and* that a population of souls endowed with free will be guaranteed to flourish for endless eons without any suffering?

A theist might say that souls in heaven will not possess free will, though I doubt that many theists would adopt that position. However, that would not circumvent the problem, which would re-emerge in this form: if souls without free will are good enough for all eternity after a certain date, why weren't they good enough for a finite period before that date? A parallel question would arise if it were claimed that souls in heaven would have 'some degree of' free will, but curtailed in some way.

I have here supposed that 'eternity' means 'for ever and ever', for an infinite future period of time. If instead we suppose that Heaven is outside time, a similar problem arises. If human souls, or those that are saved from Hell, are transported out of time to the timeless Heaven, why wouldn't it have been better to send them to Heaven as soon as they were created, and cut out all the history of the physical cosmos, with its terrible evils? A natural answer would be that souls have to go through a testing stage before being fit for Heaven, but that is incompatible with omnipotence and omniscience. An omnipotent, omniscient being could never run a test—the concept is senseless. We run tests because our knowledge is limited. The God of classical theism could have created them just as though they had been tested, and again cut out the whole messy business of space, time, and matter-energy.

Giving Up Classical Theism

Since the Free Will Defense to the Argument from Evil is a failure, the God of classical theism does not exist. Theists who understand this are compelled to modify their concept of God. The two most likely ways to do this are either to accept that God is limited in his powers, or to accept that God is not fully a person.

In 1981 Rabbi Harold Kushner, influenced by Process Theology, had a multi-million best-seller with *When Bad Things Happen to Good People*. Essential to Kushner's explanation for evil afflicting the innocent was the limited power of God and the fact that some things just happen for no reason. To the book-buying public this did not come as a shock, but to some theologians it was a scandal. Rabbi Yitzchok Kirzner responded to Kushner, with a book restating the more traditional position. Kushner's book was criticized on similar grounds by Protestants and Catholics.

The apparently orthodox Catholic Peter Geach denied that God feels any obligation to do all he can for the benefit of humans, and Brian Davies has taken this a bit further, maintaining that God is not a morally responsible agent and explicitly questioning whether God is a person at all. Contrary to Peter Parker's Uncle Ben, Davies holds that with great power comes no responsibility. If God is not a person, or if God does not truly love humans, then the Argument from Evil loses its force. It remains to be seen whether theists who adopt this position are prepared to follow through and strip their pronouncements of all references to God as a loving parent.

16

Can God Be a Person?

God is a person, an individual with a mind, someone who thinks, plans, and acts intentionally, someone who hears and understands what people say to him. Or so we are told by Judaism, Christianity, and Islam.

Genesis tells us that man was made in God's image. One way to take this is that man's mind is a kind of scaled-down copy of God's mind. The *Bible* frequently attributes emotions to God, and even more frequently attributes plans, goals, intentions, or purposes. Theists often explain that God is referred to as 'he', not because he's male but because he's a person. We can't refer to a person as 'it'.

Yet although God is a person, he's not human, and he may therefore lack certain qualities possessed by the persons we've met. And God's other qualities actually rule out many things we normally take for granted in persons belonging to the human species.

What God's Qualities Imply

God cannot be destroyed. He can't be injured against his will or made to suffer against his will, and he knows this. If this is true, then God can't be afraid of anything. He has never known fear at first hand, though he may have known fear in his imagination, the way we know fear by watching a horror movie. But if God has never been fearful, then God has never been courageous. The virtue of courage consists in overcoming or disregarding or perhaps suppressing one's fear or one's inclination to fear. Bravery, then, is a virtue that God can never achieve.

The same applies to most of the human virtues. Most virtues, like courage, involve self-control and therefore have no application to God, who experiences not the slightest flicker of appetites or impulses which might cause him to deviate from doing whatever he infallibly decides is best. God cannot be tempted, so he earns no points for resisting temptation. Nothing, to God, is an effort, so he can never become lazy or irresolute, and deserves no praise for being steadfast.[81]

If God is all-powerful and almighty, then God has never faced any onerous tasks, has never shouldered any burdens, has never had to give up one thing in order to get another (except where the alternatives are logically incompatible), has never felt involuntary pain or even a twinge of discomfort or anxiety, has never had to make a difficult decision, has never solved an intellectual puzzle (since he knows all the answers in advance). God has no curiosity, since he knows everything instantly, without making an effort to find out. God has never had to work hard at anything, has never been surprised or disappointed. God has never had to make a choice, since that would presuppose at least a moment where he had not made up his mind. God can never be careful or considerate. God can never pay particular attention. God has never experienced, at first hand, the joy of understanding an elegant theorem or experiencing a great work of art. He has heard it all before.

Creation of anything by humans, for example creation of a song or a book, has its joys and its sorrows. But for God, the Creator of the universe, there could be no joy, or sorrow, or sense of accomplishment. He created the universe just by willing it and before he willed it, he knew how it was going to turn out. Aside from that, joy and sorrow are characteristics of evolved conscious beings with bodies, forever enmeshed in the struggle to survive and reproduce. Such emotional flurries could have no place in the life of an eternal, indestructible Supreme Being.

Theists say that God is wholly good. This implies that he has never known—at first hand—malice, lust, greed, or envy. Furthermore, God, defined as God who is wholly good, is held to be necessary. If it's necessary that God is wholly good, then God could never go even slightly bad, he could never start toying with a bit of shadiness here and there. So God can't do anything even slightly evil. No credit is due to God for being good; he can't help himself.

Only a very few theists are prepared to say that God could choose to do evil, and it's easy to see why. If God is free to do something evil, then he might, at any moment, do just that. Being all-good would then be revealed as not necessarily true of God: it must have been a mistake all along to think of it as *necessarily* true. As a practical matter we could no longer depend on God to be good. How could we ever know that God had turned bad? What evidence might we find to give us an indication of any such turn of events? It does seem to be essential to the God concept that God is impotent to commit evil. Even mild naughtiness must be beyond his powers. We begin to wonder whether this entity can really be a person.

The God of Abraham, Isaac, and Jacob

Such, at any rate, is the God of classical theism. The tribal god of the Hebrews is another matter. Even his name ('I am that I am') tells us that he's a person. He is invisible and inscrutable most of the time, but that is standard with spirits. His physical form, when he chooses to assume it, is always human. He has superhuman sons who interbreed with human females (*Genesis* 6:4). He is anxious about the accomplishments of humans, because they might one day challenge his own position (*Genesis* 11:6, and remember *Genesis* 3:22). As befits a despot answerable to no one, he is moody and irritable, given to capricious changes of mind, and not inhibited by considerations of fair play. That's his prerogative; he's the Lord.

This God experiences emotions. A quick temper and an insatiable hunger for flattery are his most conspicuous weaknesses. Generally, theologians have interpreted these numerous passages as figurative, and they have assumed the same about the numerous references to God's bodily organs. Maimonides claimed that God never gets angry, but it was necessary to depict him as angry, since there was no other way to explain to the people that certain things were wrong (though Maimonides and his intended readers had no trouble in understanding this). Other theologians, including Christians and Muslims, have tended to follow Maimonides: all references to God's fits of jealous rage are meant to be taken figuratively, as are statements about God changing his mind by repenting and reversing his earlier decisions. This has the unfortunate consequence that God's word, the *Torah*, contains untruths due to

calculation rather than carelessness in transcription: false statements deliberately intended to deceive people for their own good.
If this is so, then how can we be sure where the deceptions end and
the straight talk begins?

The picture of God given to us by the Abrahamic tradition is an
uneasy amalgam of personal and impersonal elements. Starting
from a tribal god who is one god among many, but better than all
the others because he is ours, people began to develop other ideas
about this God, ideas which are ultimately difficult to reconcile
with his personhood.

He is omnipotent, omniscient, omnipresent, immutable. At
first, these ideas sounded like the usual flattery of the powerful.
The influence that transformed these ideas into the God of classical theism was Greek philosophical thought, especially Platonism,
which was widely popularized in the Roman empire. It affected
Jewish and Christian thinking. Early Christianity was impacted by
popularized Greek philosophy in two waves: this influence is
already strong in the *New Testament* itself, but a little later the
Church Fathers became steeped in Plotinus. Early Christian intellectuals were embarrassed by the crudity and barbarity of their own
ideas compared with Greek philosophy, so they instinctively tried
to defend the former by recasting it in terms of the latter.

Is God Outside Time?

We can clearly see this impact of Greek philosophy on theism when
we consider the question, 'Is God outside or inside Time?', a question the authors of the *Torah* would have found hard to compre-
hend.

All theists in the broadly Abrahamic tradition agree that God is
eternal. But this claim can mean two very different things:

**1. God is everlasting. He has always existed and always will
exist. (Eternity means endless time.)**

**2. God is outside time or timeless. He created time when
he created the universe. (Eternity means there is no time.)**

In the history of Christianity, the second interpretation has
overwhelmingly predominated. It was taken over from the pagan

philosopher Plotinus, whose thought became to the early church what dialectical materialism was to the Communist Party of the Soviet Union. Plotinus adapted this notion from Plato, who adapted it from earlier thinkers like Parmenides. It was taken up by such early Christian notables as Augustine, and later fully endorsed by Boethius and Aquinas, as well as by Maimonides.

We might have expected that the theory of the Big Bang would have given a boost to the theory that God is outside time. One interpretation of the Big Bang (before the emergence of inflationary theories at the end of the 1970s) is that time began with the Big Bang: there was no earlier time. Anything that caused the Big Bang could therefore not have preceded it in time. But perhaps the cause of the Big Bang came from outside time? In that case the timeless conception of God would seem to fit nicely with modern physics.

In fact, the past few decades have seen a collapse of the consensus among theologians that God is outside time. Though it has its defenders it is now probably a minority position. From the sixteenth century to the twentieth, Thomism (the ideas of Thomas Aquinas, including the timeless conception of eternity) was more or less the official philosophy of the Catholic Church. Pope John Paul II announced, for the first time, that the Catholic Church favors no single school of philosophy, and that philosophy must be left free to enquire without direction from the Church. But before this announcement, Thomism had already lost its firm grip on Catholic intellectuals.

The view that God is outside time has difficulties for thoughtful theists. It's not the view of the *Old Testament* or the *New Testament*. Many biblical texts clearly specify the 'everlasting' or 'endless time' interpretation of eternity, and only a few, with a bit of work, can be coaxed into harmony with the 'timeless' or 'outside time' interpretation.

The timeless theory of God is very compatible with God's immutability. If God is outside time then he can never change, not even by having a single new thought. If God is outside time, and also omnipotent and omniscient, this suggests that the whole history of the universe, or the metaverse, every bit of every spacetime, is conceived, created, and perceived by God in one great flash of intuition. The theory is also compatible with God's omnipresence. If God is outside time then he must be outside space as well, and if all points in time are accessible to him, then so are all points in space.

But the theory is not compatible with God's personhood. If God is outside time, then he cannot act in anything like the way that humans act. At most, he acts only once. He cannot deliberate, consider his options, then bring about some change in reality. Intelligent action of this kind takes time and can occur only in time. But if God is omnipotent and omniscient, then perhaps he doesn't need time. He sees everything simultaneously, and he wills everything that happens, all at once. There is no need to deliberate and certainly no need to reconsider.

The timeless conception has the appeal of incomprehensibility. It goes with the attractive notion that God is so far above us that we can't begin to figure him out. But we can see that the God of the *Old Testament* is a person because he interacts with other persons—mainly humans but also angels. He sometimes regrets his earlier decisions and goes back on them. God's active intervention in the world can be squared with the timeless theory—he wills the universe into existence and in that very act of will, wills that he intervenes in it at numerous points—but it can't be reconciled with God learning by experience or changing his mind. Proponents of the timeless view have to interpret God's conversational exchanges with Abraham, Moses, and others as interventions from outside time. In the act of making the universe, God included in it all the conversations and debates he would have with humans.

The timeless God cannot be a person. If we take God's timelessness seriously, we arrive at the theory that God does not think, in the sense of experiencing a succession of rationally connected mental events, a train of thought that occupies time, but has just one big, complex thought, once and for all and never again (so to speak), and this one big thought governs everything that has ever happened or ever will happen. But if this is so, then the one big thought is not really a thought at all. Since no deliberation could have preceded the one big thought, it's difficult to see why we should suppose that the one big thought was a good idea. If there is only *one* big thought then the having of that one big thought can only be impersonal, and we have arrived back at a brute law of nature, perhaps a quantum vacuum. This God does not love, is not conscious, and doesn't have a life.

While we can't imagine a personal God outside time, we can easily imagine a personal God outside *our* time. God is then in a sort of super-time or hyper-time, within which our spacetime universe appears as something like a motionless solid block, with time as analogous to one of its four spatial dimensions. This enables God to make plans, make decisions, and act—all of which require time before they can be possible at all. Our time would look like one physical dimension, even though the whole structure would look 'flat'. God's universe would have five or more dimensions, and the whole of our physical universe could sit on God's desk like a screensaver or a paperweight. God would be able to see our future just as easily as our past, as we can see what is on the right just as easily as what is on the left.

In this way, we can try to reconcile a personal God with a God who is outside our time. But this scenario has its puzzles. Suppose that God reaches into our universe and makes a change. This would fit Shestov's notion that God can make it true that something that has actually happened has *not* actually happened. But that actual event which God has abolished within the universe did actually occur within the universe viewed from within God's super-time. But then, it was and always will be the case (in God's time) that there was a universe within which that event did happen.

A difficulty for the timeless theory of God is that if God created the universe, he caused the universe to come into existence. But, it is usually believed, a cause must precede its effect in time. Therefore, God could not have created the universe if he were outside time. However, there is a philosophical theory that causes are actually simultaneous with effects (the effects may be processes which outlive the processes associated with the causes, but at the point of transmission, causation is considered to be always instantaneous).

Putting God in his own time (instead of altogether outside time) allows him to have a life and to be conscious while still relating to our more limited spacetime in accordance with omnipresence and immutability. But this scenario places a strain on the notion that God has no responsibility for evil, which is due to the free choices of God's creatures endowed with free will. Because of their difficulty in answering the Argument from Evil, theists have begun to emphasize human freedom much more than they used to. They want to maintain that even an omnipotent God would be simply incapable of creating a universe in which humans (and angels) would have free will without the likelihood of horrendous evils occurring.

But this limitation on God's capabilities is difficult to reconcile with God in his own super-time perceiving our universe as a timeless block, especially as, God being omnipotent, we must suppose that he can set up a simulated model of the timeless block first, tinker with it at will, and only then make it real. In this scenario, we can't begin to argue that God 'had to' allow evil if he allowed human freedom. He could have selected for kicking into actual existence one of the simulated models in which no one chose evil.

Can Theists Give Up God as a Person?

If theists abandoned their historical commitment to the personhood of God, would they be able to like what remained? Denial of the personhood of God would presumably lead in the direction of pantheism (identifying God with the universe) or deism (God as a kind of benign force, not capable of rational deliberation), both of which are roundly repudiated by the Jewish, Christian, and Muslim mainstreams.

A recent attempt to deny the personhood of God and square this denial with Christianity is by Brian Davies. Davies asserts that the "formula" of the personhood of God is quite recent (Davies 2006, p. 59), implying that it's a novelty within Christianity. But this is superficial. The word 'religion' does not occur in the *Old Testament*, nor the word 'indecisive' in *Hamlet*. A concept may long predate its expression in a formula. The *concept* of the personhood of God is continually reiterated in numerous *Old Testament* stories. God's reported dealings with Adam, Noah, Abraham, Jonah, Job, and Moses, even if we make generous allowance for figurative language, are senseless unless God acts purposively, calculates rationally, and intervenes deliberately in human affairs. The God of Abraham, Isaac, and Jacob is unequivocally and unreservedly a person.

There are many other ways in which the concept, though not necessarily the formula, of God's personhood is deeply embedded in Abrahamic culture. For example, Christians, Muslims, and Jews pray. Do they believe that anyone's listening? Listening, not in the sense in which an automatic recording machine may be said to listen, but listening with understanding of what is being said? They generally do tell us that they believe this. But if someone is listening, with understanding of what is being said, how could this listener not be a person?

Davies wants to dissolve the Argument from Evil by denying that God is a kind of entity which can be held morally responsible. But whether God can be held morally responsible depends upon how God is conceived, and it seems doubtful that Davies is prepared to discard enough of the traditional Christian conception to give God immunity from moral responsibility. Does God choose? Does God make plans and act on them? Does God ever have a preference for one outcome rather than another? Is it within God's power to shape events? Did God so love the world that he gave his only begotten son? Davies is non-committal or equivocal on these issues (within the pages of this particular book of his). If the answers are no, then Davies leaves the Abrahamic tradition behind. If the answers are yes, then Davies's God must surely be morally responsible, and gets no immunity. I can't see a middle way out.

The Christian conception of God is further complicated by the idea of the Trinity, three persons (or perhaps three personas) in one God. Davies denies that this signifies three centers of consciousness, but just what he means by this denial isn't clear either. If Jesus prays to the Father, and the Father is listening (Jesus is not talking to himself), then it's hard to see how we don't here have at least two centers of consciousness. If Davies means that God has *no* center of consciousness, that is, God is not gifted with the capacity for thought or reflective awareness, then again Davies has stepped out of classical theism into pantheism or deism.

17

What God Can't Do and What God Can't Know

What does it mean to say that God is omnipotent? The answer seems simple. It means that God can do anything.

According to classical theism, God made the universe out of nothing, by an act of will. Let's suppose that this refers to our universe which physicists say began with the Big Bang fourteen billion years ago. In that case, God made the universe as a tiny point which would rapidly expand into something very hot, very dense, and very disorderly. This universe would cool as it expanded and eventually stars would appear, and then planets.

But classical theists will deny that God had to create it this way, or even that it was any easier to do it this way than any other way: this would imply that there are general features of reality which constrain God's actions. God would then be subject to natural law (not the laws of our universe but a more fundamental law, perhaps even a law we could never hope to know) and theists insist that God cannot be subject to natural law. He is the sole author of natural law.

So God could have created the universe, exactly as it is now, five minutes ago. And whenever he made it, five minutes ago or fourteen billion years ago, he is actively sustaining it at every moment. We tend to suppose that some things just happen by themselves if no one interferes. Water runs downhill even if no one takes any interest in it. The classical theist maintains that this is an illusion. When water runs downhill, every single molecule of water is being directed, by a deliberate act of God, to take exactly the path it takes. God cannot just leave things alone to run their course, because nothing at all can happen unless God wills it.

To God, then, there is no fundamental distinction between actively intervening and letting things take their course. Both require exactly the same amount of attention and effort on his part: none.

Things God Can't Do

Can God really do anything? Can God, for example, make a square circle?

In the thirteenth century, Thomas Aquinas asserted that God cannot make a square circle. He can do nothing which is logically impossible. As Aquinas correctly argued (this is the kind of thing that makes Aquinas a great philosopher), being unable to make a square circle is not really a limitation on God's omnipotence, because if we say that something made by God is a square and is also a circle, we are making two assertions that contradict each other. When we say that God cannot make a square circle, we are not really identifying something that God cannot make: the notion of a square circle is incoherent.

In this book I often discuss whether some claim is incoherent. When I say that something is incoherent, I don't mean that it's obvious gibberish or that it makes no sense at all. I simply mean that it can't possibly be right because it leads to a logical contradiction. This may not be obvious; it may be hard to see. If I say that 'the highest prime number is less than five billion', it's quite clear what I mean. But that statement would be incoherent: mathematicians have strictly proved that there can be no highest prime number. Before that mathematical proof was worked out, my statement would still have been incoherent, but no one (except God) could have known this.

Since Aquinas, a few theists (most famously the philosopher René Descartes and the Eastern Orthodox theologian Lev Shestov) have contended that God could indeed do logically impossible things. Descartes believed that the laws of logic and arithmetic apply in our universe, but God could have decreed it differently. So God could have made a world in which $2 + 2 = 5$. Shestov maintained that God could cause it to be the case that something which has actually happened never happened. Virtually all theologians and all philosophers now disagree with Descartes and Shestov on these points.

Are there things God just can't do which don't involve logical incoherence? How about this, a puzzle raised by theologians in the Middle Ages: Can God make a rock so heavy that he himself cannot lift it? If we say yes, then there could be a rock which God could not lift, so it is not true that God can do anything. But if we say no, then there is something God cannot do: make a rock too heavy for him to lift.

We shouldn't be distracted by accidental features of this example. Of course God, if he exists, is bigger than gravity, and would not be bothered by anything being heavy (though this might not have been quite so clear in the Middle Ages). The example could equally well be: Can God make an object he cannot destroy? Can God start a process he can't control? Can God make a person who could successfully go against God's own will? These are all variants of the question: can God do something which entails God being limited?

At first, we might think that God's making a rock too heavy for him to lift is just like God making a square circle: it involves a logical contradiction and is therefore incoherent. But that can't be exactly right. You and I can't make a square circle, any more than God can. But you and I can easily make something too heavy for us to lift. Many people have made houses or boats that they could not lift. It's true that God making a rock too heavy for him to lift is incoherent, but in this case the incoherence lies not in the nature of the task but in the concept of omnipotence, if it's defined in a particular way.

But still, a theist might say, God can make a rock of any weight, without limit, and God can lift a rock of any weight, without limit, so not much has been lost by the discovery that God cannot make a rock he cannot lift. We can keep all the omnipotence worth having. I agree, but the example does alert us to the possibility that 'God can do anything' may be misleading.

Can God scratch his nose? Can God ride a bike? These actions presuppose that God has a body, and the usual theist view is that God has no body. The *Bible* tells us that God took walks in the Garden of Eden, that he has a face and ears and a backside, and that he can smell as well as see. But we can accept what most theologians say and discount these statements as figurative. It might be argued that God can create a full-grown body in an instant, and in that very instant scratch his nose and ride a bike. The question then arises whether that body is his, in the full sense that your body is yours. Probably not, as God is present everywhere throughout the universe, and your soul is presumably not present everywhere throughout the universe. Also, your body may be part of you in a stronger sense than any body could be part of God.

There may, then, be a sense in which God cannot scratch his nose or ride a bike. To avoid these problems, various attempts have been made to describe God's omnipotence in a way that excludes them. Swinburne describes God's powers to "bring about" certain states of affairs, not to "do" things. Anthony Kenny suggests that God's omnipotence can be described as possession of all logically possible powers which it is logically possible for a being with the attributes of God to possess (1979, p. 98).

This formula recognizes a conflict between unqualified omnipotence and God's other qualities. If God cannot do anything morally wrong, this is a great limitation on his powers. Some theologians have tried to say that God could do something wrong, but just never does because he is so very good. This, however, won't wash. It's part of the definition of God that he never does anything wrong, and that God as so defined is necessarily that way. If it's necessary that God never does anything wrong, then God cannot do anything wrong without ceasing to be God. But if it is also necessary that God exists, that would imply that as God ceases to be God someone else takes over that role. We can't imagine who that understudy might be, or how the instantaneous transfer of all God's powers to the understudy is guaranteed.

God Must Be Subject to Natural Law

Theists claim that God's omnipotence means that he is prior to all natural laws. Laws of nature are all determined by God, who could have chosen entirely different laws. Thus, 'impersonal' laws like $e = mc^2$ have a 'personal' origin in the mind of God. While this might conceivably be true of those laws we know, it cannot be true in the fullest sense: there must be other, more fundamental laws, to which God is subject.

Natural laws are fundamental aspects of reality, the way things are at the most general level. But God cannot exist in the first place unless reality is a certain way and not some other way. This argument was hinted at by Hume and set out by John Stuart Mill, but the force of Mill's argument was overlooked or underestimated until restated by Gilbert Fulmer in 1977.

If the God of classical theism exists, then it must be the case that everything God wills comes about. This statement, if true, is a natural law independent of God's will. It could be different: whatever God wills could come about with sixty-five percent probability, or whatever God wills comes about only roughly, with minor inaccuracies, or there is a vast mind imagining things but when this mind tries to make its imaginings real, nothing happens. God cannot make it true that everything he wills comes about. This is a pre-existing natural regularity to which God has to submit. And it's an impersonal regularity.[82] Therefore, there just is no escape from the view that impersonal law is fundamental to the universe, whether there's a God or not.

We might try to save a kind of personal origin for natural law by saying that God has existed for ever, but was originally unable to bring about anything just by willing it. Being able to bring anything about just by willing it was an achievement, a product of arduous effort and self-cultivation. God served his apprenticeship and then embarked upon his career of creating universes. This contradicts God's immutability and it contradicts the claim that God defined as omnipotent exists necessarily. But it also cannot get away from the conclusion that God exists in a context of impersonal law independent of his will. For if God could by self-cultivation develop the ability to bring about anything just by willing it, the universe had to be some particular way (even if the universe at one time was nothing but God's thoughts). The universe had to be such that God could learn how to manipulate it. This means that it exhibited regularities which confronted God as objective conditions. There is again no escape from the conclusion that at least one impersonal regularity must logically precede God. If there's a God, there has to be at least one brute, inexplicable fact which is independent of God's will and to which God, if he exists, must conform. Even if God decreed that $e = mc^2$, God could not have decreed that anything he decrees comes about. God is compelled to comply with natural law—no other possibility is even coherent.

Furthermore this God can think. But if God can think, reality (even if all of reality at this point is nothing but God's mind) is definitely some particular way and not some other way. Thinking can never be totally chaotic, even after half a bottle of Lagavulin. Thinking cannot escape being governed by pre-existing regularities. We can deny that God thinks, but then we exit classical theism, perhaps moving over to deism or pantheism. It's difficult to accept that God can think without a brain, but for God to be able to think without some general facts about his mind holding true is more than difficult to accept: it's just absurd.

Could God Limit Himself?

Some people have supposed that God, being almighty, could have deliberately placed restrictions upon himself, and even given himself a dose of amnesia so that he would be temporarily less than omnipotent. This is the idea behind the cosmology concocted by L. Ron Hubbard and made the basis of the religion of Scientology: we humans used to be nearly omnipotent beings, 'thetans', who, as a game, decided to restrict ourselves in various ways. But something went wrong: the game became a trap, and we are faced with the problem of recovering our own near-omnipotence.

It is also the idea behind the Christian story of the incarnation. God was incarnated in Jesus. Being limited in some ways, Jesus could be tempted, could experience pain, disappointment, and other human attributes. Thus, God in Christ did undergo all the stresses and discomforts of a human.

However, Jesus sometimes prays to God, sometimes even in a supplicating and once in a despairing mode. So we must suppose that while God, as one of his persons, was undergoing all the trials of humankind, he was simultaneously, as the heavenly father, performing his essential duties as sustainer of the entire universe. According to one view, popularized by Albert Schweitzer in *The Quest of the Historical Jesus* (notice the word 'of'), Jesus was born without any knowledge that he was God. He had to figure this out as he went along.

This story of the incarnation raises additional puzzles which are, however, tangential to the general God issue. Since an essential part of human learning is learning by mistakes, did Jesus make mistakes? Did he entertain some radically false theories about the world and his place in it, before arriving at the correct theory? If not, how could he learn anything—and learn in a fully human manner? Did Jesus the carpenter ever have to throw away a piece of wood that he had cut too thin? If the answer is no, then God was not really subjecting himself to all the normal human limitations, but was merely slumming on a tourist visa. If the answer is yes, then perhaps there are one or two slips in the Sermon on the Mount.

There have been billions of humans, and according to traditional Christianity, all of them, with precisely one exception, have been sinners, deserving Hellfire. Is it a pure coincidence that the one human who was not a sinner happened to be the one human who was the incarnation of God? It seems odd to say that this was pure coincidence: that it was just as likely to turn out that God's son was a sinner while Hector Stewart McRae of Dumfries was the one human without sin. We may assume, then, that there is some connection between the sinlessness of Jesus Christ and the fact that he was God. But in that case, it cannot be true to say that Jesus Christ really took on the full burden of being human. Perhaps it will be said that Jesus was in the same position as Adam: Adam could have chosen not to sin, and so could Jesus, but Adam's other descendants don't have that opportunity. But then the sacrifice of God's son was a coin toss. The whole story just doesn't hang together very well.

If God limits himself, then he is no longer omnipotent and thus ceases to be God. This suggests that the concept of omnipotence might really be incoherent, because it's a limitation not to be able to limit yourself. I have said that the classical theist view is that everything that happens is deliberately done by God. But suppose that God wanted to set up a spontaneous, undirected chain of events, with indeterminacy built in, so that even he couldn't control or predict the outcome. Would God be able to do this? If no, then God is limited by not being able to do something any kid at the beach can do with a bucket and spade. If yes, then we don't and can't know that the classical theist view of God is correct. It might be that God set off the Big Bang and then stood aside to see what would happen. And if it might be, then it probably is, because the universe does look very chaotic. And if it is, then God is not sustaining all of his Creation at all times, as the mainstream theologians have confidently maintained.

Theologians may have their doubts about whether, in general, God could limit himself by handing over parts of his Creation to undirected processes. But if we take a special case of this—giving some of his creatures free will, so that what they decide to do is not something for which God is responsible—then the theologians nearly all assert that God can do this and has done it. This is because the theologians need an answer to the Argument from Evil, and the Free Will Defense looks like their best bet. However, it seems unreasonable to say that God can create free willed persons and leave them alone to do what they want, and not also say that God can create spontaneous processes (like expanding universes or the formation of snowflakes) and leave them alone to play themselves blindly out.

It may not be obvious that God giving his creatures free will and divesting himself of moral responsibility for what they do requires God to limit his own powers. Can't God retain all his powers but just choose to let his creatures decide what to do? Not at all, for then God is still morally responsible for what they do. If I create an entity that can do what it wants to, and at every moment I am capable of effortlessly intervening to stop it doing what it wants to, then I am certainly responsible for everything that entity does (the entity may also be responsible; that's no contradiction; we're both responsible). For God to lose the moral culpability for what his creatures do, it has to become somehow impossible for him to intervene to stop them. Though even then, he's still responsible to some extent, as King Lear was responsible for what ensued when he gave up his kingdom.

If God has created a universe with genuine indeterminacy, in which even an omniscient person cannot perfectly predict the future, then this contradicts the view held by most theologians, that God knows the future. It contradicts even more strikingly the theory held by many theologians that God is 'outside time'. It may also contradict the claim that God is changeless, for if God comes to know something he did not know before, he has changed.

God's Suicide or Abdication

In Van Vogt's *The Battle of Forever*, humans have become almost omnipotent, but there's a lot they don't know, and as a result they are threatened with annihilation by comparatively puny though crafty beings. So it seems that an omnipotent being with limited knowledge would be vulnerable, but that's because we suppose he can't foresee the effects of what he does. Yet if he truly were omnipotent, the concept of 'effects' wouldn't apply, because nothing would follow from his actions except what he wanted to happen.

Another reason for thinking that a literally omnipotent God must be omniscient is that it would be part of omnipotence to become omniscient just by willing it, and why would he not have done this long ago?

A substantially omnipotent God who commits blunders and has to face unintended consequences seems unacceptable. However, just this kind of God is clearly depicted in the *Torah*. Seeing how humans have turned out, God regrets having created them (*Genesis* 6:6). The Torah repeatedly tells us that God did not foresee what would happen, and changed his mind about what to do. There has always been a current within Judaism willing to accept God's limited knowledge and limited wisdom. The Jewish theologian Yochanan Muffs depicts a very personal, very powerful God who miscalculates and learns by experience. Alan Dershowitz has contended that a distinctive merit of the *Torah* is that none of its characters, including God, is entirely worthy of emulation.

If God can limit himself, he can injure himself—with God the two concepts are hard to distinguish. And if he can injure himself, perhaps he can commit suicide. A case for the suicide of God was made by Scott Adams (of Dilbert fame) in his amusing work, *God's Debris*, which Adams calls fiction but which libraries insist on classifying as cosmology. Humans are evolving so as to reconstitute God's fragmented being.

In the Kabbalistic tradition of Judaism, Isaac ben Solomon Luria advanced the theory that God had created the world by limiting himself, by withdrawing from a certain area of existence. More recently, Hans Jonas has maintained that in creating the universe, God committed suicide, though he will eventually be reconstituted out of the end of the universe.

Things God Can't Know

Omniscience, just like omnipotence, seems at first glance clear and comprehensible. God knows everything there is to know. That means that he knows everything that all humans have known or could know, and a lot more besides. He knows whether the number of helium atoms in the Sun is odd or even, and whether it was raining or not raining precisely one thousand years ago in the area now occupied by downtown Chicago. Or at least, this is what some theists tell us. Jerome (fourth century C.E.) declared that it was ridiculous to suppose that God knows the number of fleas on the Earth—a charming example of a saint saying something that might have gotten him into hot water a few centuries later.

Knowledge is of at least three kinds: knowledge of facts, knowledge of how to do things, and knowledge by acquaintance. Most discussion of God's knowledge assumes that it is knowledge of facts. Knowledge of how to do things is a matter of skill, and therefore ultimately a matter of physiology. It seems that one can't know how to play the piano unless one has fingers. This can be resolved if God can acquire a body at any instant, and a body already equipped with favorable genes for piano playing plus the effects of thousands of hours of practice and musical training (without the actual expenditure of those thousands of hours). Someone might object that God can't play the piano at a moment when he has no body. But this could be answered by saying that he could move the keys of the piano (or, of course, of a trillion trillion pianos simultaneously), just by willing it. To demand that God play the piano with his own fingers at a moment when he has no fingers of his own would be incoherent, and therefore not a serious objection.

God's knowledge by acquaintance has struck some people as difficult. It has been objected that God cannot know directly what humans experience, and also that he cannot know lust, or greed, or envy, since he never feels these urges. But once we say that God is a spirit with intellectual and observational capacities vastly greater than anything we have detected in the physical world, I don't think there's any difficulty in giving this person all the 'knowledge by acquaintance' that all humans possess.

We must suppose that the omnipresent God not only perceives the position and trajectory of every unit of matter and energy, but also directly perceives all occurrences in anyone's consciousness. When Proust's narrator dips the petite madeleine into the tea in Combray, God knows *exactly* what it tastes, smells, and feels like. Some might say that God is not Marcel, and therefore cannot have the experiences that Marcel has. But this looks like an empty objection. If God knows exactly what those experiences are like, because

God instantly experiences perfect copies of those experiences, then that is good enough.

Similarly, if God knows directly and perfectly what greed and lust feel like to the person experiencing them, it's surely not required for God also to share in the blameworthy motivation associated with these feelings. Theists often maintain that consciousness is essentially spiritual, and we must just suppose that in the spirit world, motivational feelings can be observed dispassionately, just as particles of matter can be observed dispassionately. We can imagine this by thinking of it as 'empathy', but taken to an extreme of accuracy.

Observation in the physical world always involves exchange of energy, and therefore some degree of approximation, but we must suppose that in the spirit world, some kind of direct access to events is possible for an observer, without exchange of energy. We have to suppose, for instance, that God can directly perceive colors and shapes, and qualities like hardness and softness, without any physical or spiritual interaction between God and the objects perceived. This harmonizes well with the fact that no effects of God's perception of physical objects has been observed in physical observation of those objects. We're doing a lot of supposing without being able to test our suppositions by observation, but that's inherent in talking about an undetectable spirit world.

So we come back to knowledge of facts. It's sometimes claimed that God's knowledge is 'not propositional', but this claim cannot be sustained without giving up the core sense of omniscience. For me to know that my dinner is on the table usually means, in practice, that I can agree with the statement that my dinner is on the table. For a cat to know that its dinner is in the bowl does not imply that the cat understands any statement to that effect. If God's knowledge of facts were like the cat's it would be of a rudimentary kind, and God would be easily confused.

But there's more. As I mentioned in Chapter 6, unless God knows facts in a propositional sense (knows what is entailed in making various statements about these facts) he cannot follow the speech and thoughts of humans. Consequently, to save anything worth saving of omniscience, God's knowledge must include knowledge of many true factual propositions, and, since he's omniscient, of all true factual propositions. In *Rain Man*, when 246 toothpicks fall on the floor, the Dustin Hoffman character immediately sees that there are precisely 246. He can tell the difference between 246 and 247 just as quickly as you or I can tell the difference between one and two. This seems almost incredible, but such cases do exist. It may appear tempting to give God this kind of quick apprehension of all facts, thus freeing him of the need to go through the more involved procedures of normal humans (in this case, counting the toothpicks). Again, this won't do at all. An omniscient God has to know both ways of arriving at the number of pencils, or he cannot follow the thoughts of humans.

Among qualities commonly ascribed to God, we do not find intelligence or quick-wittedness. At first, this might seem natural, as God knows everything already, and therefore doesn't have to figure things out. However, to know anything worth knowing, you must know general theories. Otherwise you can't see the woods for the trees. To know the location of every particle in the universe would be quite useless without also knowing the relations among those particles, including large-scale phenomena like the relations among galaxies. And this means understanding the theories of physics (the true and ultimate theories, not just the ones we have now, though you would also have to know all the incorrect and inadequate theories). Although we may say that God has non-propositional knowledge as well as propositional knowledge, we can't deny him an immense store of propositional knowledge, without reducing his effective knowledge to very little.

Some critics of God's omniscience have advanced the argument that there is a large class of important things God cannot know: indexical expressions. In my view, this argument gets nowhere. According to this argument, God cannot know what is known by Jones when Jones knows that 'I have spilled my soup'. He also cannot know what is known by Smith, when Smith knows at a particular time that 'the final exams are now over'. Some atheists have seen this argument as important, but it strikes me as trivial. If God knows that Jones has spilled his soup, then God knows everything we can expect an omniscient God to know on the matter. It's true that God cannot apply to himself the pronoun 'I' as it applies to Jones, but this merely means that he knows the same facts as Jones without suffering from the delusion that he is Jones. God can know just as well as Smith that 'the final exams are now over', if God is in our time. If God is timeless, or in a different super-time, he knows that 'given Smith's precise position in that particular spacetime universe, it correctly appears to Smith that the final exams are now over'. Since God (by supposition) knows Smith's situation, he knows precisely what Smith means by 'now'. I can't see in these examples any information that God is ignorant of.

To be literally omnisicient, God would have to be aware of all truths, but Patrick Grim has advanced an argument from set theory, showing that a set of all truths is incoherent. Grim developed this idea into a book-length treatment of the necessary limitations of knowledge of the truth.[83] A theist might respond to this in one or both of two ways: suggesting that paradoxes and other curiosities of logic and set theory merely indicate the imperfections in existing versions of these theories, or insisting that God's failure to know what logically cannot be known is not a serious limitation on omniscience. If God knows all events that occur, at every level of generality, then it doesn't seem to matter much that he doesn't know certain facts about the membership of power sets.

God's Knowledge of the Future

Many theists have held that God knows the future in perfect detail. If true, this means that when God created humankind, or created the universe knowing exactly how humankind would evolve, he foresaw everything that every human would do. But theists usually also believe that humans have free will or—a more modest requirement—that humans make genuine choices.

The *New Testament* seems committed to both God's perfect foreknowledge of future events and human freedom of choice. Throughout the history of Christianity since the fourth century C.E., some Christians have seen this as a problem. Some have held that God is omniscient and that we're not really free. Others have argued that we are free and that God doesn't know the future.

The problem is not that there's a simple contradiction between the two Christian beliefs: there is no contradiction.[84] That A knows in advance what B will do does not immediately imply that B could not have done something different. But, taken in conjunction with the traditional Christian and Muslim belief that we will all be rewarded or punished after death because of what we have done in this life, there is something here that Christians and Muslims have found troubling.

The theory that God sees exactly what everyone will do helps to destroy the Free Will Defense to the Argument from Evil. If God knew, before he made the world, exactly what everyone would do, then God cannot be absolved from responsibility for what they do. This is not a matter of shrewdly forecasting what people will probably do (though even that makes God culpable to some extent for what they do; he didn't have to create them); it's a matter of knowing with certainty exactly what they will do. And this implies that God could foresee the exact outcomes of all the possible worlds he might have created and did not create. In that case, God could have selected, from all the infinity of possibilities, one which had all humans behaving in such a way that many appalling evils would not have come about, and also had all humans making the necessary commitment to avoid damnation. If I know that someone who goes into a certain building at a certain time will make choices which will lead to that person having a nasty accident, then by making them go into that building at that time, I am responsible for their nasty accident. It's no defense that they were free.

Another problem arises when we consider *how* God knows the entire future including the precise actions of all humans. Either this means that God is 'outside time' or 'outside our time' (and we've seen in Chapter 16 that this theory can't be squared with God as a person) or it means that God is living through time with us, and this means that God cannot directly perceive what happens in the future, but can only deduce it from what has happened so far, along with theories such as laws of nature. But this means that determinism is true, and this means that the Free Will Defense to the Problem of Evil cannot even get started.

Omnipotence and omniscience both turn out to be less clear-cut than they look. It cannot be true that God can do anything logically possible and it cannot be true that God knows everything it is logically possible for him to know. Yet theists might be able to incorporate many of these conclusions without giving up what they view as the essential core of omnipotence and omniscience. It's obviously possible for someone to be able to do vastly more than I can do, and to know vastly more than I know. God can be able to do a lot, and know a lot, without bumping up against the limit of what can be done or known. There's no practical or observable difference to humans between a God who can do and know an immense amount and a God who can do and know everything. This suggests a concept of workable omniscience and workable omnipotence, defined to avoid the contradictions and other difficulties. It would not be literal omnipotence or omniscience, but as close to those as is conceivable.[85]

However, God's omnipotence is untenable in one important way. God cannot be the author of natural laws. The universe (or the metaverse) must have some general properties which had to be in place before God could exist. Those laws are more fundamental than God. However ineffably lofty God may be, he's an actor on the stage, like the rest of us. Some people may view this also as a matter of little consequence. It could still be the case that God is so tremendously powerful by human standards that we can hardly begin to conceive of his powers. But I suspect that many theists view their belief that God is more fundamental than any other general properties of reality as crucial.

18

Is There a Spirit World?

In the cloudy heights
Live the gods.
Valhalla is their home.
They are spirits of light.

—Richard Wagner, *Siegfried*, Act I, Scene 2

All theists agree that God is a spirit. An atheist does not need to deny that there are spirits. There could be a multitude of spirits and no God—that seems to have been the opinion of the majority of humans throughout most of history, if we restrict the word 'God' to the God of classical theism.

Yet anyone who denies that there are any spirits automatically denies that there's a God, and, like most atheists today, I do deny that there are any spirits.

Let's first look at direct evidence of spirit activity. Today many theists or generic believers in a spirit world appeal to near-death experiences as evidence, while very few now appeal to ghosts, spirit séances, or demonic possession.

In considering all such phenomena, there are two ways to proceed. We can collect anecdotes and compile a lot of evidence indicating the existence of phenomena that are difficult to explain if we don't accept the existence of a spirit world. This kind of thing is being done all the time, and is obviously worthless. The problem is that anecdotes get better with retelling and remembering. There is an inbuilt tendency to turn an account into a 'good story', by emphasizing confirming aspects and overlooking awkward aspects.

The media routinely do this with 'the news', but we all do it; it's only human.

What is needed is to interrogate all the witnesses, looking for fraud or flights of fancy, and setting aside anything that is unreliable (for example, because it was not recorded as having been observed until weeks or months after the event).

Near-Death Experiences

Sometimes someone suffers an injury, comes close to death, and is apparently unconscious, but later recovers. And sometimes someone who survives this experience tells a story like the following:

> I seemed to be hovering outside my body, observing what was going on, including the efforts of doctors to save my life. I felt an overwhelming sense of peace. I saw a dark tunnel and at the end of it a light. Many incidents from my life were swiftly re-enacted in my memory. I had a strong sense of making a decision on whether to 'return' to life or not. A being dressed in white appeared and informed me that it was not yet time for me to go. The whole episode was intensely vivid and 'real'—much more 'real' than a dream—but also somehow different from ordinary waking life.

In some cases, individuals who have undergone a near-death experience, though formerly skeptical about religion or afraid of death, find the experience transforming, and become committed to some religious organization or ideology. In other cases, people report merely that they have become less afraid of death.

Near death experiences are one type of out of body experiences. The experience of floating above one's body and being able to witness it as if from outside also occurs in other cases, without any suggestion of being near death. It is sometimes prompted by heavy doses of drugs like marijuana, but most people who take such drugs do not have out of the body experiences and most people having out of the body experiences have not taken any such drugs.

What catches the imagination of journalists, of enthusiasts for the paranormal, and of some theists, are reports that the 'disembodied' person, floating above their body, is able to accurately describe what is going on. Newspaper accounts often emphasize that the person witnesses accurate details that *they could not possibly have known about* if the experience were purely imaginary. They may, for example, give precise descriptions of the conversation of the doctors and of the equipment in the emergency room. A much cited example is that of Maria, who in her wanderings outside her body, saw a tennis shoe stuck in the third-floor ledge of the hospital building, with a worn patch by the little toe and the lace stuck under the heel. Later an investigator, after a very thorough search, *found the tennis shoe, just as described!* Or so the story goes.

These references to external corroboration show that everyone understands what would count as evidence in this area. If people really could leave their bodies and float away, visually perceiving things without the use of their eyes, as demonstrated by their ability to accurately describe things they could not have otherwise known about, this would indicate an unknown aspect of human beings which would open up a marvelous new field for investigation and overturn many assumptions scientists have made.

There's abundant evidence that out of the body experiences, including near-death experiences, actually do occur. People are not making up these experiences: they are real. Though details of the experiences are colored by prevalent beliefs, some features of the experiences are common across different cultures and at different historical periods, as anyone who has read *The Egyptian Book of the Dead* and *The Tibetan Book of the Dead* already knows. But as to whether some part of the person has really left the body, and is able to accurately describe what happens from a vantage point outside their body, here there is no good corroboration. Years of investigation by researchers have failed to verify a single well-documented case of any such phenomenon. This is, of course, rather sad. But it is true.

The experiences can be explained by various physiological causes, such as deprivation of oxygen to the brain.[86] But what of the supposed accuracy of observations made by people undergoing these experiences?

When investigators have followed up and interviewed the subjects of experiences and other witnesses, they have found that accounts in newspapers and in books committed to belief in a spirit world tend to omit contrary facts and over-emphasize confirming facts. For example, a person while out of the body may describe a number of details, some of which would be easy to arrive at by guesswork and some of which are incorrect, and perhaps one or two of which are both unusual and accurate. A newspaper account will fail to mention the incorrect observations, and report the correct ones as though they were typical. This occurs because an inexplicable or paranormal event is, in journalistic terms, 'a good story', whereas someone's imagination playing tricks on them under the impact of unusual stresses to the brain is not much of a story.

Some cases of correct observations can be explained by the fact that people judged to be 'unconscious' may not be completely closed off from picking up some clues. Unconsciousness is a matter of degree, and it has been shown that people under anesthesia, or otherwise supposed to be unconscious, do sometimes observe what is going on near them, or what is being done to their bodies. For example, a person who correctly reports 'seeing' the doctors doing something to a part of her body might in fact be able to sense that medical procedure through the affected body part, and then translate this into a 'vision from above' in which they imagine themselves seeing the doctors do something in that area.

As for the really striking cases of accurate observation, like Maria and the tennis shoe, it has never been possible to confirm any such case.[87] Investigators have always found that the original witnesses are untraceable or refuse to be interviewed, or that the episode was enhanced by whoever reported it. I'm sorry, I really am.

An account of investigations into near-death experiences is given by Susan Blackmore. Blackmore herself had an intense out of the body experience in her youth, and went on to become a research psychologist, devoting decades of her life to research into out of the body and near-death experiences, and other paranormal phenomena. Her book, *Beyond the Body* (1982) became the standard work on out of the body experiences, and then her book *Dying to Live* (1993) became the standard work on near-death experiences. She started out with a strong inclination to believe in the possibility of paranormal phenomena, but gradually came to the conclusion that no convincing evidence for such phenomena can be found.

It has recently been reported that out-of-body experiences can be produced by electrical stimulation of a specific region of the brain,[88] though the findings of a single study like this should be viewed with suspicion until it has been confirmed independently.

If any good evidence that near-death experiences were accurate, in the sense that the personality was leaving the body and roaming around able to observe what was going on, this would compel us to take more seriously the hypothesis of an afterlife. It would not, however, be very congenial to traditional Christianity or Islam. Near-death experiences, with the same overwhelming sense of peace, security, and freedom from anxiety, occur to individuals of all religious affiliations and none. Hellish experiences have been reported, but are very rare (and confined to cases studied by those investigators committed to a belief in Hell). The notion that nearly everyone is going to Heaven regardless of their prior religious affiliation is quite popular today. But it is very much at odds with both the *New Testament* and the *Quran*. Furthermore, if there were an afterlife, it would not by itself indicate the existence of a God.

GHOSTS

Close study of hauntings or reported appearances of ghosts have failed to find any serious evidence of anything that lacks a natural explanation.

Both Britain and America have a classic case of haunting, in both cases thorough investigation showed that the haunting was due to fraud. The British case was the haunting of Borley Rectory, popularized by psychic investigator Harry Price in the 1940s. It was later shown that Price and the wife of the rector had staged many of the ghostly doings, and Price lavishly embellished other reports he received.[89] The American case is the 'Amityville Horror'. Six people were murdered in a house in Amityville, New York, in 1974. A couple who later moved into the house reported terrifying and spectacular manifestations of supernatural entities. It was later shown that the entire Amityville episode was a money-making scheme concocted by that couple in collaboration with the lawyer who had defended the 1974 murderer.[90]

SPIRIT SÉANCES

There was a huge boom in spiritualism from the mid-nineteenth century until the 1920s. It was repeatedly demonstrated that mediums who could produce appearances of spirits on stage were doing this by trickery. The most publicized exposure—though it was only one of many—was the sustained effort by the superb stage illusionist and escapologist Harry Houdini. Large cash prizes were awarded (and are still there for the taking) for anyone who can generate these effects in a way which cannot be exposed by practiced stage magicians.

Most Christian denominations have always denounced spiritualism and have usually claimed that the effects are produced, not by the spirits of deceased relatives, but by demons masquerading as these departed souls. This theory is equally contrary to the evidence. The effects are produced by unscrupulous trickery, to make money from credulous dupes.

DEMON POSSESSION

Demon possession continues to occur in communities where belief in possession remains powerful. Observers are sometimes impressed by the fact that the personality of the possessor is so different from the personality of the possessed person. A similar phenomenon occurs in some cases of 'multiple personality disorder', where no one claims that demon possession is involved. That a person can switch from one personality to another doesn't seem to demand a supernatural explanation. If the alleged possessing entity demonstrated knowledge the possessed person could not have acquired, this would be evidence of something very unusual, perhaps showing the existence of a spirit world. But no such case has been documented.

The general conclusion on all these different types of spirit manifestations is that investigators looking for spirits have failed to find them. The more precise their instruments and the more forearmed they are against fraud (perpetrated by fleshly humans), the more thoroughly they are able to rule out any indications of spirits. Spirits, then, either have almost nothing to do with the physical world, or they are shyer than hobbits, and especially liable to be scared off by scientific scrutiny.

Researchers into spirit doings, if they are at all rigorous, always find one of the following three outcomes:

1. The reported phenomena do not occur when the investigators are looking.

2. Strange phenomena are observed, but they can be explained by non-spirit causes other than deliberate fraud.

3. Strange phenomena are observed, but are results of fraud.

It's a reasonable surmise, and I believed it's the truth, that these three categories exhaust the phenomena.

Purported spirit activity belongs to a broad class of reported occurrences that used to be labeled 'supernatural' and are now usually called 'paranormal'. I don't like either of these terms. If the phenomena do really exist, then they are natural and even 'normal'.

So-called paranormal activity encompasses a range of very different phenomena, all more or less independent of each other. For example, astrology could imaginably be real and telepathy ('extrasensory perception', a form of 'psi') not real, or the other way round. The evidence so far indicates that neither of them is real. Neither of these two, or of many other paranormal claims, has anything inherently to do with spirits or with God.

What Are Spirits Like?

Sometimes the spirit world is seen as rather like the physical world, only in a different area of reality, separate from the physical world. A wraith or phantom is supposed to look and sound like a living human body. Folklore has it that a ghost usually or routinely cannot interact like a physical body with other physical bodies. For example, in many ghost stories, the ghost can be seen and heard, but not touched.

If the intangible ghost looks and talks like a human, does it have the internal physiology of a human? Does it eat, breathe, and defecate? The spirit world of Miyazaki's *Spirited Away* seems to be a fully realized physical world, but (to employ the conventional terms of fantasy fiction) on a different plane or in a different dimension from our familiar physical world. Movement from one plane to the other is rare and unusual; normally the two planes co-exist, the spiritual plane imperceptible to those in the familiar physical plane.

There are different views on the relation of spirits to bodies. Some people seem to think that the human personality is the spirit, with the body worn like a suit of clothes. Others take the view that something essential to our identity is inherently bodily. Aquinas famously stated: "I am not my soul," and one strand of Christian tradition views bodies as essential for the expression of the soul.

While some early Christians thought of the resurrected Jesus as a phantom, and some thought he had always been a phantom, the belief of the sect of Christianity which managed to displace all the others and become Orthodoxy was that 'resurrection' meant literal bodily resurrection. Jesus's body disappears from the tomb; it does not remain there while his ghost appears to others. The resurrected Jesus eats and drinks, and asks Doubting Thomas to feel the wounds of his crucifixion. These elements of the story may have been added precisely because of sectarian disputes with Christians who held a more 'spiritual', less carnal, conception. The book of *Revelation* foresees a literal bodily resurrection, in which bodies are recovered from burial in the ground and from drowning at sea, and brought back to life.

There's no mention in the *Torah* of a general resurrection of the dead. It makes its appearance in later Hebrew scriptures, such as *Ezekiel* and *Daniel*. The mainstream of Judaism before the appearance of Christianity, known to Christian tradition as "the Pharisees," had come to accept such a resurrection and this belief was incorporated into Christianity. Such Jewish and Christian thinking sees it as very important that the actual physical substance of the dead persons shall be restored to them, something that now seems outlandish, because we know that every atom in our bodies is periodically replaced. Aquinas felt obliged to argue in detail that, even in the hypothetical case of a man who ate nothing but the flesh of other humans, it would be feasible for every human body to be literally reconstituted and resurrected.

Maimonides held that people in the afterlife don't have bodies. To reconcile this with the general resurrection, he maintained that those resurrected continue to live for a while, and eventually die, whereupon their spirits enter the afterlife. Christians have usually held that the resurrected are given new bodies, "spiritual bodies," dispensing with some bodily functions such as eating, but still possessing some sort of physical body for all time. Catholics, for example, hold that Jesus even now has a body, though not one that performs embarrassing functions. If the resurrection body is an utterly new body, we wonder why Jesus's crucifixion wounds persist in his post-resurrection body.

If we move away from the quasi-physical spirit-world of traditional Christianity, and yet accommodate such phenomena as 'seeing ghosts', we arrive at the idea that ghosts look and sound like human bodies and yet lack internal physiologies. Why, then, would they look and sound like live human bodies? Why would they nearly always appear clothed?

An obvious answer would be that ghosts have a human bodily appearance because that's the appearance they had in their former earthly life, or perhaps in the case of non-human spirits like angels, they can adopt a human or quasi-human appearance, the better to communicate with humans. Perhaps ghosts are a projection of what we consider the mental. In other words, the ghost of a dead person is that person's mind, or a projection of the mind, and the way we see the ghost is as that person's mind visualizes itself, like Neo's "residual self-image" in *The Matrix*.

One conception of the relation of spirit and body is that the spirit is like a software program. The program can only be run on some piece of hardware (a body), but it could conceivably be filed away when no body was available, and run on a different body at some later date. It could even be destroyed and then reconstituted, provided someone knew all the code. But we have no confirmation of this: we haven't found any database where everyone's souls might be on file.

The world of subjective experiences—the world of hopes, fears, dreams, emotions—does certainly exist. The capacity to love other people exists, and the ability to respond to music exists. These things comprise what some people call 'the soul'. But, as far as we have been able to determine, these things are entirely dependent on the continuing existence of intact brains. If, for instance, the brain is damaged, the subjective experiences can become restricted, and if the brain is very badly damaged in specific ways, these experiences fizzle out completely, as far as we can tell. If the brain is deprived of oxygen for a few minutes, the person has gone, forever beyond recall. Alzheimer's Disease is a disease of the brain, and it leads to the disappearance of all fine and noble qualities formerly manifested by the body's occupant (however passionate and virtuous the occupant may have been before the onset of the disease).

Where has this person's spirit gone? Where's the flame of a candle once it's been blown out? The believer in a spirit has to maintain that the spirit still exists, only its ability to use the body as its instrument has been lost. (It seems to follow that we could dispose of that body without doing anything wrong, but the believer in spirits rarely draws this conclusion.) The brain damage is like the damage to a radio that prevents it from picking up broadcasts, though the broadcasts are still out there. This would be a reasonable hypothesis to pursue if we had some way of detecting that broadcast signal, but we don't.

God's Brainless Mind

If the core notion of a spirit is a disembodied mind, then we have to consider the possibility that there just are no spirits: that the universe is completely empty of minds, except where these happen to spring into existence in association with brains. No one is likely to dispute that this is true of other subjective experiences: pain or the sensation of being tickled do not exist all by themselves before animals develop nervous systems, and the sensations yellowness or blueness do not exist all by themselves before animals develop eyes.

The problem for people who insist that there are spirits is that these spirits are always totally undetectable. The spirit world is supposed to interact with the non-spirit world in numerous and definite ways, yet aside from the assertion that these interactions occur, no other spirit activity is observed. This somehow doesn't seem very likely.

Spirits are supposed to have something to do with the thoughts that go through people's minds. But if this is true, one way of thinking about spirits is closed off: we can't say that they don't have physical effects. Spirits, then, must be able to affect physical events in regular ways. But in that case, it becomes simply astounding that spirits apparently never have any *other* physical effects, beyond those that we assume to fill in the gaps in our knowledge of how thoughts relate to events in brains. If we were to propose searching for spirit activity using highly sensitive instruments, in the way that scientists searched for the cosmic background radiation, believers in spirits would laugh at us, and say that we hadn't gotten the point. But why are they so sure that spirits will never have detectable physical consequences, if they also believe that spirits routinely and reliably have physical consequences in our brains?

Most versions of theism propose that God is a bodyless and therefore brainless mind. At one time some people thought they might be able to locate God's enormous brain. We tend to smile at this, yet no one has ever observed a brainless mind. All the minds of which we have any knowledge are somehow intimately associated with those body parts we call brains.

A Parable of Reflections

We sometimes see reflected images, in mirrors, water surfaces, and the like. Suppose an ideological movement were to arise, called Reflectivism, contending that what we see in these reflections is a glimpse of a superior world, even the fundamentally real world, while our apparently 'real world' is actually generated by the world seen in reflections, and dependent upon it. We ought to govern our lives by paying close attention to what we see in the reflected images, since these are more momentous than anything on this side of the reflective surface. The actual real world, the origin and source of our seemingly real world, is the looking-glass world. How could we conduct a discussion with the Reflectivists?

- We could point out that the world behind the surface seems to tally quite well with the world this side of the surface. The Reflectivist will respond that this is just what we should expect, if the world on the other side generates the world on this side.

- We could then say that in some respects the world on the other side is not quite so crisp and clear as the world this side, and is sometimes distorted. But (the Reflectivist will point out) this could be due to our imperfect way of looking, our enslavement to the depraved point of view that over-rates the ephemeral world on this side. What look like distortions are really glimpses of a higher reality.

- We could argue that the world on this side is here all the time, while very special conditions are required to make the world on the other side appear. The Reflectivist's answer is obvious: the world on the other side is there all the time, in fact it was there before the world this side, brought it into being, and will outlast it. But special receptive conditions are needed on our side so that we can peer into that more wondrous other world.

- We could say that there really is no 'other side', and look behind the surface (at the back of the mirror, for instance), to reveal that the reflected objects aren't really there, but the Reflectivist will tut-tut and say that this isn't the way to look, and simply exposes our obsession with the superficial.

- We could assert that we know the laws of optics, and we can therefore explain how the image apparently on the other side is produced, without there really being another side. To this the Reflectivist has two replies. First, any little detail of the reflective image we couldn't fully explain would be cited as proof that our much-vaunted laws of optics don't tell the whole story. Second, the Reflectivist would say that these optical laws are indeed the laws governing our ability to get in touch with the real world on the other side. These optical laws are therefore all very well in their way, but what appalling arrogance to suppose that they can truly get to the heart of what is going on, behind the mirror!

Asked to comment on this parable, the believer in spirits would point out that the laws of optics are very well understood whereas the laws governing the relations between consciousness and processes in the brain are still largely a mystery.

This is perfectly true, but so far, neuroscience has not turned up *anything* that indicates generation of thoughts from something located outside the brain. We can easily imagine that in the future, brain scientists might begin to make discoveries which would compel them to entertain the hypothesis that consciousness is projected into brains by spirits. This would be a reversal of direction: up to now, science has kept shrinking the area of observed reality in which spirits might be hiding. If it did happen, it would be wonderful and exciting, like all those revolutionary occasions when scientific investigation opens up a whole new world of knowledge. But it hasn't happened yet.

Can Science Explain Everything?

Theists commonly say that science 'can't explain everything'. How arrogant it would be to suppose that it could!

In the English language, there's a common tendency to use the word 'science' to mean empirical science, and even more narrowly, empirical science as it applies to aspects of reality which do not involve the effects of consciousness. Thus, 'science' may be taken to mean physics, chemistry, astronomy, and biology, but not economics, psychology, or history—which empirically investigate human activities—nor logic, mathematics, or philosophy—which are not empirical disciplines at all. Science thus defined also excludes such pursuits as interpreting *Moby-Dick* or the U.S. Constitution.

Can physics, chemistry, biology, and the like explain everything? Of course not, and neither should the specific techniques of these disciplines be uncritically copied by other disciplines. We don't want people to use Bunsen burners or particle accelerators to decide whether Hamlet's madness is entirely feigned or to identify the causes of the French Revolution. Each area of reality should be investigated by appropriate methods.

There's a broader sense of the word 'science', more closely corresponding to the scope of the German word 'Wissenschaft', which includes these other disciplines. It includes the social sciences, mathematics, and philosophy, as well as the natural sciences. Science, in this broader sense, is concerned with getting at the truth, finding out about reality. Science in this sense does not exclude any detectable phenomena from consideration. Some branches of science, as a matter of practical convenience, may of course give up on an endless quest for phenomena which have so far not been detected.[91]

Various arguments are offered for the existence of God. Sometimes, more rarely now than in the past, the arguments make claims which physicists, chemists, or biologists are competent to test. More often the arguments are of a very general nature which does not lend itself to empirical testing. This means that the arguments can be tested by philosophical reasoning (most often metaphysics, but occasionally other branches of philosophy, such as epistemology or ethics).

Theists often suggest that since empirical natural science can't explain everything, something is left over for metaphysics, which they then equate with religion or 'the spiritual', which in turn they identify with theism. But the correct response to this is straightforward: we do indeed need metaphysics, and within metaphysics atheism is a possible theory, which happens to be true.

A commonly held view is that science excludes certain kinds of question from the outset. It doesn't, for instance, acknowledge the existence of miracles, and so miracles, if they occur, are to be investigated by different methods. Both theists and scientists often give voice to this view. I think it's mistaken. Science doesn't usually investigate miracles for exactly the same reason that it doesn't usually investigate the once-popular canals on Mars: because preliminary investigation has drawn a blank, and it therefore looks very much as though there is nothing to investigate.

Many of the types of phenomena now accepted within 'science' are areas which people in the past might have considered supernatural, paranormal, or occult. Gravity was once viewed with suspicion because it involved action at a distance, regarded as occult. (Galileo refused to accept that the Moon caused the tides, partly because of this distaste for occult qualities.) Magnetic fields and hypnosis are examples of areas which were once viewed with a similar kind of suspicion. Blindsight, in which people who believe that they are blind can see things, without being aware that they can see them, has recently been demonstrated to be a reality.

If we tried to explain these phenomena to someone living in, say, ancient Egypt, he might easily conclude that we were talking about something spiritual or supernatural. The reason that gravity, magnetic fields, hypnosis, and blindsight are no longer viewed as 'non-material' is because they have been found to exist. Their effects are detectable; they can be investigated. When some people unwisely say that 'science is only concerned with what is natural', *this means no more and no less than that science will not expend resources on investigating entities which are totally undetectable by any means whatsoever.* But this follows trivially from the fact that science is serious about getting at the truth. It's quite wrong to infer that there is some area of reality which science would refuse to investigate if the opportunity arose.

The fact that phenomena which would once have been considered occult are now embraced by natural science illustrates that even natural science does not permanently and irrevocably rule out any imagined entity. But obviously, if science is to make progress, to extend our acquisition of true or approximately true theories, it must arrive, at least provisionally, at conclusions which deny the existence of some entities. Science, as the pursuit of truth, would be nothing but a sham if scientists were not allowed to arrive at the conclusion, on the basis of their enquiries to date, that certain types of entities just don't exist. No one reproaches natural science with narrow-minded dogmatism because it denies the existence of the philosopher's stone, phlogiston, the ether, protoplasm, or the life force. To spend time and money on endlessly searching for

Sidebar: Natural and Supernatural

Theists sometimes say that science is committed to a naturalistic or physicalist worldview. Some theists think that this is a prejudice on the part of scientists. Other theists say that it's only right: the scientists are experts on the natural or physical world, while other people (usually the theologians of whichever sect the theist adheres to) are experts on the spiritual world.

Some scientists are quite ready to let the theists have the spiritual world, because they see it as a tactful way to avoid any appearance of a conflict between 'religion' and 'science', which they feel would be bad for the social status of science.

How do we mark the distinction between natural and supernatural? There are two ways we might do this:

1. We might count as supernatural all those entities which proponents of the supernatural call 'supernatural'. So, spirits of all kinds, demons, jinns, poltergeists, God, godlings, and angels would be included in the supernatural.

2. We might try to define the difference between 'natural' and 'supernatural'. For example, we might say that natural phenomena conform to laws of nature whereas spiritual phenomena don't.

Now let's consider the spirit world, first as demarcated in #1 and then as demarcated in #2.

My opinion about spiritual or supernatural entities as demarcated in #1 is that they don't exist. This is the conclusion of past investigations. So far, all serious attempts to detect any spirits have drawn a blank. *At any moment this conclusion might be overturned by new evidence.*

There are numerous episodes in the history of science where a whole new world of enquiry is opened up by the demonstration that hitherto denied phenomena do, after all, exist. There was a time when scientists did not believe that rocks fall from the sky, or that continents move. There was a time when scientists did not suspect that there were types of light (infra red and ultra violet) invisible to human sight, though visible to some other animal species. Prior to 1895, scientists had no suspicion of the existence of x-rays or any other nuclear radiation. There's no reason to assume that the age of big surprises is past.

So the non-existence of spirit and other supernatural phenomena is not something we have to accept before we begin to investigate the world around us. It's something we have to accept, provisionally, after we have done a lot of such investigation. In the sense of #1, then, 'naturalism' is thrust upon us by the evidence, but we are not wedded to it at the deepest level. We don't believe in 'the supernatural'—for exactly the same reason that we don't believe in cold fusion. If new evidence came to light, we might be forced to accept that spirits exist and that 'naturalism' (defined in this way) is false.

> Now consider the matter in terms of #2. Here, I maintain that we cannot define the 'supernatural' because there can be nothing outside nature. I am definitely *not* saying that there can be no spirit world because it would be outside nature. I am saying that if there is a spirit world, *and it is just the way believers in the spirit world say it is,* then it can only be part of nature. It must operate according to regularities which we call laws of nature (though they might be laws very different from those we now apply to non-spirit reality).
>
> This is clear just from what believers in the spirit world tell us. Consider ghosts. They appear to humans and they often appear in human form. Obviously, spirits could not appear to humans unless those spirits conformed to regularities, and somehow those regularities in the spirit world could be made to mesh with regularities in our physical world. The spirit world, then, cannot be totally chaotic or without any order. Its laws may be very different from what we now call the 'physical' world, but this is what we would expect: so are chemical laws very different from electromagnetic laws.

these entities would be pointless. Exactly the same goes for gods, angels, and demons.

At one time it looked as though telepathy (extra-sensory perception) might be demonstrated to exist, but more stringent attention to experimental design has eliminated the earlier positive (though very slight) results. It now seems clear that they were bogus: there's no such thing as telepathy. But if telepathy had been shown to be real, no one would have cared that it was not 'material', it might even have been redefined as 'material' or 'natural', just as hypnosis has been. If poltergeists were demonstrated to exist, they would probably come to be seen as 'material'; be that as it may, no scientist would say they should not be investigated because of their supposed non-materiality. Blackmore was behaving in exemplary 'scientific' (that is, honest and reasonable) fashion when she compared and tested all the theories of out-of-body and near-death experiences), including the frankly spiritualistic ones, before deciding that these experiences must have their basis in human physiology.

Sometimes people who say that science is committed to a naturalist ideology have in mind the fact that in various branches of science there are conventions limiting what may be accepted as evidence. For instance, in most areas of physics and chemistry, it's accepted that an experiment must be capable of being repeated many times under strictly controlled conditions for its results to become accepted. However, in such disciplines as astronomy and history, there is no such requirement. The conventions shift from area to area, and which conventions are best for a particular problem is always a matter open for discussion and review.

We can imagine a race of beings who would be curious about the world around them without being able to perform experiments. They might be a species of fish, unable to manipulate materials to any appreciable extent, but intelligent enough to conduct discussions about the behavior of water, rocks, and other observable things. In testing their speculations about physics and chemistry, they would be confined to sporadic, uncontrolled, observation, much as ancient astronomers were. Though unable to perform repeatable experiments under uniform conditions, they would (provided they had excellent memories) be able to develop a steadily improving theory of physical reality. Over time they would tend to converge on the same theories formulated by human scientists on dry land, though in some cases probably by different routes.

People sometimes say that science searches for laws, and miracles, being exceptions to laws, are therefore outside the domain of science. But first, science does more than search for laws. The discovery that the Moon's light is the reflected light of the Sun was, in its day, a great scientific achievement, but it is not a law. Much of science is not laws or putative laws. Second, if there are miracles, they must conform to laws, even if these are laws of which we do not currently have any inkling. If there's a spirit world, it's a world with its own spirit laws.

A miracle is sometimes defined as a contravention of laws of nature, and this is assumed to occur because of intervention by God, who can over-ride laws of nature. This definition, however, is a recent development; it is certainly not the way miracles were seen by the authors of the *Tanakh*, the *New Testament*, or the *Quran*. In the Ancient world it was widely believed that miracles could be performed by a number of powerful prophets, priests, or magicians. According to the gospel story, Jesus, when accused of casting out demons with the help of the Prince of Demons, replied to his detractors by asking, rhetorically, how their favored magicians were able to cast out demons (*Matthew* 12:27-30; *Luke* 11:19-23; see Ehrman 1999, p. 198). The miracle-worker Jesus did not challenge the factual claims made for his competition.

But isn't there a fundamental clash between science, with its search for regularities, and the miraculous doings of an omnipotent God? Not in principle. Science is very used to the procedure of finding a supposed 'law', which then turns out to hold only under special circumstances, not under all conditions. In such cases, science looks for a wider law to explain all the observations. If theism were correct, then that wider law would be that whatever God wills happens. This would be the one universal regularity with no exceptions. It would be the true 'theory of everything'.

Nothing prevents a scientific-minded person from entertaining such a possibility, and nothing would prevent such a person from reaching such a conclusion—nothing except the actual evidence.

Bad or Feeble Arguments
Against God

In this book I've gone briskly through the most important arguments for and against the existence of God, to explain why we can reasonably conclude that God does not exist. It's only fair to mention a few arguments employed by atheists which I regard as inadequate or worse.

One of the reasons why atheism is getting more of a hearing right now than it did a few years ago is the murder of innocent civilians by Muslims in acts of terror such as 9/11. The three spectacular best sellers advocating atheism (*The End of Faith*, *The God Delusion*, and *God Is Not Great*) all rely heavily on the claim that murder and other wicked deeds are the fruits of theistic belief.

If it's true that theism leads to mayhem, this would do nothing to show theism false. But the atheist may say that the God theory is false on other grounds, and that the appalling consequences of theism are mentioned only to show that this is an urgent issue. Yet it doesn't seem to be true that theism has exceptionally bad consequences, by comparison with other ideologies. Communists have tortured and killed far more people in the name of Communism than Christians in the name of Christ or Muslims in the name of Allah. Ideological commitment can encourage people to perpetrate enormities, but it doesn't seem to make much difference whether the ideology includes belief in God.

Furthermore, the story that Muslims commit suicide bombings because they think this will give them the regulation seventy-two virgins in Paradise is entertaining for the American public but has little to do with reality. As Robert Pape has shown in careful detail, suicide bombers reflect all kinds of personal backgrounds and beliefs, and many of those of Muslim background are far from devout. The single organization perpetrating the most acts of suicide terrorism is the Tamil Tigers, made up entirely of atheists from Hindu backgrounds.[92] Suicide terrorism always has a *political* program. It is a response from militarily weak ethnic communities to setbacks inflicted on them by much stronger forces.

Some atheists try to show the influence of 'religion' in atrocities where its involvement is not obvious. But the same argument can work the other way: 'religion' is often largely a badge of ethnic or national identity, and much 'religious' conflict is fundamentally a manifestation of nationalism.

A popular theme of atheist propaganda is that the person being addressed (usually a Christian) doesn't believe in Zeus or Allah, so it is only taking it one step further to disbelieve in the Christian God. I grant that something similar to this may sometimes be useful as a rhetorical goad to get people to look at the fleeting nature of all ideologies, including theistic ones, and mentally to step outside their own cultural milieu. But it doesn't cut very deep. Christians, of course, do believe in Allah, which is simply the Arabic word for 'God' (Arabic-speaking Christians call God 'Allah'—what else?). God, Allah, and Yahweh are just different labels for the same hypothetical entity.

Even Zeus could be defended as another label for God, by claiming that he is more powerful than the Greeks supposed. It was presumably this train of thought which led Kierkegaard to say that a man who worships an idol in the right spirit may be worshipping God. But can the Christian God really be the same as the Jewish and Muslim God, if he is 'three persons in one'? Yes, just as many people can agree on the existence of some historical personage, while only some of them adhere to the theory that this personage was a case of multiple personality disorder.

An atheist argument that was popular sixty years ago, but no longer, is that 'God' is a meaningless expression. You will still come across this claim, arising from the philosophical theory known as verificationism, in some older books. It was popularized in Ayer's *Language, Truth, and Logic*, but was only briefly held by some philosophers. The verificationists hoped to get rid of metaphysics, leaving only logic and empirical science. However, metaphysics is here to stay. Even empirical science cannot do without metaphysics.[93]

The argument of the verificationists was that a statement which appears to make a factual claim is strictly meaningless if it cannot in principle be verified by observation—by the evidence of our senses. Statements containing the word 'God' are thus meaningless; they are strictly speaking mere nonsense. The Ayer of 1936 held that theism and atheism are both untenable, since asserting or denying the existence of God are equally meaningless utterances. But if atheism means 'lacking any belief in God', then atheism should not have been ruled out, as not believing in something meaningless does not commit the non-believer to any meaningless utterances.

To see what's wrong with verificationism, consider this question: When some of the ancient Greeks (folks like Democritus and Epicurus), over two thousand years ago, put forward the theory that matter is composed of atoms, was this meaningless? It did not seem then as though anyone would ever be able to see or otherwise observe an atom. If it was meaningless at that time, then it must have become meaningful at some point in history, but it would be difficult to agree on exactly when that was. To take a contemporary example, is the theory of superstrings meaningless?

It's true that I have shown that the God of classical theism is self-contradictory and therefore cannot exist. I would say that 'God' is incoherent, but I do not accept that an incoherent assertion is meaningless. For example, 'There is a way of squaring the circle' is incoherent, but not meaningless.[94] My claim of incoherence is based on logical contradictions, not on lack of verifiability, and I don't say that 'God' is meaningless.

Some atheists claim that they do not know what is meant by the word 'God'. This was the position of the nineteenth-century atheist Charles Bradlaugh (who was forcibly prevented from taking his seat in the British Parliament because of his atheism). But as I have tried to show in this book, there's no problem about knowing what's meant by 'God'. 'God' certainly means different things to different people, and some people may hold unclear notions of God, but each concept of God can be spelled out and examined.

Some discussion by atheists suggests that belief in God is 'irrational', and tries to lay down criteria of rationality, by which theism can be excluded. Occasionally, theists return the favor and contend that atheism is itself irrational. Discussions of the irrationality of theism or atheism are often associated with discussions of what we are rationally entitled to believe.

However, belief is always involuntary. You can't choose to believe one thing or another. The evidence strikes you a certain way, and you spontaneously reach a conclusion: you can do nothing about that. And you shouldn't try. You can certainly study logic and philosophy, and thus improve your skill at detecting bad arguments. You can also search for new factual evidence. These accomplishments might cause you to evaluate evidence differently so that you find yourself with new beliefs, but you can't guarantee in advance which of your beliefs will have to be jettisoned following this process of self-education. You can never choose your beliefs, though you can choose to pretend that your beliefs are other than they really are.

'Irrational' is often used to mean 'ill-advised', 'unwise', or 'mistaken'. In this sense, if we pick holes in an argument, say, for the existence of God, we add nothing by then saying that this argument is irrational. There's something wrong with the argument, that's all, and if that's so, we can say what's wrong with it. But if 'irrational' is to mean more than that, it suggests that we can classify whole categories of quite persuasive arguments as more than just mistaken, as evidence of some kind of intellectual sickness. I think this is muddled and encourages a dogmatic outlook.

Some atheists try to suggest that theism is unsound because of the motives leading people to accept it. This atheist stratagem is actually quite rare: theists often respond to it where it doesn't exist. For instance, Freud gave an explanation—a pretty ludicrous one—for the origin of theistic ideas, and theists often treat this as an argument for atheism. Freud, however, probably thought atheism sufficiently warranted by the findings of natural science, and was taking atheism for granted when he attempted to explain theism's supposedly unconscious psychological origins.

On the rare occasions when any such argument is deployed against theism, it commits the Genetic Fallacy—trying to discredit a belief by making a claim about how its adherents came to hold it. The history of how someone came to hold a belief has no bearing on whether that belief is true or false.

IV

God or the Truth?

AUNT MAY: Are you telling me you prefer God over the truth?

SOL: If necessary, I'll always choose God over the truth.

—From the Woody Allen movie, *Crimes and Misdemeanors*

19

Atheism Is Irresistible

Whether or not there actually is a God, it's very popular to claim that people naturally feel a need to believe in a God. Even some atheists hold this view, with the implication that most people are just irrational.

There's a flourishing popular literature arguing that humans are biologically programmed to believe in God. The two most conspicuous examples are *Why God Won't Go Away* by Newberg, d'Aquili, and Rause, and *The God Gene* by Dean Hamer. Each of these books begins with the anecdotal account of a person who follows a spiritual path and has mystical experiences. We can assume that these reports were selected as particularly apt examples to introduce the argument of each book; they are prize exhibits. But guess what? Both books, it so happens, have as their prize exhibits a person who does not believe in God.

The 'spiritual' person described at the beginning of *Why God Won't Go Away* is a Tibetan Buddhist, who would therefore believe in devas or godlings, but would reject the existence of a Creator or Supreme Being. The first chapter, which talks about scans of this person's brain, is titled "A Photograph of God?" The question is wildly misleading. The example given in *The God Gene* is that of a Zen Buddhist, who might not even believe in devas.

What's going on here is that the authors of both books present evidence for the fact that some humans display an appetite for the experience of enlightenment through meditation or, loosely speaking, the 'spiritual'. Presumably for marketing reasons, the authors find it convenient to refer to these matters loosely with the term 'God'. Consider these two statements:

1. A minority of people are prone to mystical experiences and this tendency has to do with their brain chemistry and is partly genetic in origin.

2. People have an innate need to believe in God.

The first statement is pretty obvious, and I doubt that it would surprise anyone. The second statement is quite outlandish, even if we amend "people" to 'a minority of people'. There's just no evidence for this second statement in the Newberg or Hamer books.

Hamer confronts this issue directly. Defending his choice of the phrase "the God Gene", he remarks that "Some of the most spiritual people I've interviewed and discuss, such as Tenkai [his prize exhibit of the God Gene], don't believe in a deity at all. Nevertheless I felt it [the term 'God gene'] was a useful abbreviation of the overall concept" (pp. 8–9).

Newberg and his co-authors proceed rather differently, referring to God as a "metaphor" and as "unknowable." The implication of their whole argument seems to be that mystics really do perceive something real and external to themselves, something the authors are content to call 'God', but that this God is remote from the God of classical theism. Remarkable as it may seem, neither *Why God Won't Go Away* nor *The God Gene* really have much to say about belief in God.

Is There a God Gene?

Belief in God, affiliation to a religious association, and susceptibility to mystical experiences are three different things, yet the authors slide easily from one to the other. Hamer's theme is that something he calls 'God', but admits may have nothing to do with belief in God, is good for people. He tells us that mystical experiences and hallucinations are correlated, may be induced by drugs, and even when not induced by drugs are associated with the release of certain chemicals in the brain.

Hamer quotes the research indicating that people who go to church are healthier. Hamer presents no evidence that people who go to church are more likely to have mystical experiences, and doesn't show any correlation between genetic susceptibility to mystical experiences and health or wellbeing. But if such a correlation were ever to be found, there would be two likely explanations:

that genes for susceptibility to mystical experiences are also genes for aspects of health and wellbeing, or that mystical experiences are themselves conducive to health and wellbeing (regardless of the beliefs which may accompany them).

A lot of people are prone to mystical experiences and a few of them get some kind of satisfaction out of methodically cultivating these experiences. Whether these folks connect their experiences with God is a matter of the beliefs they hold before the mystical experiences occur.

Almost every month a new book comes out conveying the message that people have an innate need for God, and occasionally one of these books sells very well. Nearly all of them, like the two mentioned here, trade on the confusion between belief in God and spiritual experience much more broadly defined.

Is there a God Gene? It goes without saying that in this context 'a gene' may mean a combination of genes, perhaps dozens, acting together. If we could test the DNA of people who joined the Communist Party in the 1930s or bought a hula hoop in the 1950s, we would undoubtedly find statistical genetic differences between these people and the rest of the population. In that sense there is always 'a gene' for anything we care to investigate, which is to say: if there are things people might or might not do, their genes will always have some measurable effect on whether they do or don't do that thing. There's just bound to be 'a gene' for being a baseball fan, 'a gene' for joining a rock band, and, yes, 'a gene' for believing in God. By the same token, there's 'a gene' for *not* doing any of these things.

But what advocates of a God Gene mean is something different. They mean there's something 'in the genes' which ensures that most people believe in God, or have an appetite for belief in a God. Now if there were any such gene, it would have to be absent from most of present-day China and Japan, and must have been absent from the vast majority of human populations until at the earliest 1,500 years ago. And in those populations where this gene does prevail, it must still be absent from a large proportion of the population. Now that Pentecostalism is rapidly becoming the world's biggest religious denomination, I expect we'll soon have someone claiming there's a Speaking in Tongues Gene.

Prior to the rise of Christianity, belief in numerous limited gods or nature-spirits was prevalent in many places, though the Chinese, a fifth of the world's population, had little belief in any personal gods. Although Christianity and Islam have made some inroads in China, 'traditional Chinese religion', a blend of Confucianism, Daoism, and Buddhism (all three religions which have no place for anything close to the God of classical theism) is still the predominant Chinese belief system. I haven't met anyone who maintains that the God Gene was a mutation which began to spread in the population only two thousand years ago and has not yet moved into China or Japan.

When we look at history, we always observe that ideological enthusiasm of any kind is something that animates a minority of the population. Most people are affected by the ideological enthusiasm of the few, and may go along with it for various motives. Most people adapt themselves to whatever verbal and ceremonial formulas are imposed by the state or by pressure from other powerful institutions. Most people do not have specifically a God Gene, a Communism Gene, or a Fascism Gene but they do possess a Don't Go Against the Herd Gene.

We also observe that rising real incomes are accompanied by a decline of belief in God and of religious observance generally. God's biggest enemy, on the practical level, is economic growth. Economic growth brings with it improved access to information and greater scope for free debate. Give people rising real incomes, and most people spontaneously prefer the disco, the bar, or the Internet to the church or the mosque. In all industrialized countries without exception, there's a slow, long-term decline in reported religious observance and belief.

Disbelief in God Has Always Been Endemic

There's a popular impression that disbelief in God is peculiarly modern. Some folks claim that people in past ages did not doubt the existence of God.[95] It's true that, contrasted with medieval society, Christian or Muslim, belief in God measurably erodes with economic, technological, and scientific advances. However, atheism has always been there. Wherever there are theists, there are people who doubt their claims.

If atheists are not free to argue their case, there will be fewer atheists in the population, just as, anti-Marxists not being free to argue their case in Soviet Russia, there were fewer anti-Marxists in the population. And those who do exist will be less vocal; they will often pay lip service to the official ideology or at least keep their mouths shut. But there will still be some such dissident thinkers.

What has changed since the Middle Ages is not so much the private questioning of God's existence as the possibility, in a liberal legal framework, of being able to publicly deny God's existence without hazard to life and limb. To say that we can't find much atheism in medieval Europe is like reporting that we can't find much homosexuality in Colonial New England or much in the way of demands for free speech in 1950s Russia.

In all cultures, at all stages of history, most people are not imbued with zeal for the official doctrine imposed by the government. It makes no difference whether this doctrine is Christianity, Hinduism, Atheism, Communism, or Fascism. Most people go along with it, especially if painful penalties are inflicted for failure to toe the line, but they are not deeply enthusiastic. Ideological zeal, including religious zeal, never seizes more than a small minority of the population, though they may for brief periods sweep others along with them in their excitement. No doubt we'll eventually find the group of genes responsible for susceptibility to ideological zeal.

Most people are not by temperament attracted to abstract intellectual systems of any kind, and when they encounter some such system, will pay it lip service if this is helpful to them in their everyday lives, and otherwise ignore it. Thus, most people in the United States today would never dream of identifying themselves with atheism, precisely because they attribute so little importance to the God question. Today's atheists are atheists because they care far more about the God issue than most nominal theists do. Most Americans simply don't care enough about God to get worked up about his existence, one way or another, so naturally they are horrified both by outright atheism and by 'fanatical' religiosity. It's partly a matter of tact. Since the small minority of enthusiastic believers in God are known to be terribly touchy, ordinary people believe in God in the same way that they believe their best friend's wife doesn't look her age.

Historical Traces of Grassroots Skepticism

Psalm 14 informs us: "The fool has said in his heart, there is no God."[96] This was written no later than the second century B.C.E., perhaps a good bit earlier. The poet recognizes the existence of closeted atheists, even while abusing them, and since he goes on to attribute all kinds of immorality to this private denial of God's existence, he must judge discreet atheism to be widespread. The "fool" referred to is not such a fool as to declare openly that there is no God, for then he and his family would probably be physically attacked by theists.

In pagan Greece and Rome, though those cultures were far more tolerant than medieval Christendom or Islamdom were later to be, atheism was generally punishable by death. 'Atheism' at this time usually meant denial of the numerous traditional gods, and so the early Christians were often denounced as atheists by those in power.

Several ancient thinkers, especially Democritus (around 460–370 B.C.E.), Epicurus (around 341–270 B.C.E.), and Lucretius (around 99–55 B.C.E.) propounded basically materialist views of the universe, and have often been suspected of atheism, though their atheism is not unanimously accepted by classical scholars. Epicurus explicitly stated that there are gods, but they don't care about humans and have nothing to do with us. I find it difficult to read Lucretius's great work, *On the Nature of Things*, without judging him to be an atheist through and through.

In Plato's *The Laws*, composed around 346 B.C.E., the character known as the Athenian Stranger begins his exposition of the Cosmological Argument by explaining that an argument for the gods' existence is necessary, because some people don't accept it:

> Fire and water and earth and air, they say, all exist by nature and chance, and none of them by art . . . in this way and by these means they brought into being the whole Heaven and all that is in the Heaven, and all animals, too, and plants, . . . not owing to reason, nor to any god or art, but owing, as we have said, to nature and chance.[97]

Medieval Europe was a near-totalitarian society in which the media were completely controlled by one institution, which harbored no namby-pamby inhibitions about burning or dismembering any dissenters. Anyone who (for example) contended that life after death would not literally restore the physical stuff of the original bodies of the deceased, or that Jews and Muslims might not end up in Hell, would be set upon by the Church's hired thugs and tortured to death unless they promptly recanted. Medieval Europe was an 'age of belief' in precisely the sense that Russia between 1918 and 1980 was an age of belief: state terror was routinely employed to stamp out deviations from the official line. The fundamental reason why you and I have even heard of Christianity is centuries of state terror in its behalf. Christians were less than ten percent of the population of the Roman empire at the time of the conversion of Constantine in 312 C.E., and they might never have become very much bigger by purely peaceful persuasion.

Some time around 1200 C.E., Peter of Cornwall (Prior of Holy Trinity, Aldgate) wrote:

> There are many people who do not believe that God exists. They consider that the universe has always been as it is now and is ruled by chance rather than by Providence. Many people consider only what they can see, and do not believe in good or bad angels, nor do they think that the human soul lives on after the death of the body.

This is quoted by the historian Robert Bartlett, who comments on this case and that of a Scottish Cistercian lay brother who concluded that there is no life after death: "simple materialism and disbelief in the afterlife were probably widespread, although they leave little trace in sources written by clerics and monks."[98] Few except clerics and monks could write. The records cited by Bartlett are rare written traces of an ever-present reality: disbelief in God and in survival after death are, always and everywhere, simple common sense. This does nothing to show that these views are correct: simple common sense can easily be wrong and often has been. We just ought to face the fact that privately conceived atheism is always endemic at the grass roots, whatever official ideologues may say.

The most brilliant philosopher of the fourteenth century, William of Ockham, maintained that we should not try to use philosophical reasoning to prove the existence of God, which he thought should be based purely on faith. In the course of defending this position, Ockham wrote:

> The proposition 'God exists' is not known by itself, since many doubt it; nor can it be proved from propositions known by themselves, since in every argument something doubtful or derived from faith will be assumed; nor is it known by experience, as is manifest. (Ockham 1990, pp. 139–140)

Later the Church made it obligatory for Catholics to believe that the existence of God can be proved by reason alone. Reading these remarks by Ockham, we can see how they might assist the Devil in putting skeptical doubts into the minds of believers.

Thomas Tailour was a fuller by trade, though apparently literate, in fifteenth-century England. He was disciplined for uttering the following heresies: calling people "fools" for going on a pilgrimage, saying it was pointless to worship images of saints, disparaging the learning and the moral behavior of priests, questioning the need for baptism, and maintaining that the soul dies with the body, as the flame of a candle dies when blown out.

Tailour had to publicly renounce these views and each day for the rest of his life say the *Pater Noster* five times, the *Ave Maria* five times, and the *Credo* once. If he didn't stick to this, or if he again voiced his heretical beliefs, he would be burnt to death. He was made to carry around with him the firewood that would be used for this purpose. Tailour's explicit heresies did not include denial of God's existence, or he might not have gotten off so lightly.

The historian John Arnold comments that this case was exceptional in that a record of it happened to survive (Arnold 2005, pp. 2–3). Arnold footnotes a number of specialized scholarly articles on medieval unbelief and skepticism and cites several actual cases (pp. 216–229). I like the reports of people who argued that if Christ's body had been the size of a mountain, it would long ago have been completely devoured by Christians celebrating the eucharist. Amidst the bloody nightmare that was Christendom, some bright sparks of critical intelligence alleviate the general gloom.

In the sixteenth century John Calvin argued that everyone is aware of God, but acknowledged that "there were some in the past, and today not a few appear, who deny that God exists."[99] Calvin knew that there were more than a few atheists around, even though anyone owning up to being an atheist was taking his life in his hands. Calvin himself, as advisor to the government of Geneva, was prepared to have people executed for much less than atheism, for example for denying that Jesus was the son of God. In its early years, Protestantism was even more violently intolerant than Catholicism. The persecution of dissidents got much worse in the sixteenth and seventeenth centuries, in both Protestant and Catholic countries, than it had been in the Middle Ages.

The fact that confessing one's atheism would lead to one's body being incinerated or vivisected without anesthetic naturally meant that many individual atheists would be reticent, or would publicly deny their atheism. In some cases this was so obvious a possibility that it was generally rumored at the time. Very likely Thomas Hobbes and Francis Bacon were atheists, for all their protestations to the contrary, and their contemporaries certainly believed it of them. We can never be sure just which eminent thinkers were closeted atheists, though I have my own suspicions about some outwardly very pious personages. David Hume barely tried to conceal his atheism, though he was still a little cautiously irenic: even in eighteenth-century Britain, people had been executed for heresy within living memory.

Why Does Classical Theism Rule the World?

The worldwide dominance of classical theism is a feature of only the last fifteen hundred years. It's essentially a consequence of the spread of Christianity and of Christianity's imitator, Islam. Christianity and Islam are still making converts; both are expanding as a proportion of the world's total population. Both are strongest among the poor of the Third World, and both lose support wherever there is economic development.

If people do not have an innate need to believe in God, why has theism become so dominant?

From the getgo, Christianity was different from earlier religions in that it included an explicit command to preach to the entire world (a project favored by the existence of the Roman empire and the freedom of movement within it). People conquered by Assyria or Egypt, for example, adopted Assyrian or Egyptian gods, but the Assyrian and Egyptian priesthoods didn't send out missionaries beyond their empires. Christianity was spiritually imperialist: the world must be remade in our image; everyone must think as we do. Islam emulated Christianity in this, as in so much else, though whereas Christianity had three centuries of dissemination by personal persuasion before it took up the sword, Islam was born sword in hand.

Thus there is a specific historical explanation for the fact that the world is now dominated by theism. But there's also a more general explanation of what has made theism attractive to so many.

People have innate tendencies which may, in the appropriate cultural circumstances, strongly favor belief in God. Among these innate tendencies are the following five:

1. An appetite for satisfying explanations.

People are born programmed to make sense of the world, to fit everything that interests them into a meaningful pattern. This appetite is a powerful influence in both religion and science.

What makes an explanation satisfying? One important element is finding unity in diversity. There is something deeply gratifying in discovering, or thinking one has discovered, that different things are somehow really the same. This is the insight of Emile Meyerson's Identity Principle, which Meyerson propounded to account for the development of science.

Meyerson argued that all attempts to explain anything spring from a basic tendency of the human mind: to deny diversity and insist upon sameness, in both space and time. This tendency is resisted by the details of experience, so it takes the form of looking for something constant behind the fleeting appearances. The Identity Principle successfully explains the impetus behind Einstein's search for a unified field theory in physics, but it is also active in the development of religious ideas.

2. A tendency to attribute intentions to all observed entities.

Divining other people's intentions is a basic human skill. Divining the intentions of other animals, both those you want to eat and those who want to eat you, is also valuable. It's more costly to fail to attribute intentions where these exist (in a prospective mate, a sexual rival, or a bear) than to attribute intentions where they do not exist (in a storm, a river, or a corpse).

People instinctively impute intentions to objects. They become angry with an electronic appliance or even a piece of furniture that misbehaves. Poker players can often be heard pleading: 'Give me a ten, a ten on the river', even when these players are quite well aware, at the level of sober reflection, that this supplication is totally ineffective.

This spontaneous mental impulse to suppose that things have purposes, or can be changed by mere words, is at the heart of magic, and elaborate magical thinking always permeates any culture in which theistic religion is born. Today we witness the power of magical thinking in such everyday expressions as 'if looks could kill' and in the popularity of books and movies in which the heroes have 'super powers', powers usually exercised by mental acts of will.

3. A tendency to treat elements of the imagination as though they were external entities.

A hallucination, a dream, a daydream, or a 'weird experience' may be interpreted as a perception of something external to the mind, when it is in fact (as far as we can tell) purely internal. Occasional minor hallucinations are extremely common, especially in the transition between wakefulness and sleep. Most people, at one time or another have 'heard a voice' when falling asleep or waking up, for example they hear someone calling their name. More intense hallucinations are less common, but by no means rare. Attempting to make sense of such experiences may easily lead a person to classify them as perceptions of another world, a different realm of existence.

4. A tendency for imaginary structures to be modeled after familiar human social structures.

If a person is familiar with the institutions of aristocracy or royalty, and also believes in spirits, he will tend to attribute these human institutions to the world of spirits. Spirits will tend to be conceived of as being aristocratic in relation to ordinary humans, and to being arranged hierarchically with a king at the top.

The emergence of the great monotheistic religions followed on centuries of glorification of absolute human rulers—Sargon, Nebuchadnezzar, Xerxes—who styled themselves "king of kings." In Islam as well as Judaism and Christianity, God sits on a throne. 'Islam' means 'submission' and 'Christ' means 'anointed', which is to say, a king. "Every knee should bow" to Christ (*Philippians* 2:10).

5. A tendency, in any belief-system, to move to more extreme positions on those points deemed important.

It has been observed that sometimes, particularly in times of economic depression, people are led by an invisible hand to act more concerned about their dress than they would ideally like to act. If a person typically feels that his prospects for advancement are influenced by his appearance, and if he judges the penalties of being 'over-dressed' as less serious than the penalties for being 'under-dressed', then he will tend to 'dress up'. Thus he becomes part of the perceived reference of other people who are thereby impelled to dress more formally, and in this way the interaction of everybody's observations and actions acts as feedback, to push everyone toward more dressiness.

A similar interpersonal process occurs in groups committed to a belief system. Once it's accepted that a particular point of doctrine is important, and that defectiveness on that point is serious, individuals have an incentive to err on the side of greater emphasis, rather than less, on that point of doctrine. Once they do this, the whole reference for each individual shifts up: now the perceived consensus on this point of doctrine is at a higher or 'more extreme' level: to be regarded as doctrinally sound, a person has to escalate their commitment to that point of doctrine, and it is safest to escalate a bit further, to outdo anyone who might become personally critical. Because of this bidding war for orthodox accreditation, the whole group moves toward ever increasing emphasis on that point of doctrine.[100]

Such points of doctrine may include the estimable qualities of the leader. At first the adherents of the belief-system may feel that the leader has valuable insights they can learn from. Gradually they are made to feel uncomfortable if they assert any shortcomings whatsoever in the leader. As this process unfolds, the community of believers moves toward the position that the leader is the most exalted of beings. Thus we move by stages from the view that Mao is, under the circumstances, the best man for the job of party chairman, to the position that Mao is the greatest all-round genius in human history and that pondering brief quotations from his writings can enable you to play better table tennis.

This is the process that led so many people from the view that one god is more exalted than all the others, to the view that there is just one very powerful God, and then to the view that this God is all-powerful, all-knowing, and all the rest of it. This doctrine surely did not emerge because evidence or arguments were found in its favor, but it becomes understandable as the outcome of a process of interpersonal interaction among committed ideologues competing with each other for approval. If we just take all the most impressive things about a God and make them as extreme as we can, we arrive at classical theism. It's the same interpersonal process that exalts the status of Sargon, Caesar, Lenin, Mussolini, Hitler, Stalin, and Mao, as well as Osho and L. Ron Hubbard. Once it becomes hazardous to one's health to hold a less exalted conception of God than the consensus of other believers, an automatic interpersonal process ensues, driving this consensus towards ever more expansive claims, culminating in the God of classical theism.

All these five tendencies are inherent in the human condition. #1 through #3 are genetically programmed tendencies of psychology, varying in intensity with individuals, while #4 is a typical exercise of the imagination, and #5 arises spontaneously within any group defined by enthusiastic adherence to a set of ideas. It becomes clear, just by making a few obvious extrapolations from these tendencies, that there exists the possibility that belief in God will emerge in a culture, if certain cultural conditions happen to come about.

I reject the view that that there is some specific human appetite for a God, while accepting that there are innate human tendencies which can easily lead to belief in God. Add those innate human tendencies to the specific historical circumstances of the origin and spread of Christianity, and we have the skeleton of an adequate explanation of the dominance of theism today.

20

Disillusioned and Happy

It's often claimed that belief in God makes life better, but the evidence for this is pretty darn feeble.

One popular view is that belief in God gives life meaning. Now, anything can seem to give life meaning to some people. Belief in the supreme wisdom of Stalin appeared to give meaning to life for a lot of people in the 1930s. Humans often like to kid themselves that something they value is something they can't live without. Very often, an individual's life seems to require the love of a specific other individual. When they lose that love, they feel that life has lost all meaning. But if they can get along for a while without committing suicide, they wake up one morning and notice that that other individual suddenly seems a bit shallow.

There's a misconception involved in this notion of God giving your life meaning. After all, why should the existence of God have anything to do with whether you find your life meaningful? It has no possible bearing on the matter.

Only you can give your life meaning. No one else can do it for you. If you feel that you need a God—or other people's favorable opinion, or a World Poker Tour bracelet, or your sweetheart's continued love, or good health, or revenge on your enemy, or a lot of money—to give your life meaning, this merely shows that you have decided to demand this of life and to go on strike if your demand isn't met. If you believe in God, and find life meaningful, and are convinced that without God your life would be meaningless, still it's *you*, and you alone, who are doing all this. It's not the existence of God that affects the meaningfulness of your life, but your insistence that there be a God.

Does Belief in God Make Life Better?

Research has been done by social scientists into the effects of religious affiliation on such matters as happiness, health, and crime. Such research is worthwhile and could be helpful, but there are peculiar difficulties.

This kind of research cannot be experimental: for obvious reasons, the researchers cannot pay people to take up a religious commitment, and then measure the results. Researchers must look at the religious choices various groups of people actually happen to have made, and then test those people for other things going on in their lives. But this means that it's hard to disentangle the effects of various influences.[101]

For instance, if churchgoers of denomination *x* are mainly farmers, they will be different in many ways from the population as a whole, and if you find that these churchgoers are rarely convicted of fraud, this could be just because farmers (let's suppose) are rarely convicted of fraud, compared with other occupations. There are ways to disentangle the effects of different influences, but it's quite a tricky exercise in statistics, and it's easy to put a foot wrong.

Another difficulty is that social scientists can't examine people's souls and measure the type of religious commitment they have. So what they do is try to find out whether people are affiliated with a church and whether they go to services regularly. This is something concrete and measurable, whereas the depth of someone's religious faith or commitment is something hard to pin down. Even this may not be accurate, however, for most studies merely ask people how often they attend services. It's too expensive to follow them around and find out how truthful their answers are.

For several decades numerous studies were reported showing that people who attend religious services have lower crime rates than people who don't. The same research also persistently showed that people attending Protestant services have lower crime rates than people attending Catholic services, while those attending Jewish services have even lower crime rates than the Protestants. It was often speculated that there might be a 'hellfire effect', that people who believed in God's retribution for sin would have an added deterrent against breaking the law (despite the fact that Jews pay less attention to the afterlife than Christians).

Then in work published in 2006, an economist named Paul Heaton looked more closely at the results of some of these earlier studies and came up with a different conclusion.[102] Heaton found an overlooked flaw in the design of these studies: they had failed to control for the fact that high crime in a locality causes reduced church attendance.

When this was corrected for, Heaton found that church attendance was associated with *more* crime, not less, though the observed difference was 'not significant', meaning that it was so small it was likely to be due to chance. Essentially then, Heaton found that church affiliation has no measurable effect on the crime rate.

If you think about religion in relation to anti-social behavior the following striking and quite well-known facts are liable to occur to you. Europe, Canada, Australia, and New Zealand have much lower levels of religious involvement than the United States—and also much lower levels of most kinds of crime, especially violent crime. Japan has even lower levels of religious involvement than Europe (and what religious observance there is, is mainly nontheistic), and Japan has astonishingly low crime rates, even by European standards.

In 2005 Gregory Paul published a study comparing eighteen industrially advanced nations.[103] He concluded that a higher level of religious belief within a country goes along with higher homicide rates, higher young-adult suicide rates, higher abortion rates, higher rates of sexually transmitted diseases, lower life expectancy, higher infant mortality, and lower acceptance of the theory of evolution.

Paul's study was criticized by several social scientists, who argued that it was inconclusive because of allegedly lax statistical procedures, and because Paul did not attempt to look at different types of religious belief. Partly in response to Paul, Gary Jensen produced a study in 2006 looking at over forty nations and distinguishing between 'dualistic' and 'God-only' religions.[104] His conclusion was that dualistic religion (belief in the Devil as well as God) was associated with more violence as well as other social evils, while God-only religion (belief in God without belief in the Devil) was no more associated with these evils than non-religion.

The difficulties in disentangling the actual influences at work are especially great when doing comparisons between entire nations, and I don't have much confidence in Paul's conclusions or Jensen's.

Can God Improve Your Health?

For the last twenty years the media have been buzzing with stories that research has demonstrated that 'religion' contributes to good health. If these claims were accurate, it would not indicate that theism is true. It could conceivably be more conducive to good health to believe in falsehoods, and that would be rather sad. Yet if you're reading a book like this, you probably agree with me that truth is more important than some small statistical increment of better health.

Contrary to an impression given in the popular literature, the studies aimed at finding whether religious belief leads to better health are very few. All the relevant studies up to 2006 are summarized and criticized by Richard Sloan,[105] who points out the shortcomings of these studies and identifies the many ways in which they are misrepresented—sometimes by the people who do the studies, more often by journalists and theistic propagandists. However, attempts to find some health benefits of religious adherence will continue, and no doubt some rigorous studies will be done which take us closer to an understanding of what the actual health effects of different forms of religious commitment are.

A 1972 study by George Comstock found that church attendance is correlated with quicker recovery from illnesses. This result continues to be cited by theists, though Comstock himself subsequently withdrew the conclusion that church attendance could be beneficial for health. The problem is that his analysis didn't control for the possibility that people with serious or worsening illness may find it harder to get to church. In that case, we could explain the correlation by saying that worsening illness reduces church attendance, rather than by church attendance benefiting health.

Recently there has been a huge growth of research studies of how happy people actually are.[106] These studies show a very slight advantage in happiness ('subjective well-being' or SWB) among churchgoers. This should be seen in the context of the more conspicuous findings of this research: that most people in all the advanced industrial countries are happy, that the countries with the happiest populations are Switzerland, Holland, and the Scandinavian countries, that having a higher real income is strongly correlated with happiness, and that freedom is also strongly correlated with happiness. There's also powerful evidence that once various extreme sources of wretchedness are removed by economic growth, while most people are then happy, their level of happiness stays close to a 'set point' which is largely governed by their genes.

What are we to make of all this? After decades of reports that belief in God had good effects, the last few years have seen a spate of reports that theistic belief has evil effects or no significant effects. I think we should take all these findings with a large pinch of salt, while not in any way decrying the efforts of social scientists to arrive at a more accurate picture of what is really going on in human cultures. I've heard atheists say that the percentage of atheists in prison is much lower than in the general population, but I immediately think that there may be ways in which it pays prisoners to profess a religious affiliation.

Suppose that in the future some new correlations are found between churchgoing and various good things. I don't think this would mean much as a practical guide. Whenever such research has looked at different religious denominations, it has always found differences among the denominations. Shall we then convert to that religious denomination which has the best health record (Seventh-Day Adventism?) or the lowest crime rate (Judaism?) or the highest real income (Unitarian Universalist?)? (The denominations in parentheses are just my first guesses.) But if we're not going to do that, why support theism in general because of such side-benefits?

If churchgoing is beneficial, it could be that churchgoing is correlated with healthier lifestyles like not smoking. In that case, it's possible to get the benefits without going to church, by opting for the healthier lifestyle (or accepting increased health risks as part of the cost of the enjoyment yielded by the less healthy lifestyle). It could be that people who go to church receive benefits from taking part in community activities, and that what they believe is immaterial (except insofar as it helps to motivate them to participate). It could be that religious devotion is beneficial but has nothing to do with belief in God: maybe Buddhists, Jains, or Unitarian Universalists gain as much from attending services as Jews, Christians, or Muslims.

Above all, there is the problem that an association between churchgoing and something good doesn't show which is cause and which is effect (or whether both are the effect of some third factor). Perhaps, for example, married people are more likely to go to church than single people (there is much evidence that married people are happier and healthier than the unmarried). Or perhaps, in a culture where most people believe in God, extreme misfortune causes people to cease to believe in God and thus stop going to church, and extreme misfortune is associated with numerous material and moral evils.

We can hope that these purely factual questions will eventually be settled by research and by improved social science theory. But right now, despite centuries of theory and research, the study of the actual social and medical effects of theistic and other belief-systems is in its infancy.

What we can say is that those effects are probably not large. Any connection between belief in God and good or bad health or behavior is not so dramatic that either theism or atheism is going to cause the social order to collapse or to degenerate into general misery.

Beyond Theism and Atheism

Both belief in God and commitment to organized religion decline in countries which become wealthy. In the long term, improved education and greater personal freedom, both associated with economic growth, promote atheism and irreligion.[107]

Rational discussion is not an all-powerful force shaping the way people think, but neither is it a negligible force. Free debate tends to lead to the growth of those ideas favored by reason and by the evidence. Since atheism is so favored, it will always win out against theism wherever there is free debate.

Most of the world's people still live in low-income countries, and in most of these theistic belief is tremendously powerful. Yet people in low-income countries want the benefits of economic growth. As they get these benefits, their religious commitment, or at least that of their grandchildren, declines. I am speaking here in the perspective of centuries, not election cycles: there can be irritating flare-ups of theistic ideology during the course of modernization.

Among industrialized countries, the United States stands out as a solitary and quite remarkable exception. Its level of belief in God or of any important religious ideas and its level of regular visits to a place of worship are vastly higher than Europe's or Japan's, and fit the usual profile of a third-world country.

Although the U.S. is the great exception among industrialized countries, in the sheer scale of its theistic activity, the *trend* in the U.S. is just the same as in Europe: active commitment to theistic religion declines with every passing decade. The U.S. has recently experienced massive immigration of comparatively devout theists from third world countries, yet the decline in religious participation has overwhelmed the effect of immigration.

Many people have become alarmed by the rise of the Christian Right. It's easy to overlook the fact that the Christian Right, by strictly dispassionate standards, has been an almost total failure.[108] None of its major objectives has so far been achieved, and evangelical involvement in politics has further discredited evangelical Christianity. Viewed from within the history of American Protestantism, the Christian Right is one more manifestation of decay.

In the United States, the proportion of people polled who say they have no religion is very low by European standards, but it rises ineluctably. Of course, some of those who say they have no religion do believe in God, just as some who identify with a religion have no belief in God. But precise statistics on theistic belief are harder to obtain for a long period, and statistics of religious affiliation give a rough indication.

America's periodic waves of religious revival should not be feared but viewed with sympathy. Each wave recruits young enthusiasts for theistic religion. They tend to have a high level of honesty: they care deeply about the truth of their ideas. The best and the brightest of them think for themselves, criticize the received doctrine, repudiate it, and eventually become atheists.

America's loss of theistic commitment has been slow but has now reached a tipping point. Over the next fifty years, we will witness a more rapid shrinkage of organized religion and theistic belief in the United States. Half a century from now, the U.S. will probably still have higher levels of theistic belief and religious practice than Europe or industrialized Asia and Latin America, but the difference will be modest. If I were a real-estate speculator I would be checking out church buildings, as most of those that now exist will soon have to be assigned to other uses.

In the immediate future we can expect to see an intensified American preoccupation with 'atheism', hence the demand for books like this one. But in a longer perspective, as belief in God dwindles, people will just stop talking about God or atheism, unless they are historians of ideas who study such vanished ideologies as Mithraism or Marxism.

There was a time when all decent people were horrified at the thought of cutting open dead bodies but today no one bothers to label themselves 'pro-autopsy'. Atheism is like pro-autopsyism: when it's universal, people will no longer talk about it or even have a name for it.

Does this mean that there's nothing to do except wait for theism to disappear?

Clear thinking about God, which I believe this book encourages, can be a valuable exercise and can save numerous individuals much emotional discomfort. It has therapeutic value for as long as theism remains a conspicuous feature of our cultural landscape. For some, it's also a fascinating way of getting into philosophy and the history of human culture.

Ultimately, atheism is limited. Atheism is like a clean water supply: very elementary and purely negative. It doesn't tell us how to conduct our personal lives or how to organize our social order. But then, despite first impressions, neither does theism.

Notes

¹ On Armstrong, see Campbell 2004; Asimov, Asimov 1995, pp. 314–320; Barry, *Fort Worth Star-Telegram* (25th November, 2001); Bartók, Demény 1971, pp. 76–83, 84–86; Buffett, Lowenstein 1995, p. 13; Penn and Teller, Gagnon 2006; Hepburn, *Ladies Home Journal* (October 1991); Mencken, his *Treatise on the Gods*; Orwell, *Complete Works*, Volume 16, pp. 437–442, Volume 19, pp. 63–64; Rand, Rand 2005, pp. 149–150; Sartre, Sartre 1965; Szasz, his 'An Autobiographical Sketch', in Schaler 2005; Twain, his *Letters from the Earth*; Wells, Wells 1934, pp. 568–578; Whedon, Nussbaum 2002.

² See the discussion of Galactus in Taliaferro and Lindahl-Urben 2005.

³ Orwell, *Complete Works*, Volume 19, p. 379.

⁴ Among many other writers who include agnosticism as a variety of atheism are Smith (1974) and Martin (1990)—and of course anyone at all before 1869.

⁵ *Genesis* was probably assembled and edited from several earlier documents around 700 B.C.E. Very likely, the people who first compiled *Genesis* knew perfectly well that the position of the Sun accounts for day and night, but included some passages already hallowed by great antiquity. Thus, the story of day and night existing before the Sun may well be a folk tale inherited from a primitive early stage when the dependence of day and night upon the Sun, though known to the astronomers of Mesopotamia and Egypt, was not known to the Hebrews.

⁶ Or, if you *really* want to get literal, "gods" [*elohim*].

⁷ 'Darwinism' is the name both for a scientific theory and for what Popper calls a "scientific ideology." I use the term 'ideology' to mean system of beliefs, without any implication that the beliefs are necessarily false (or true).

⁸ For several decades after Darwin's death, his theory of natural selection was widely disbelieved, while *Origin of Species* was admired as a

highly eloquent case for the fact of gradual evolution. Only in the period 1900–1940 was it finally recognized that Darwin had been right about natural selection, which fit beautifully with the new science of genetics.

[9] For example, one can read the first sentence of *Genesis* as a kind of heading summarizing the next few sentences, rather than as an event preceding them.

[10] See Whitcomb and Morris, Appendix II.

[11] See Woodmorappe 1996.

[12] Darwin's and Wallace's theories are not identical. Where they differ, Darwin is right and Wallace wrong.

[13] The same goes for the *Bible*.

[14] Eiseley 1979.

[15] Adams 2001, pp. 69–70.

[16] A simple way to make the distinction is that monkeys have tails; apes don't.

[17] Cairns-Smith 1985, pp. 58–61.

[18] Miller 2004.

[19] Estabrooks 1941. Olshansky, Carnes, and Butler 2001. See the discussion in Williams 1997, pp. 124–141.

[20] Dawkins 1986, p. 93; Williams 1997, pp. 138-141.

[21] The stages are laid out very simply in Smith and Szathmáry, Chapters 3–6.

[22] Musgrave 1998.

[23] This doesn't mean that one report of an event contrary to the proposed law will cause scientists to abandon it. In some branches of science, the convention is that decisive experiments be repeatable. This should be viewed as an attempt to make really sure that at least one contrary event has been observed, not as acceptance of the view that more than one contrary event is required. The *logic* of refutation by a single contrary instance is unaffected.

[24] Leoni 1961.

[25] The majority of American scientists either disbelieve in God or express agnostic doubt. Among scientists of the highest caliber ("greater" scientists), the atheist majority is overwhelming. A 1998 study of greater scientists found that 7.0 percent believed in a personal God, 72.2 percent disbelieved, while 20.8 percent were doubtful. The level of belief in God was much lower than for comparable data in 1933. Larson and Witham 1998.

[26] Stenger has devised a computer program enabling anyone to randomly 'create' their own virtual universes. The program is based on minimal physical assumptions. Stenger claims that most virtual universes generated last long enough for planets with heavy elements to form.

27 The probability of a tossed coin coming up heads is one-half. The probability of its coming up heads twice in two tosses is one-quarter, which we get by multiplying one-half by one-half. We would not be able to do this if there existed some mechanism making it more (or less) likely that the second toss would yield the same result as the first. The two tosses would not then be independent.

28 According to a popular legend, medieval philosophers debated how many angels could dance on the point of a needle (or, even more fatuously, 'on the head of a pin'). Medieval philosophers were not so idiotic. The legend of such debates probably arose because some philosophers argued that angels had no spatial dimensions which, put picturesquely, means that any number of them could dance on the point of a needle.

29 There are other possibilities, such as independent universes not commensurable in time, but this doesn't affect the argument here.

30 For a fuller discussion, see Sorabji 1983, pp. 219–223; Craig 2002; Guminski 2003.

31 Craig 2003, p. 25.

32 This is different to terms like 'multiverse' or 'megaverse' which have been used as names for a bunch of universes of which ours is one. Conceivably physicists might find that the multiverse or megaverse is part of a larger conglomeration, whereas I want to *define* 'metaverse' as the totality of everything that exists.

33 For something to be a conceivable thing, we don't have to be able to picture it in our minds, and being able to picture it in our minds does not make it a conceivable thing. We may really believe we can picture a square circle, but a square circle is not a conceivable thing. We may be unable to picture a world with many more than three spatial dimensions, but as long as we can specify such a world in a consistent set of equations, that world is a conceivable thing.

34 My view is that while the structure of moral theory is just as objective as the structure of, say, medical theory, practicing morality, like practicing medicine, requires an input of subjective values. In the case of morality, these values derive from empathy for other conscious beings. This empathy is, as a matter of fact, almost but not quite universal among humans. Among many atheists who disagree with me and favor 'moral realism' are Martin (2002); Wielenberg (2005).

35 Here and throughout the book, I sometimes simplify by saying 'matter' instead of 'matter and energy'.

36 The book I have found most helpful on this is Ellis 1995.

37 Yes, this is what Plantinga says. Plantinga 1993, pp. 225–26.

38 Most recently in Mawson 2005, pp. 163–64.

39 H. Benson *et al.* 2006; Sloan 2006, pp. 168–69.

40 See the discussion in Kenny 2004, Chapter 9.

[41] Pascal 1966, p. 150.

[42] O'Leary-Hawthorne, pp. 124–28.

[43] This statement is probably false. We all make mistakes. And while it would be illogical to assert something and then add that it is false, it's not necessarily illogical to say that somewhere, among a whole slew of assertions I assert, there are probably some which are false, as long as I don't know and can't specify which ones they are.

[44] For instance Paul quotes a line from the comic writer Menander at *1 Corinthians* 15:33.

[45] Some verses in the New Testament refer to scriptures which have not survived. If you think that all scripture is infallible, then you think God guaranteed the infallibility of certain documents and then quite soon permitted them to be lost.

[46] See the discussion in Wells 1999, pp. 196–200.

[47] The erudite Christian scholar Origen (around 185–254 C.E.) refers to Josephus in a way that suggests that possibly neither of these passages was in the copy of the *Antiquities* he read, though there was another mention of Jesus, presumably a scribal interpolation which did not survive later Christian editing.

[48] See the discussion by Wells (1996, pp. 43–44).

[49] Like the incompatible genealogies of Jesus (*Matthew* 1; *Luke* 3:23–38) or the incompatible datings of the crucifixion in relation to the Passover (*Mark* 14–15; *John* 13–19).

[50] Several examples are given in Nineham 1969.

[51] Asimov, Introduction to Evans and Berent 1988, p. xiv.

[52] Brown 1993. And see Wells 1999, pp. 115–122.

[53] Later church tradition ascribed some early epistles to Paul which were not in fact by Paul. Letters now accepted by most scholars as genuinely by Paul are *Romans, 1 Corinthians, 2 Corinthians, Galatians, Philippians, 1 Thessalonians,* and *Philemon.* The others are all disputed and (except for *Colossians,* a borderline case) considered by most scholars to be not by Paul. Claims that these letters were not really by Paul go back to before the formation of the *New Testament* canon. Some of the disputed letters are significantly later than the ones genuinely by Paul, others are almost equally early.

[54] This is a standard fundamentalist argument. For one example see Collins 1995, p. 58.

[55] There is one likely exception to this, the reference to a still-living person, "James, the Lord's brother" (*Galatians* 1:19; see *1 Corinthians* 9:5). This is usually taken to refer to a male sibling of Jesus who was personally known to Paul. But "the Lord's brother" could easily mean something else. G.A. Wells has proposed that there might have been a sect or order known as 'Brethren of the Lord'.

56 If the canonical gospels were at least roughly accurate, then Jesus and his closest companions would have been illiterates who knew only Aramaic.

57 Early in World War I, there were numerous reports attributed to British soldiers, that angels had been seen in the heavens over the town of Mons, fighting against the Germans, and that this angelic intervention had saved the day for the Allies. These 'sightings' originated in a short story published six months earlier, 'The Bowmen', by Arthur Machen.

58 For instances, rubbing spittle into a blind man's eyes before miraculously curing him of blindness.

59 'Cephas' is Aramaic for 'stone'. 'Petros' (Peter) is Greek for 'stone'. Both words were used as personal names before the appearance of Christianity.

60 Hume 1992, pp. 78–83.

61 Victor 1993.

62 A simple and familiar example of this universal process is the story of the 'wise men' (astrologers) who presented gifts to the baby Jesus, recorded in *Matthew* 2:1–12. Later the astrologers, of indeterminate number, became three (presumably suggested by the fact that the gifts mentioned are gold, myrrh, and frankincense). They then became kings, though their kingdoms have never been found, and in time acquired names: Caspar, Balthasar, and Melchior in the western churches, totally different names in the eastern (where there were supposed to be twelve of them). These later legends accumulated after *Matthew* was written (or at least, there is no earlier trace of them), so Protestants have generally rejected them. But such legend-building did not begin on the date that *Matthew* was compiled. Notice that 'Matthew' assumes that astrology is true.

63 'What Shape Is the Earth?' www.islaminfo.com.

64 Brooks and Brooks 1998.

65 See Moeller 2007.

66 Boller and George 1989.

67 For an interesting example, see Dummett 2007, pp. 5–6.

68 Hume 1992. This is explicitly part of an argument, voiced by the character Cleanthes, that we do get evidence like that, but Hume undermines that argument.

69 Swinburne 1991, pp. 211–12; Van Inwagen 2006, pp. 146–48; Murray 2002, pp. 69–76. This defense is similar to the 'soul-making' defense advanced by John Hick.

70 Technically known as a 'theodicy'.

71 Mackie 1982, p. 161–62.

72 Suppes 1984.

[73] There is a theory that when we think we make choices we're always deluded, but since no theist is likely to accept that, I won't take up space here to argue against it.

[74] He doesn't explicitly state this, but his argument fails if he accepts that it isn't true. Reichenbach 1982, pp. 87–118.

[75] I question this theist belief here, but since it is the overwhelmingly predominant theist assumption, I also accept it, for purposes of argument, in my further objections below.

[76] For example, Reichenbach 1982, pp. 131–33.

[77] My argument on page 201 can be completely answered by accepting that God is confined within 'our' time, and is not capable of knowing the future. This would also rule out Molina's 'middle knowledge'— God's knowledge of what choices persons would freely make in any hypothetical circumstances.

[78] That is, I'm assuming that one of the following three things is true: a. that these two conditions are all that free will means; b. that free will means something more than these two conditions, but that these two conditions are reliable markers for free will; or c. that free will means something more, and that these two conditions are not reliable markers, but that in all the examples where I mention free will and these two conditions hold, it's clear that there is or there might be free will.

[79] A conclusion of economic theory: financial intermediaries increase output and therefore income.

[80] Swinburne 1996, p. 113.

[81] Carneades (around 213–128 B.C.E.) apparently argued that, since God is defined as all-virtuous and yet cannot exercise virtue, this proves that God doesn't exist. Carneades's argument is developed by Douglas Walton (1999). I prefer not to include virtue in the definition of God, and simply to point out that God, if he exists, cannot be virtuous or vicious, and therefore departs from what we normally expect of a person.

[82] Fulmer 1977. To say that this law is "a pre-existing natural regularity," is not to say that this regularity existed before God did. If God has always existed for infinite time, or if God exists outside time, it remains necessary that this law must exist if God is to exist. This natural regularity is logically prior to God's existence (there could be no God without it) not necessarily prior to God's existence in time. Similarly, we can say that 'if any person understands square roots then he must understand multiplication, whereas a person can understand multiplication without understanding square roots'. This is necessarily true, even if the person in question, along with his understanding of square roots, has existed for infinite time past.

[83] Grim 1991.

[84] Everitt 2004, pp. 290–91.

[85] There might not be a unique solution, and God might have to choose one of many, but to humans the difference would be imperceptible.

[86] Blackmore 1993, 49–66, 81–93, 106–110.

[87] Blackmore 1993, pp. 127–28.

[88] Blanke, Ortigue, Landis, and Seek 2002.

[89] Dingwall, Goldney, and Hall 1956; see Hines 1988, pp. 62–64.

[90] Hines 1988, pp. 64–65.

[91] For brevity's sake, I have to move without warning between two uses of the word 'science', roughly science as it ought to be if it is to make the best stabs at the truth, and science as a real human institution, which is prone to various errors, sometimes caused by bias from various ideological preconceptions. I do not recommend that any of us uncritically accept the pronouncements of 'scientific experts' on anything whatsoever. On this see Steele 2005a.

[92] Pape 2005.

[93] Zahar 2007.

[94] Squaring the circle means constructing a square the same area as a circle, using standard equipment like compasses and a setsquare. It has been proved to be impossible.

[95] A view voiced by Jacob Joshua Ross, in Howard-Snyder and Moser, p. 183.

[96] *Psalms* 14:1 and also 53:1. The whole of *Psalm 53* is a slightly different draft or variant of *Psalm 14*.

[97] Plato 1926, p. 312.

[98] Bartlett 2000, p. 478.

[99] Calvin 1960, Volume 1, p. 45.

[100] This tendency has aroused most comment when it occurs in 'cults'. In my view, there is an element of the cult in all associations united by a common set of ideas, including professional societies, academic disciplines, families, business corporations, and nation-states.

[101] In other words there are no clinical trials in this area, but only epidemiological studies. When testing drugs, clinical trials are generally considered more decisive than epidemiological studies. If a clinical trial fails to confirm the findings of an epidemiological study, it's usually concluded that the findings were spurious.

[102] Heaton 2006.

[103] Paul 2005.

[104] Jensen 2006.

[105] Sloan 2006; see also Sloan, Bagiella, and Powell 1999.

[106] I have summarized some of the high spots of this research in Steele 2005b.

[107] 'Secularization' is associated with various sociological theories, some of which I don't endorse. The *fact* of declining theistic belief and declining religious participation in the more industrially developed countries is documented by a vast weight of evidence, such as that assembled in Norris and Inglehart 2004.

Recent increases in theistic activity in a few European countries are due either to the removal of Communist governments or to Muslim immigration.

[108] Bruce 2002, pp. 214–17.

Bibliography

Adams, Scott. 2001. *God's Debris: A Thought Experiment.* Kansas City: Andrews McMeel.

Anders, Timothy. 1994. *The Evolution of Evil.* Chicago: Open Court.

Aquinas, Thomas. 1989. *Summa Theologiae: A Concise Translation.* Allen: Christian Classics.

Armstrong, Karen. 1993. *A History of God.* New York: Ballantine.

Arnold, John H. 2005. *Belief and Unbelief in Medieval Europe.* London: Hodder.

Asimov, Isaac. 1988. Introduction to Evans and Berent 1988.

Asimov, Stanley, ed. 1995. *Yours, Isaac Asimov: A Lifetime of Letters.* New York: Doubleday.

Augustine. 2003. *The City of God.* London: Penguin.

Ayala, Francisco J. 2007. *Darwin's Gift to Science and Religion.* New York: Joseph Henry.

Ayer, Alfred Jules. 1946 [1936]. *Language, Truth, and Logic.* London: Gollancz.

Barrow, John D., and Frank J. Tipler. 1986. *The Anthropic Cosmological Principle.* Oxford: Oxford University Press.

Bartlett, Robert. 2000. *England Under the Norman and Angevin Kings, 1075–1225.* Oxford: Clarendon.

Bechert, Heinz, and R. Gombrich, eds. 1984. *The World of Buddhism: Buddhist Monks and Nuns in Society and Culture.* London: Thames and Hudson.

Beckmann, Petr. 1974 [1971]. *A History of π (Pi).* New York: St. Martin's Press.

Behe, M. 2006 [1996]. *Darwin's Black Box: The Biochemical Challenge to Evolution.* Tenth anniversary edition. New York: Free Press.

Blackmore, Susan J. 1989. *Beyond the Body: An Investigation of Out-of-the-Body Experiences.* Chicago: Academy Chicago.

————. 1993. *Dying to Live: Near-Death Experiences.* Buffalo: Prometheus.

————. 1996 [1986]. *In Search of the Light: The Adventures of a Parapsychologist.* Amherst: Prometheus.

Blanke, Olaf, Stephanie Ortigue, Theodore Landis, and Margritta Seek. 2002. Neuropsychology: Stimulating Illusory Own-Body Perceptions. *Nature* 419:6904 (19th September).

Boller, Paul F., and John George. 1989. *They Never Said It: A Book of Fake Quotes, Misquotes, and Misleading Attributions.* New York: Oxford University Press.

Brooks, E. Bruce, and A. Taeko Brooks. 1998. *The Original Analects: Sayings of Confucius and His Successors.* New York: Columbia University Press.

Brown, Raymond E. 1993 [1977]. *The Birth of the Messiah: A Commentary on the Infancy Narratives in the Gospels of Matthew and Luke.* New York: Random House.

Bruce, Steve. 2002. *God Is Dead: Secularization in the West.* Oxford: Blackwell.

Bucaille, Maurice. 1987. *The Bible, The Quran, and Science: The Holy Scriptures in the Light of Modern Knowledge.* Tripoli: The Great Socialist People's Libyan Arab Jamarihiyah.

Cairns-Smith, A.G. 1985. *Seven Clues to the Origin of Life: A Scientific Detective Story.* Cambridge: Cambridge University Press.

Calvin, John. 1960 [1536]. *Institutes of the Christian Religion.* Two volumes. Philadelphia: Westminster.

Campbell, Alastair. 2004. A Legend? I'd Rather Be Remembered as a Dad. *The Times* (London, 28th February), www.lancearmstrongfan-club.com/uktimesonline.html.

Carrier, Richard. 2000. Are the Odds Against the Origin of Life Too Great to Accept? www.infidels.org/library/modern/richard_carrier/addendaB.html.

————. 2002. Did Jesus Exist? Earl Doherty and the Argument to Ahistoricity. www.infidels.org/library/modern/richard_carrier/jesuspuzzle.html.

Ching, Julia. 1993. *Chinese Religions.* Maryknoll: Orbis.

Collins, Steven. 1995. *Championing the Faith: A Layman's Guide to Proving Christianity's Claims.* Tulsa: Hensley.

Comstock, George W., and Kay B. Partridge, 1972. Church Attendance and Health. *Journal of Chronic Disease* 25:12 (December).

Cook, Michael. 2000. *The Koran: A Very Short Introduction.* Oxford: Oxford University Press.

Cowdrey, Wayne L., Howard A. Davis, and Arthur Vanick. 2005. *Who Really Wrote the Book of Mormon? The Spalding Enigma.* Saint Louis: Concordia House.

Craig, William Lane. 1979. *The Kalām Cosmological Argument*. London: Macmillan.

———. 2002 [1991]. The Existence of God and the Beginning of the Universe. www.leaderu.com/truth/3truth11.html.

———. 2003. The Kalam Cosmological Argument. In Pojman 2003.

Craig, William Lane, and Walter Sinnott-Armstrong. 2004. *God? A Debate between a Christian and an Atheist*. New York: Oxford University Press.

Crone, Patricia. 1987. *Meccan Trade and the Rise of Islam*. Princeton: Princeton University Press.

Crone, Patricia, and Michael Cook. 1977. *Hagarism: The Making of the Islamic World*. Cambridge: Cambridge University Press.

Cupitt, Don. 1981. *Taking Leave of God*. New York: Crossroad.

Darwin, Charles. 1998 [1859]. *The Origin of Species by Means of Natural Selection, Or, The Preservation of Favored Races in the Struggle for Life*. New York: Modern Library.

Davies, Brian. 2006. *The Reality of God and the Problem of Evil*. London: Continuum.

Davis, Stephen T. 1983. *Logic and the Nature of God*. Grand Rapids: Eerdmans.

———. 1997. *God, Reason, and Theistic Proofs*. Grand Rapids: Eerdmans.

Dawkins, Richard. 1986. *The Blind Watchmaker: Why the Evidence of Evolution Reveals a Universe Without Design*. New York: Norton.

———. 2006. *The God Delusion*. New York: Houghton Mifflin.

Dembski, William A. 2006. *Darwin's Nemesis: Philip Johnson and the Intelligent Design Movement*. Downers Grove: InterVarsity.

Dembski, William A, and Michael Ruse, eds. 2004. *Debating Design: From Darwin to DNA*. Cambridge: Cambridge University Press.

Demény, János, ed. 1971. *Béla Bartók Letters*. New York: St. Martin's.

Dershowitz, Alan M. 2000. *The Genesis of Justice: Ten Stories of Biblical Injustice that Led to the Ten Commandments and Modern Morality and Law*. New York: Warner.

Dingwall, E., K. Goldney, and T. Hall. 1956. *The Haunting of Borley Rectory*. London: Duckworth.

Doherty, Earl. 1999. *The Jesus Puzzle: Did Christianity Begin with a Mythical Christ?* Ottawa: Canadian Humanist Publications.

Donner, Fred M. 1998. *Narratives of Islamic Origins: The Beginnings of Islamic Historical Writing*. Princeton: Darwin Press.

Drange, Theodore M. 1998. *Nonbelief and Evil: Two Arguments for the Nonexistence of God*. Amherst: Prometheus.

Drees, Willem B. 1990. *Beyond the Big Bang: Quantum Cosmologies and God*. Chicago: Open Court.

Dummett, Michael. 2007. Intellectual Autobiography. In Randall E. Auxier and Lewis Edwin Hahn, eds., *The Philosophy of Michael Dummett* (Chicago: Open Court).

Ehrman, Bart D. 1999. *Jesus: Apocalyptic Prophet of the New Millennium.* New York: Oxford University Press.

———. 2004. *Truth and Fiction in the Da Vinci Code.* New York: Oxford University Press.

———. 2003. *Lost Christianities: The Battles for Scripture and the Faiths We Never Knew.* New York: Oxford University Press.

———. 2006. *Misquoting Jesus: The Story Behind Who Changed the Bible and Why.* San Francisco: Harper Collins.

Eiseley, Loren C. 1979. *Darwin and the Mysterious Mr. X: New Light on the Evolutionists.* New York: Dutton.

Ellis, Ralph D. 1995. *Questioning Consciousness: The Interplay of Imagery, Cognition, and Emotion in the Human Brain.* Amsterdam: Benjamins.

Estabrooks, G.H. 1941. *Man: The Mechanical Misfit.* New York: Macmillan.

Evans, Rod L., and Irwin M. Berent. 1988. *Fundamentalism: Hazards and Heartbreaks.* La Salle: Open Court.

Everitt, Nicholas. 2004. *The Non-Existence of God.* London: Routledge.

Feldman, Louis H., and Gohei Hata. 1987. *Josephus, Judaism, and Christianity.* Detroit: Wayne State University Press.

———. 1989. *Josephus, the Bible, and History.* Detroit: Wayne State University Press.

Flank, Lenny. 1995. Can Noah's Flood Account for the Geologic and Fossil Record? www.geocities.com/CapeCanaveral/Hangar/2437/sorting.htm.

Fulmer, Gilbert. 1977. The Concept of the Supernatural. *Analysis* 37. Reprinted in Martin and Monnier 2003.

———. 2001. A Fatal Flaw in Anthropic Principle Design Arguments. *International Journal for Philosophy of Religion* 49.

———. 2003. Faces in the Sky: The Anthropic Principle Design Argument. *Journal of American Culture* 16:4 (December).

Gagnon, Geoffrey. 2006. Faces of the New Atheism: The Illusionists. *Wired* (November).

Gale, Richard M. 1991. *On the Nature and Existence of God.* Cambridge: Cambridge University Press.

Geach, Peter T. 1977. *Providence and Evil.* New York: Cambridge University Press.

Ghiselin, Michael T. 1984 [1969]. *The Triumph of the Darwinian Method.* Chicago: University of Chicago Press.

Glasenapp, Helmuth von. 1970 [1954]. *Buddhism: A Non-theistic Religion*. New York: Braziller.

Glynn, Patrick. 1999. *God—The Evidence: The Reconciliation of Faith and Reason in a Postsecular World*. Rocklin: Prima.

Greene, Brian. 2004. *The Fabric of the Cosmos: Space, Time, and the Texture of Reality*. New York: Vintage.

Griffin, David Ray. 1976. *God, Power, and Evil: A Process Theodicy*. Philadelphia: Westminster.

Grim, Patrick. 1991. *The Incomplete Universe: Totality, Knowledge, and Truth*. Cambridge, Ma: MIT Press.

Guminski, Arnold. 2003. The Kalam Cosmological Argument Yet Again: The Question of the Metaphysical Possibility of an Infinite Temporal Series. www.infidels.org/library/modern/arnold_guminski/kalam2.shtml.

Guth, Alan. 1997. *The Inflationary Universe: The Quest for a New Theory of Cosmic Origins*. Reading, Ma: Perseus.

Hamer, Dean H. 2004. *The God Gene: How Faith Is Hardwired into Our Genes*. New York: Doubleday.

Harris, Sam. 2004. *The End of Faith: Religion, Terror, and the Future of Reason*. New York: Norton.

Hartshorne, Charles. 1964 [1941]. *Man's Vision of God and the Logic of Theism*. Hamden: Archon.

Haught, John F. 2008 [2000]. *God After Darwin: A Theology of Evolution*. Second edition. Boulder: Westview.

Heaton, Paul. 2006. Does Religion Really Reduce Crime? *Journal of Law and Economics* 49 (April).

Hick, John, and Arthur C. McGill. 1967. *The Many-Faced Argument: Recent Studies on the Ontological Argument for the Existence of God*. New York: Macmillan.

Hines, Terence. 1988. *Pseudoscience and the Paranormal: A Critical Examination of the Evidence*. Amherst: Prometheus.

Hitchens, Christopher. 2007. *God Is Not Great: How Religion Poisons Everything*. New York: Hachette.

Holbach, Paul-Henri Thiry, Baron d'. 1970 [1770]. *The System of Nature or Laws of the Moral and Physical World*. New York: Franklin.

Howard-Snyder, Daniel, and Paul K. Moser, eds. 2002. *Divine Hiddenness: New Essays*. Cambridge: Cambridge University Press.

Hume, David. 1992. *Writings on Religion*. Edited by Antony Flew. Chicago: Open Court.

Jensen, Gary F. 2006. Religious Cosmologies and Homicide Rates among Nations: A Closer Look. *Journal of Religion and Society* 8.

Jonas, Hans. 1966. *The Phenomenon of Life: Toward a Philosophical Biology*. New York: Dell.

Jones, Steve. 2000 [1999]. *Darwin's Ghost: The Origin of Species Updated.* In Britain titled *Almost Like a Whale.* New York: Random House.

Kauffman, Stuart A. 1993. *The Origins of Order: Self-Organization and Selection in Evolution.* New York: Oxford University Press.

Kapitan, Tomis. 1991. Agency and Omniscience. *Religious Studies* 27. Reprinted in Martin and Monnier 2003.

———. 1994. The Incompatibility of Omniscience and Intentional Action: A Reply to David P. Hunt. *Religious Studies* 30. Reprinted in Martin and Monnier 2003.

Kenny, Anthony. 1979. *The God of the Philosophers.* Oxford: Clarendon.

———. 1980 [1969]. *The Five Ways: St. Thomas Aquinas's Proofs of God's Existence.* Notre Dame: University of Notre Dame Press.

———. 2005. *The Unknown God: Agnostic Essays.* New York: Continuum.

Kirzner, Yitzchok. 2004. *Making Sense of Suffering: A Jewish Approach.* New York: Mesorah.

Kushner, Harold S. 1981. *When Bad Things Happen to Good People.* New York: Random House.

Lahav, Noam. 1999. *Biogenesis: Theories of Life's Origin.* Oxford: Oxford University Press.

Larson, Edward J., and Larry Witham. 1997. Scientists Are Still Keeping the Faith. *Nature* 386 (3rd April).

———. 1998. Scientists Still Reject God. *Nature* 394 (23rd July).

Leoni, Bruno. 1991. *Freedom and the Law.* New York: Van Nostrand.

Lester, Toby. 2002 [1999]. What Is the Koran? In Ibn Warraq 2002. Reprinted from *Atlantic Monthly* (January 1999).

Lewis, C.S. 2001 [1952]. *Mere Christianity.* New York: HarperCollins.

Lindsey, Hal. 1970. *The Late Great Planet Earth.* Grand Rapids: Zondervan.

———. 1980. *The 1980s: Countdown to Armageddon.* King of Prussia: Westgate.

Lowenstein, Roger. 1995. *Buffett: The Making of an American Capitalist.* New York: Doubleday.

Lucretius. 1997. *On the Nature of the Universe.* Oxford: Oxford University Press.

Mack, Burton. 1995. *Who Wrote the New Testament? The Making of the Christian Myth.* San Francisco: HarperCollins.

Mackie, J.L. 1955. Evil and Omnipotence. *Mind* 64. Reprinted in Martin and Monnier 2003.

———. 1982. *The Miracle of Theism: Arguments for and Against the Existence of God.* Oxford: Clarendon.

Maimonides, Moses. 1956. *The Guide for the Perplexed*. New York: Dover.

Martin, Michael. 1990. *Atheism: A Philosophical Justification*. Philadelphia: Temple University Press.

———. 2002. *Atheism, Morality, and Meaning*. Amherst: Prometheus.

Martin, Michael, and Ricki Monnier, eds. 2003. *The Impossibility of God*. Amherst: Prometheus.

———, eds. 2006. *The Improbability of God*. Amherst: Prometheus.

Mawson, T.J. 2005. *Belief in God: An Introduction to the Philosophy of Religion*. Oxford: Clarendon.

Mencken, H.L. 1946 [1930]. *Treatise on the Gods*. New York: Knopf.

Mesle, C. Robert. 1993. *Process Theology: A Basic Introduction*. St. Louis: Chalice.

Meyerson, Emile. 1989. *Identity and Reality*. New York: Gordon and Breach.

Mill, John Stuart. 1969 [1874]. *Three Essays on Religion*. New York: Greenwood.

Miller, Kenneth R. 1999. *Finding Darwin's God: A Scientist's Search for Common Ground between God and Evolution*. New York: HarperCollins.

———. 2004. The Flagellum Unspun: The Collapse of 'Irreducible Complexity'. In Dembski and Ruse 2004.

Moeller, Hans-Georg. 2007. *Daodejing: A Complete Translation and Commentary*. Chicago: Open Court.

Morison, Frank. 2002 [1930]. *Who Moved the Stone? A Skeptic Looks at the Death and Resurrection of Christ*. Grand Rapids: Zondervan.

Morris, Thomas V., ed. 1988. *Philosophy and the Christian Faith*. Notre Dame: University of Notre Dame Press.

Muffs, Yochanan. 2005. *The Personhood of God: Biblical Theology, Human Faith, and the Divine Image*. Woodstock: Jewish Lights.

Munitz, Milton K. 1974. *The Mystery of Existence: An Essay in Philosophical Cosmology*. New York: New York University Press.

Murray, Michael J., ed. 1999. *Reason for the Hope Within*. Grand Rapids: Eerdmans.

Musgrave, Ian. 1998. Lies, Damned Lies, Statistics, and Probability of Abiogenesis Calculations. www.talkorigins.org/faqs/abioprob/abio-prob.html.

Neher, Andrew. 1990 [1980]. *Paranormal and Transcendental Experience: A Psychological Examination*. New York: Dover.

Newberg, Andrew, Eugene d'Aquili, and Vince Rause. 2002 [2001]. *Why God Won't Go Away: Brain Science and the Biology of Belief*. New York: Ballantine.

Nineham, Dennis E. 1969 [1963]. *The Gospel of St Mark*. Pelican New Testament Commentaries. Harmondsworth: Penguin.

————. 1977. *Explorations in Theology 1: D.E. Nineham*. London: SCM Press.

Norris, Pippa, and Ronald Inglehart. 2004. *Sacred and Secular: Religion and Politics Worldwide*. Cambridge: Cambridge University Press.

Nowacki, Mark R. 2006. *The Kalam Cosmological Argument for God*. Amherst: Prometheus.

Numbers, Ronald L. 1993. *The Creationists: The Evolution of Scientific Creationism*. Berkeley: University of California Press.

Nussbaum, Emily. 2002. Must-See Metaphysics. *New York Times* (22nd September).

Ockham, William of. 1990. *Philosophical Writings: A Selection.* Indianapolis: Hackett.

O'Leary-Hawthorne, John. 1999. Arguments for Atheism. In Murray 1999.

Olshanksy, S. Jay, Bruce Carnes, and Robert N. Butler. 2001. If Humans Were Built to Last. *Scientific American* (March).

Orwell, George. 1986–2001. *The Complete Works of George Orwell*. Twenty volumes. London: Secker and Warburg.

Paley, William. 2006 [1802]. *Natural Theology: Evidence of the Existence and Attributes of the Deity, Collected from the Appearances of Nature*. Oxford: Oxford University Press.

Pape, Robert A. 2005. *Dying to Win: The Strategic Logic of Suicide Terrorism*. New York: Random House.

Papineau, David. 2002. *Thinking about Consciousness*. Oxford: Clarendon.

Pascal, Blaise. 1995. *Pensées*. London: Penguin.

Paul, Gregory S. 2005. Cross-National Correlations of Quantifiable Societal Health with Popular Religiosity and Secularism in the Prosperous Democracies: A First Look. *Journal of Religion and Society 7*.

Perakh, Mark. 2004. *Unintelligent Design*. Amherst: Prometheus.

Pickover, Clifford A. *The Paradox of God and the Science of Omniscience*. 2001. New York: Palgrave Macmillan.

Plantinga, Alvin. 1967. *God and Other Minds: A Study of the Rational Justification of Belief in God*. Ithaca: Cornell University Press.

————. 1993. *Warrant and Proper Function*. Oxford: Oxford University Press.

————. 1998. *The Analytic Theist: An Alvin Plantinga Reader*. Grand Rapids: Eerdmans.

————. 2000. *Warranted Christian Belief*. Oxford: Oxford University Press.

Plato. 1926. The Laws. *Plato in Twelve Volumes*, XI Laws, Volume II: Books VII–XII. Cambridge, Ma: Loeb Classical Library.

Plotinus. 1975. *The Essential Plotinus.* Indianapolis: Hackett.

Pojman, Louis P., ed. 2003. *Philosophy of Religion: An Anthology.* Fourth edition. Belmont: Wadsworth.

Popper, Karl R. 2000 [1983]. *Realism and the Aim of Science: From the Postscript to The Logic of Scientific Discovery.* London: Routledge.

Price, Robert M. 2003. *The Incredible Shrinking Son of Man: How Reliable Is the Gospel Tradition?* Amherst: Prometheus.

Psillos, Stathis. 1999. *Scientific Realism: How Science Tracks Truth.* London: Routledge.

Rahula, Walpola Sri. 1974 [1959]. *What the Buddha Taught.* New York: Grove.

Rand, Ayn. 2005. *Ayn Rand Answers: The Best of Her Q&A.* New York: New American Library.

Rawlinson, Andrew. 1997. *The Book of Enlightened Masters: Western Teachers in Eastern Traditions.* Chicago: Open Court.

Reichenbach, Bruce R. 1982. *Evil and a Good God.* New York: Fordham University Press.

Russell, Bertrand. 1945. *History of Western Philosophy.* New York: Simon and Schuster.

Russell, D.S. 1963. *Between the Testaments.* Philadelphia: Fortress.

Sartre, Jean-Paul. 1965 [1947]. The Humanism of Existentialism. In Sartre, *Essays in Existentialism* (Secaucus: Citadel).

Schaler, Jeffrey A., ed. 2004. *Szasz Under Fire: The Psychiatric Abolitionist Faces His Critics.* Chicago: Open Court.

Schweitzer, Albert. 1956. *The Quest of the Historical Jesus: A Critical Study of Its Progress from Reimarus to Wrede.* New York: Macmillan.

Searle, John R. 1992. *The Rediscovery of the Mind.* Cambridge, Ma: MIT Press.

Shermer, Michael. 2003 [2000]. *How We Believe.* New York: Holt.

Shestov, Lev. 1977 [1905]. *All Things Are Possible and Penultimate Words and Other Essays.* Athens, Oh: Ohio University Press.

Sloan, Richard P. 2006. *Blind Faith: The Unholy Alliance of Religion and Medicine.* New York: St. Martin's.

Sloan, Richard P., E. Bagiella, and T. Powell. 1999. Religion, Spirituality, and Medicine. *The Lancet* 353: 9153 (20th February).

Smith, George H. 1974. *Atheism: The Case Against God.* Los Angeles: Nash.

Smith, John Maynard, and Eörs Szathmáry. 1999. *The Origins of Life: From the Birth of Life to the Origin of Language.* Oxford: Oxford University Press.

———. 2002 [2000]. *Three Roads to Quantum Gravity.* New York: Basic Books.

Smolin, Lee. 1997. *The Life of the Cosmos*. New York: Oxford University Press.

Sorabji, Richard. 1983. *Time, Creation, and the Continuum: Theories in Antiquity and the Early Middle Ages*. Ithaca: Cornell University Press.

Southwood, Richard. 2003. *The Story of Life*. Oxford: Oxford University Press.

Steele, David Ramsay. 2005a. The Atkins Diet as an Alternative Theory. In Lisa Heldke, Kerri Mommer, and Cindy Pineo, eds., *The Atkins Diet and Philosophy: Chewing the Fat with Kant and Nietzsche* (Chicago: Open Court).

———. 2005b. Life, Liberty, and the Treadmill. *Liberty* (February).

Stenger, Victor J. 2006. *The Comprehensible Cosmos: Where Do the Laws of Physics Come From?* Amherst: Prometheus.

———. 2007. *God: The Failed Hypothesis*. Amherst: Prometheus.

Strobel, Lee. 1998. *The Case for Christ: A Journalist's Personal Investigation of the Evidence for Jesus*. Grand Rapids: Zondervan.

Suppes, Patrick. 1984. *Probabilistic Metaphysics*. Oxford: Blackwell.

Susskind, Leonard. 2005. *The Cosmic Landscape: String Theory and the Illusion of Intelligent Design*. New York: Little, Brown.

Swinburne, Richard. 1977. *The Coherence of Theism*. Oxford: Clarendon.

———. 1991 [1979]. *The Existence of God*. Oxford: Clarendon.

———. 1996. *Is There a God?* Oxford: Oxford University Press.

———. 1986. *The Evolution of the Soul*. Oxford: Clarendon.

Taliaferro, Charles, and Craig Lindahl-Urben. 2005. The Power and the Glory. In Tom Morris and Matt Morris, eds., *Superheroes and Philosophy: Truth, Justice, and the Socratic Way* (Chicago: Open Court).

Thrower, James. 1971. *A Short History of Western Atheism*. London: Pemberton.

Twain, Mark. 1962 [1938]. *Letters from the Earth: Uncensored Writings*. New York: Harper and Row.

Van Inwagen, Peter. 2002 [1993]. *Metaphysics*. Boulder: Westview.

———. 2006. *The Problem of Evil: The Gifford Lectures Delivered in the University of St Andrews in 2003*. Oxford: Clarendon.

Victor, Jeffrey S. 1993. *Satanic Panic: The Creation of a Contemporary Legend*. Chicago: Open Court.

Vilenkin, Alex. 2006. *Many Worlds in One: The Search for Other Universes*. New York: Hill and Wang.

Walker, Jeff. 1998. *The Ayn Rand Cult*. Chicago: Open Court.

Walton, Douglas. 1999. Can an Ancient Argument of Carneades on Cardinal Virtues Be Used to Disprove the Existence of God? In Martin and Monnier 1999.

Wansbrough, John E. 2004 [1977]. *Quranic Studies.* Amherst: Prometheus.

Warraq, Ibn. 1995. *Why I Am Not a Muslim.* Amherst: Prometheus.

———, ed. 2000. *The Quest for the Historical Muhammad.* Amherst: Prometheus.

———, ed. 2002. *What the Koran Really Says: Language, Text, and Commentary.* Amherst: Prometheus.

Weinstein, Steven. 2001. *Facing Up: Science and Its Cultural Adversaries.* Cambridge, Ma: Harvard University Press.

Wells, G.A. 1996. *The Jesus Legend.* Chicago: Open Court.

———. 1999. *The Jesus Myth.* Chicago: Open Court.

———. 2004. *Can We Trust the New Testament? Thoughts on the Reliability of Early Christian Testimony.* Chicago: Open Court.

Wells, H.G. 1934. *Experiment in Autobiography: Discoveries and Conclusions of a Very Ordinary Brain (Since 1866).* New York: Macmillan.

Whitcomb, John C., and Henry M. Morris. 1961. *The Genesis Flood: The Biblical Record and Its Scientific Implications.* Philipsburg: Presbyterian and Reformed.

Wielenberg, Erik J. 2005. *Value and Virtue in a Godless Universe.* New York: Cambridge University Press.

Williams, George C. 1997. *The Pony Fish's Glow: And Other Clues to Plan and Purpose in Nature.* New York: Basic Books.

Woodmorappe, John. 1996. *Noah's Ark: A Feasibility Study.* El Cajon: Institute for Creation Research.

Index